Implementing Credit Derivatives

Other Titles in the Irwin Library of Investment and Finance

Convertible Securities
by John P. Calamos (1-55738-921-7)

Pricing and Managing Exotic and Hybrid Options
by Vineer Bhansali (0-07-006669-8)

Risk Management and Financial Derivatives
by Satyajit Das (0-07-015378-7)

Valuing Intangible Assets
by Robert F. Reilly and Robert P. Schweihs (0-7863-1065-0)

Managing Financial Risk
by Charles W. Smithson (0-7863-0440-5)

High-Yield Bonds
by Theodore Barnhill, William Maxwell, and Mark Shenkman
(0-07-006786-4)

Implementing Credit Derivatives

DR. ISRAEL "IZZY" NELKEN
Super Computer Consulting, Inc.
www.supercc.com

With a contribution by **Claude Brown** *of Clifford Chance*

McGraw-Hill

New York   San Francisco   Washington, D.C.   Auckland   Bogotá
Caracas   Lisbon   London   Madrid   Mexico City   Milan
Montreal   New Delhi   San Juan   Singapore
Sydney   Tokyo   Toronto

Library of Congress Cataloging-in-Publication Data

Nelken, Israel.
    Implementing credit derivatives / by Israel Nelken.
      p. cm.
    ISBN 0-07-047237-8
    1. Credit derivatives. 2. Risk management. I. Title.
    HG6024.A3N45   1999
    332.63'2—dc21   99-13976
                                  CIP

McGraw-Hill

*A Division of The **McGraw·Hill** Companies*

2 3 4 5 6 7 8 9 0 DOC/DOC 9 0 9 8 7 6 5 4 3 2 1 0 9

ISBN 0-07-047237-8

The sponsoring editor for this book was Stephen Isaacs, the editing supervisor was Fred Dahl, and the production supervisor was Modestine Cameron. It was set in Palatino by Inkwell Publishing Services.

Printed and bound by R.R. Donnelly & Sons Company.

This publication is designed to provide accurate and authoritative information in regard to the subject matter covered. It is sold with the understanding that neither the author nor the publisher is engaged in rendering legal, accounting, or other professional service. If legal advice or other expert assistance is required, the services of a competent professional person should be sought.
—*From a declaration of Principles jointly adopted by a Committee of the American Bar Association and a Committee of Publishers.*

McGraw-Hill books are available at special quantity discounts to use as premiums and sales promotions, or for use in corporate training programs. For more information, please write to the Director of Special Sales, McGraw-Hill, 11 West 19th Street, New York, NY 10011. Or contact your local bookstore.

 This book is printed on recycled, acid-free paper containing a minimum of 50% recycled de-inked fiber.

This book is dedicated to my son, Jason Benjamin Nelken, a shining light.

Contents

Preface   *xvii*

CHAPTER 1
Introduction   1

Credit Derivatives   *1*
Relationship Issues   *2*
The Credit Paradox   *3*
The One-Sided Nature of the Market   *4*
The Basic Structure   *5*
The Search for Yield   *5*
Risk Measurement   *6*
Globalization and Democratization   *7*
The Potential Market for Credit Derivatives   *8*
Market Size   *9*
Growing Pains   *10*
The Players   *11*
Rationale of the Market   *11*
Buyer and Seller   *12*
A Bit of History   *14*

CHAPTER 2
The Structures   15

Typical Credit Swap   *15*
The Premium   *16*
Correlation   *18*
The Contingent Leg   *20*
Recovery Value   *21*
Secrecy Issues   *21*
Legal Test and Market Test   *22*
Moral Hazard   *23*
Hedging   *23*

Downgrade Options   26
Credit Intermediation Swaps   26
Default Substitution Swaps   28
    Total Return Swap   29
    Credit Risk in a TROR   31
    Maturity   33
    Exposure to a Credit Desired   34
    Credit Spread Options   34
    An Example of a Credit Spread Put   36
    Credit Spread Forwards   38
    Volatility   40
Standardization   41
Special Requests   42
Use of Total Return Swaps by Corporation   42
Credit-Linked Notes   43
    The Investor in a CLN   47
    The J.P. Morgan—Wal-Mart CLNs   48
    Sovereign   49
Convertibility Risk Products   50
An Example of a Trade   51
Summary of Products   52

CHAPTER 3
Legal and Regulatory Aspects (by Claude Brown of Clifford Chance)   53

Types of Credit Derivative Instruments   54
Credit Spread Products   55
Total Rate of Return Swaps   55
Convertibility Products   59
Credit Default Products   59
Payout Profile   61
    Credit Event upon Merger   63
    Cross Acceleration and Cross Default   63
    Downgrade   65
    Failure to Pay   66
    Restructuring   67

Repudation   67
Publicly Available Information (PAI)   68
Notices   69
Materiality   71
Settlement Terms   72
Physical Settlment   73
Cash Settlement   74
Summary   78
Regulatory Capital Treatment of Credit Derivatives   78
The United Kingdom   80
The FSA's Chapter CD   82
FSA Banking Book Treatment for Credit Derivatives   83
Funded or Unfunded   84
Payout Structure   85
Asset Mismatch   86
Currency Mismatch   87
Maturity Mismatch   87
Basket Products   88
FSA Trading Book Treatment   89
General Market Risk   90
Specific Risk   91
Counterparty Risk   93
Risk Transfer Requirements   94
Regulatory Capital Treatment of Credit Derivatives in Germany   95
BAKred and the Banking Book   95
Regulatory Capital Treatment of Crdite Derivatives in France   96
Summary   98
Conclusion   99

CHAPTER 4
Analysis of Credit Spreads   101

An Example of a Spread Curve   101
Computation of the Forward Spread   102
Estimation of Volatility   104
Probability of Default, Recovery, Value, and Credit Spreads   105

CHAPTER 5

Revenue-Neutral Diversification   109

Credit Risk Measurement   *109*
Background   *110*
The Trade   *111*
Equivalent Position   *113*

CHAPTER 6

Examination of Term Sheets   115

Put Credit Spread   *115*
Digital Spread Options   *118*
Asset Swap Put Credit Spread   *119*
Zero-Premium Collars   *122*
Combining Credit and Foreign Exchange   *126*
Very Structured Products   *129*
Binary Bonds   *129*
Basket Credit-Linked Notes   *134*
Total Return Swaps   *139*
More Structures Using Credit Derivatives   *141*
    Credit Default Swap Trade   *141*
    Credit Exposure Default Swap   *158*
    One-Year Default Swap   *160*
    Asset Swap Put   *164*
Summary   *166*

CHAPTER 7

Credit Derivatives and the Repo Markets   167

Classic Repo   *167*
Repo vs. a Total Return (TR) Swap   *169*
Similarities   *171*
Balance Sheet Considerations   *172*
Selling Credit Risk   *172*
What is a Credit Derivative?   *173*
Summary   *173*

CHAPTER 8

Collateralized Bond Obligations 175

Introduction 175
CBO and MBS 175
Junk Debt 177
Some History 178
Difficulties 179
CBOs as Complementary Vehicles to Credit Derivatives 179
Financial Engineering 180
Market Size 180
Fees 181
The Junior Tranche 181
    Size of the Junior Tranche 183
    The Sweetener 185
A Sample CBO Deal 185
Credit Rating Agencies 187
Summary 187

CHAPTER 9

Locating the CD Function within a Bank 189

Introduction 189
Requirements 189
Summary 191

CHAPTER 10

Credit Risk Management in Asia 193

Introduction 193
    Dearth of Data 193
    Lower Credit Quality 194
    Loose Disclosure Requirements 194
    Recovery Rates 195
Courts 195
Default Models 195
Illiquidity 196

Bankers Trust   197
Government Intervention   197
Collateralization   197
Speculation   198
Staff   198
How to Deal with These Issues   199
Credit Derivatives   199
Credit Mediation   200
Asia after the Catastrophe   200
Credit Neutral Strategies   202
Credit Derivatives Help the Asian Markets—In Theory   203
Summary   203

CHAPTER 11

CreditMetrics   205

Introduction   205
CreditMetrics   205
Credit Risk vs. Market Risk   207
Skewed Distribution   208
Acceptance   208
The Methodolgy   209
Credit Risk of a Swap   210
Probability of Default, Downgrade, or Upgrade   211
The Value of a Bond   212
A Portfolio   214
Markov Chains   215
Credit Risk or Market Risk?   216
Probability of Default   216
What-If Questions   217
Risk Limits   218
Historical Data   218
Traditional Credit Allocation   219
Advantages of Portfolio Approach   219
Architechture of the System   220
Recovery Values   221
Correlation   222
Summary   223

CHAPTER 12

CreditRisk+ 225

What Are the Risks in Designing the Model? 225
Credit Risk in Loans 226
Default Rate 226
Time Horizon 227
Output of the Model 227
Current Management Practices 227
Model Inputs 228
Default Rates and Correlation 229
Default Events and Default Losses 232
Sector Analysis 233
Use of the Model 233
Economic Capital 234
Credit Provisions 235
Summary 237

CHAPTER 13

Credit Derivatives and Bank Loans 239

Introduction 239
The Role of Credit Derivatives in the Loan Book 239
Improving Returns 240
Using Credit Derivatives for Risk Management 241
Volatility of Defaults in a Loan Book 242
Big Exposures to Single Names 243
Risk Capital 245
Originators of Loans 246
Holder of Loans 247
The Attraction of Loans 248
Opening the Loan Market to Nontraditional Investors 249
Economic Capital Example 1 249
Economic Capital Example 2 251
Regulatory Capital Example 1 252
Regulatory Capital Example 2 253
An Internal Conflict 255
Joint Default 256

The Credit Paradox   *257*
Addressing Credit Line Constraints   *258*
Swap Guarantees   *259*
Relative Value   *260*
Increasing Off-Balance-Sheet Credit Risk   *260*
Cultural Changes within a Bank   *261*

CHAPTER 14
Creation and Analysis of Structured Credit Derivatives   265

Analysis of a Note   *265*
The Creation Process of a Note   *267*
   Conceptual Stage   *267*
   Identification Stage   *269*
   Structuring Stage   *273*

CHAPTER 15
The Valuation of Credit Derivatives   275

Introduction   *275*
   Equity Value Models   *275*
   Spread-Based Models   *276*
   Ratings-Based Models   *277*
The Academic Question   *278*
   Evidence from the Market   *278*

CHAPTER 16
Analysis and Pricing   281

Binary Structure   *281*
   Analysis   *282*
   Motivation   *287*
   Hedging   *288*
A Credit Default Swap   *289*
   Notation and Assumptions   *289*

Analysis   *289*
Moral Hazard   *293*
CBO Creation   *294*
Analysis   *295*
Comparison   *298*
Commission   *298*
A Structured Note   *298*
Analysis   *299*
Chances of Spread Increase   *301*
The Longstaff and Schwartz Model   *302*
Surprising Results   *304*
Back to Our Problem   *305*
Summary   *305*

Glossary   *307*
Index   *309*

Preface

Credit derivatives are generating a lot of interest within the financial community. Simply put, these instruments allow the transfer of credit risk between market participants. There is a distinction between "credit risk" and "market risk." *Market risk* is the risk that the market may move against your position. *Credit risk* is the risk that a counterparty will not pay amounts owed to you due to financial distress. Consider the holder of an over-the-counter call option of a stock. The owner of a call option faces market risk as the underlying stock price may decline and the call will expire out of the money. The owner of the call also faces credit risk. The stock price may go up, so the option expires in the money. At the same time, the writer of the call option may default and not pay the amount due on expiration.

Every market participant accumulates credit risk. An employee of a company gets paid once a month. If the company were to default before the month is over, the employee will not get paid. A merchant ships an item to a client and the client may default before the invoice gets paid. Hence credit is the largest source of risk and it impacts all market participants.

While the concept of credit risk is quite old, instruments for trading this risk are a very recent development. As with any developing field, there are some "growing pains." However, credit derivatives as an asset class can only grow in importance.

This book is a compilation of our "Credit Derivatives" course taught to many delegates all over the world. In the course we tend to emphasize the intuitive understanding of the concepts rather than show formal or cumbersome mathematical proofs. The book follows the same format. Wherever possible, we concentrate on the essence of the products and their implications.

The material in the book comes from many sources.

- Newspaper articles.
- Magazines, such as *Risk Magazine* or *The Economist*.
- Websites, internet discussion groups, and web-based magazines (webzines).
- Private discussions and interviews.

By far the most important sources of information are the delegates that have taken the "Credit Derivatives" course. They come from a variety of backgrounds and disciplines and have different interests and capabilities. All the delegates have one thing in common: the strong desire to understand and develop this asset class and fully comprehend its implications.

I wish to thank Claude Brown of Clifford Chance who has kindly volunteered to write Chapter 3. Claude is a specialist in the legal issues surrounding credit derivatives and has the unique ability to explain complex legal terms to anyone. The people at McGraw-Hill and especially Stephen Isaacs also deserve a big thank you for making this book possible.

ISRAEL NELKEN

Implementing Credit Derivatives

CHAPTER 1

Introduction

CREDIT DERIVATIVES

There are many types of credit derivatives. They are a new way to look at and hedge credit risk. In this book, we look at how financial engineering is used to create many different types of structures. We discuss many different structure types: default swaps, default options, total return swaps, credit link notes, etc. We connect the credit derivatives and the repo trades. An important point is to focus on the design of credit derivatives from the investor's point of view. A financial engineer can design a very beautiful and a very interesting structure with a lot of bells and whistles, but at the end somebody has to buy it. So any type of structure has to answer a need, whether perceived or real. With credit derivatives, one also has to worry about the legal issues, the precise definitions of "default," "cross acceleration," and so on. In this book we also compare the J.P. Morgan CreditMetrics system with CreditRisk+ by Credit Suisse Financial Products (CSFP). We also discuss pricing models of credit derivatives and review several examples, and look at the appropriate use of a pricing model.

The field of financial engineering is exploding. In addition to derivative products in equities, currencies, commodities, or interest rates, we now have derivatives in weather, catastrophe-linked bonds, and so on.

Morgan Stanley, for example, was rumored to be designing volatility and correlation derivatives. For each day that market volatility is above a certain amount, the writer will pay the holder of the volatility option.

The point is that all different kinds of derivatives are appearing on the scene. Until recently, there was no way to unbundle the credit risk from the interest rate risk of a bond, or the credit risk from the interest rate risk of a loan. There was no way to take a view on the interest rate without also taking a view on the credit risk, or, the danger that a borrower would simply fail to meet its interest payment or repay its debt. You bought a bond and you got the total return of that bond, but you were also exposed to the credit risk of that borrower, and there was no way to unbundle them. On the other hand, there was a way to unbundle the market risk of the bond, because if you received fixed income payments on the bond, you could swap them into floating rate payments, for example. But there was no way to unbundle the credit risk of the bond, and that's what we are talking about. How do you unbundle that?

Now, think about the growing market for derivatives on all different kinds of underlying instruments. Some companies have currency exposures, but not all of them. Some have interest rate risks but, again, not all of them. On the other hand, everyone has credit risks.

As you know, we started talking about credit derivatives in the early 1990s. A conference was held in New York, and a few people attended. Each bank sent one or two people, to test the waters, and then the topic died out for a while.

There are many different estimates for the size of this market. We will look at all kinds of estimates and how they are arrived at. It's hard to get precise numbers for the credit derivatives market because:

- They are over-the-counter transactions. Hence, there are no precise numbers reported from an organized exchange.
- Banks may define the same product in different ways. For example, one reports a repo trade while another reports a total return swap, a type of credit derivative.
- The market itself is changing from day to day. New structures are being created, bought, and sold. New players are constantly entering the market, so we are trying to estimate the size of a "moving target."

RELATIONSHIP ISSUES

Banks are in the business of lending money. But many banks have developed specific niches, often because their portfolios of loans are too heavily concentrated in a single geographical region or industry. In such cases, when times are hard for one borrower, the chances are that all of them are suffering, leaving the bank exposed to widespread defaults. So the bank finds itself in a difficult position: The relationships that the bank has successfully built and the niche that it specializes in may hurt it the most.

The bank may wish to offload some of its heavily concentrated loans in the secondary market. This will hurt the relationships the bank has successfully built. Its clients are very sensitive to a developing relationship. Borrowers are not going to be very pleased with the bank selling off their loans.

Assume that you are a banker who has loaned a lot of money to your top corporate client. You are very nervous about whether the client will succeed or not. If you sell off the client's loans, they are going to be very upset with you because you are their top banker, you work together, and you are supposed to be in a solid relationship. In addition, the clients always come to you with their business—equity underwritings, bond issuances, and structured finance deals. You are their main banker and now you are saying, "I like being your main banker, but I don't exactly trust you." That is not a very relationship-enhancing attitude.

Borrowers have resisted the development of a secondary market for bank loans. The market exists, but it is a tiny one and it has to do with troubled loans, usually involving companies that are almost in default. Banks are also not very happy sellers of loans, because selling loans is a relationship issue and causes a potential loss of lucrative advisory work.

THE CREDIT PARADOX

The "relationship versus credit exposure" dilemma is sometimes known as the credit paradox. Assume that you are a bank manager. One of your employees, the relationship manager who deals with your top client, comes to you and says, "Our top client has already borrowed 200 million pounds and now they want to borrow another 100 million. They want another big line and we have to approve it because they're our key client, and they might take the business from us to somewhere else." On the other hand, out comes your credit risk manager who says, "You know, they already borrowed 200 million and now they want another 100 million and if they go under, we are going to have a serious problem." Now, you are the manager. There is a dispute between the relationship manager and the credit risk manager, and it is up to you to resolve it.

Now think of a bank in Tennessee. Its top clients are located in the same place geographically, in Tennessee. They are all exposed to the Tennessee financial climate, they make similar products, and they are exposed to the same political climate, population shifts, and so on. The Tennessee bank ends up being exposed to one particular sector or one particular segment. Of course, that bank would prefer to diversify its risk. How can it do that?

Credit derivatives have the potential of allowing you and the Tennessee bank to download some of the credit risk in a confidential manner. That's the premise of the market instrument. However, as we shall see, it doesn't always work that way in practice.

THE ONE-SIDED NATURE OF THE MARKET

Consider U.S. dollar and Deutsche mark (now Euro) investors. As you know, some of them have exposure in U.S. dollars, others have exposure in Deutsche marks. Some are U.S. companies exporting to Germany and some are German companies exporting to the U.S. Just as there are as many writers of exchange traded call options as there are buyers of them the currency exchange is more or less an even market. The profit and loss line is evenly distributed. For example, if the dollar moves up German exporters are going to make a profit; if the dollar moves down they are going to lose. So there is almost a symmetrical profit and loss effect with spot transactions to a specific underlying currency.

On the other hand, what happens with a loan? There is a high probability of a small gain as you earn the spread, and there is a small probability of a huge loss if the borrower defaults. The theory is that people who are investing want to diversify their risk. What happens in the market in real life is that everybody is happy to lend money until some trouble hits the sector. Recall the situation in the 1990s of the declines in a number of Asian economies. Lending is a much more one-sided type of transaction than other investment decisions. Everybody wants to lend money and then all of a sudden almost everybody becomes nervous or paranoid about the risk. The credit market tends to be one-sided because of the one-sided nature of the distribution: The lenders earn a spread unless a catastrophe occurs.

For example, currently many investors want to buy credit derivatives on the Russian government, but few would sell them; an investor needs to have a very strong risk appetite to sell credit protection on Russia. So there is not an equal number of buyers and sellers. Who would sell you a credit derivative on the Russian government? A Russian bank would sell it to you, because it can earn the premium and if the Russian government goes into default, so does the bank. Credit derivatives have the potential to reduce the concentration in the market, but at times they actually increase concentration in some sense, because the only people who are willing to insure are the people who are highly correlated to the risk they are insuring. It's like my young daughter promising to repay my credit card: If I go bankrupt, she won't have anything to pay the debt with.

THE BASIC STRUCTURE

The mechanics of credit derivatives can be quite complicated but what they achieve is simple enough. If a bank thinks it is overexposed to a big borrower, it can use a credit swap to reduce its risk. Basically, the bank pays a regular fee to its counterparty on the credit swap. If the borrower in question defaults, then the counterparty compensates the banks for the losses. All this can be done without the borrower even knowing about it. A credit derivative works very much like an insurance policy. You keep on paying the premiums and nothing happens until all of a sudden there is a catastrophe—a default—and then the insurer pays you. What do they pay you? They pay you the amount you lost. When you crash your car, an insurer pays the value of the car before the crash minus the remaining value after the crash. In loan terms, the insurer pays the value of the loan before default minus the value after default, or the recovery value. The credit swap market is very similar to the insurance and reinsurance markets. Just as the reinsurance market grew out of the insurance market, after the credit market develops a little more, it's going to grow.

Right now, however, credit is a very one-sided market. Everybody has the same view: If Kmart goes into trouble, everybody wants credit derivatives on the retail sector in the U.S. On the other hand, if everything is fine, then nobody needs them.

THE SEARCH FOR YIELD

The credit derivatives market has grown a lot. We think it is due to the search for yield. As you well know, in the past few years, credit spreads have become razor-thin. In the past you could earn 600 basis points for Italian government bonds over U.S. Treasury bonds; then it became 120 basis points; now the yield enhancement is 60 basis points to flat. The point is that you used to get compensated very much for holding risky debt. Take the BBB sector or BB sector. When credit spreads were such that the compensation for holding these risky assets was very big, you did not have to be too concerned because, even if some defaulted, you were still okay. Now that the margins are much thinner, you really have to discern who exactly each BBB borrower is and what exactly is its probability of default. You must differentiate between different BBB borrowers, not just go blindly and buy their debt.

Currently we are at the intersection of two powerful trends.

- First of all, banks want to be insured that they won't lose because they can't afford to lose. If a bank gets 200 basis points over the relevant risk-free rate, then it can afford to lose some of its loans and still make a profit. If it gets 50 basis points over, it has to be very careful. At 50 basis points, even if one single borrower does not pay, the bank is going to hurt a lot. So banks have to be much more careful about how they lend, and they are ready to insure themselves much more against borrower default.

- On the other hand, investors, especially institutional investors, are searching for yield. They used to invest in BB securities and earn a fat spread and everything was fine. But now credit spreads are razor thin. Where are investors going to find yield? The answer, is in the form of structured finance deals. If the investor can earn a premium for insuring the bank against a default, and the default *does not happen*, then the investor will earn an increased yield.

RISK MEASUREMENT

Banks have developed increasing sophistication in measuring market risk first and credit risk next. There is still a lot more work to be done in this area. Ask the president of a big bank, "What is your exposure to a specific counterparty?" For example, take Credit Suisse. Citibank borrows from Credit Suisse, but Credit Suisse also borrows from Citibank. Is Credit Suisse a client of Citibank, or is Citibank a client of Credit Suisse?

Think of another example, a commercial bank that has multiple branches. It has some retail loans and some small business loans. What is its total exposure to a geographical location? Just collecting the data is an information technology nightmare. Just to put a figure on the exposure to each of its customers is tough. Then it's necessary to also decide whether to off-lay this risk or not, what the diversification effect is, and how something will hurt or not hurt the bank. Credit analysis systems have become a lot more important and have developed a lot, as we shall see.

GLOBALIZATION AND DEMOCRATIZATION

Why have risk management systems developed so much recently? They have developed because of two big trends in the market: globalization and democratization of finance.

By globalization we mean that anyone can invest anywhere. Consider an investor from a town in rural Utah. Fifteen years ago that investor could invest in U.S. stocks or U.S. bonds and not much else. It was very difficult for individuals to invest in overseas companies. Now the investor in Utah connects to the Internet and accesses the latest annual report and quarterly statement of a Japanese company, written in English. Everything is available. The local investor has a much wider range of investment choices. That's what we call globalization of finance. Trade barriers are coming down, and almost everybody can invest everywhere.

Let's look at an example of the democratization of finance. Consider a corporate client and a bank. Fifteen years ago, the relationship manager at the bank would call up the counterparty at the corporation and say, "Here's what the dollar mark did yesterday; let's have lunch." Now if you call a client with that information, the client is going to hang up the phone. The client has exactly the same information you have. The client receives research from the bank, and also gets research from the six other banks in its banking group. The client may even have more information than the bank has. Calling clients and giving them more information probably does not really help them very much. Clients can connect to the Internet and get any stock price or market information from anywhere in the world.

Here's an analogy: Fifteen years ago I was walking in the desert and I had no water. Can someone please give me a drop of water? Can someone please give me market information? Now it's the other way around. Now I am drowning in a sea, like the *Titanic*. Can somebody give me a life jacket? I have so much information, and it's coming at me from every which way. Can somebody please help me with a system for making sense of the information?

Can you help me with a way of analyzing my risks and taking preventive measures? I'm a small company and I'm growing in so many different directions and investing in so many different parts of the world. Can you help me understand my market risk and my credit risk? This is where the banks come in. The system is the value added that a bank can bring, and it can build a relationship on the system. That's why banks are almost giving away risk management systems. That's how they are going to offer something of worth to their clients. Years ago it was the information that used to be the gold mine. Now the information is available to everybody. What the bank can offer is not the information itself, but *how to use* the information. That's why risk management systems are being developed and offered free to the major clients of the bank.

THE POTENTIAL MARKET FOR CREDIT DERIVATIVES

What is the potential market for credit derivatives? Currently the market for credit derivatives is tiny. Whether it's $40 billion or $60 billion, it's tiny compared to the approximately $47 trillion of over-the-counter derivatives that are sold in the market today. It's a tiny drop in the bucket. However, loan portfolios represent the main exposure everybody has to deal with. Not everybody has dollar–mark exposure, but everybody in any business has exposure to credit risk. So credit represents a much bigger source of risk. Literally any business you can think of is exposed to credit risk. A corporation delivers products to a client and the client owes the company money for a month until the invoice is paid. Every company has credit risk all the time. It's the most universal risk factor. So the growth of credit derivatives can be huge. That is what all the banks are hoping for. The market for credit derivatives could outstrip everything else we've seen so far.

Furthermore, the very nature of banking itself will change. You can now lend money without taking on the credit risk of the borrower, so the whole idea of relationship banking or what it means to lend money will radically change from the ground up.

That is already happening with the European Union. A French company does not have to borrow from a French bank. I can borrow from anywhere and I can lend to anyone. So what is the differentiation?

Market Size

In 1995–96 the notional volume of deals outstanding has grown from approximately $5 billion to more than $50 billion, according to Blythe Masters of J.P. Morgan. "It is a very young, innovative market. Everyone is still exploring new opportunities."

In London, the British Bankers' Association's October 1996 "Credit Derivatives Report" estimated that there were $20 billion outstanding CDs. They estimate that the number will grow to $100 billion by the year 2000.

Six banks in a 1998 survey estimated credit derivative volumes in the range of $140 to $325 billion. The brokers' estimates are in the range of $50 to $80 billion. It is estimated that by the year 2000, global volumes will reach $1 to $1.5 trillion. Broker's estimates are lower since many deals are done "directly" between dealer and client. The brokers only see part of the market.

In the U.S., the Office of the Comptroller of the Currency (OCC) reported its official findings for the first three quarters of 1997:

1997Q1	$19 billion
1997Q2	$26 billion
1997Q3	$39 billion

Nineteen of the 475 banks reporting derivatives activity had traded CDs in 97Q3, as compared with five in 97Q2. The size of the market is growing and so is the number of participants. J.P. Morgan had $24 billion on its books in 97Q3; Chase Manhattan and Banker's Trust were runners up with around $4 billion each.

Currently the credit derivatives market is small compared to the global OTC derivative market, but it is expected to grow to something much larger if it develops according to predictions. The reasons we have difficulty in assessing the size of the market are:

- It is a growing market, a "moving target."
- The Bank for International Settlements (BIS) and the International Swaps and Derivatives Association (ISDA) do not collect statistics on the market.

- Banks define credit derivatives differently, so we don't know exactly what to count as a credit derivative. For example, an OCC survey asks the size of your credit derivative deals. You might have one answer to that question on one day, and on another day you might answer in a different fashion. This may be due to the fact that a division of your bank has decided to move credit derivatives from the high-yield desk to the repo desk. So the precise definition of what gets counted as a credit derivative is shifting and changing, especially as banks merge and their internal organization is rearranged time and again.

Growing Pains

The credit derivative market is experiencing what are called "growing pains." Who wants to buy credit protection? As we've said, very few players. You are happy to receive the extra income lending provides and you are comfortable with the risk, until you begin to worry about it. But by that time, everybody else is also worried about it and no one wants to sell the protection.

Another problem with this market is the way deals are priced. There is very little transparency in the pricing. In established markets, you can put your parameters into a Black-Scholes equation and arrive at the price of a call option. Alternatively, you can ask six dealers for the price of the cap and if they all come in within 0.1 basis points, you are quite sure that the price is correct. Credit derivatives have not been turned into commodities and there is very little transparency in their pricing.

In addition, there isn't a liquid secondary market for credit derivatives. Holders of credit derivatives who want to get out in the middle sell them and find that very hard. Who is going to buy it back from you? Maybe the market maker will, but at what price?

This lack of liquidity is a general problem with structured notes. The market makers who sold you the structured note in the first place might buy it back from you. Rather than revealing to you the bid–ask spread, they will buy it from you after the market moves, when they can blame the much lower price on the market movement. That's standard technique. They say, "The market moved from 300 to 298, therefore the price of your structure moved from 100 to 80." Rather than reveal that there is a wide bid–ask spread, they just blame the price on the market move. Because it is a credit derivative and very few people can price it precisely, the dealers can charge hefty spreads.

We also note that regulators have not yet finished working on the issues: regulatory issues, netting and capital adequacy issues, and so on. The ISDA has completed a master document for default swaps.

The Players

The big players in the credit derivatives market are:

J.P. Morgan

Bankers Trust

Chase Manhattan

Credit Suisse Financial Products

Swiss and German banks are entering the market and some U.K. banks are expected to follow. Japanese banks are also entering the market.

A quick and easy way of gaining entry into the market is to hire the chief of an established team, who then brings on the entire team. This is called the "poaching mechanism." In this fashion, a bank can "poach" the entire CD desk of its competitor.

Rationale of the Market

Just as interest rate derivatives were destined for success because they can separate and restructure interest rate risk, credit derivatives serve to separate credit risk from an underlying financial instrument. This virtually guarantees the market's potential success.

Paul Hatory of Dressner Bank says: "The credit derivatives toolkit will revolutionize credit risk management and fundamentally modernize the credit market from the ground up."

Credit derivatives also redefine the relationship between supply and demand for credit. Blythe Masters of J.P. Morgan says: "Traditionally, credit was sourced in the new-issue market and placed with end investors, where it remained irrevocably linked to the asset with which it was originally associated. But now it is possible to unbundle credit risk from loans, bonds, and swaps and place it in a different form into different markets."

Traditionally, what did you do if you wanted to obtain credit? Credit was sourced at the new-issue market. A certain company issued a bond and an investor purchased it. The end investor who held the bond basically ended up holding the credit risk. There was no way to separate one from the other, no way to share the credit risk with somebody else. If you held the bond, you held the entire credit risk yourself. The credit risk remained irrevocably linked to the asset to which it was originally associated. Now, however, "it is possible to unbundle the credit risk from loans, bonds, and swaps and place it in a different form and into different markets."

In Chapter 13 we provide examples of regulatory capital and economic capital that demonstrate that if you add a credit derivative to a loan or a bond, your regulatory capital requirements are reduced by quite a bit. Part of the rationale for the CD market is the effect of CDs on regulatory capital issues.

Buyer and Seller

For the risk manager, CDs offer an important means of stripping out the credit risk from the market risk of an instrument. For the institutional investor, they present a new asset class with potentially very high returns.

For the credit derivative market to develop, we need a culture shift. Credit risk managers traditionally come from an accounting background and are not schooled in derivatives. They may not even know that you can reduce your credit risk by paying somebody. They are used to making yes or no decisions, to saying "Yes, we increase your limit and we approve your loan," or "No, we decline your application and we don't grant you the loan."

Credit risk managers typically assess each creditor individually. They are not used to considering credit at the portfolio level and taking diversification effects into account. They are not used to thinking, "This is an airline, but it is actually good for us to lend to an airline because we have some exposure in the oil industry." That is to say, if oil prices go up, then the airline suffers and the oil company does well; if oil goes down, the oil industry suffers but the airline does well. There is a negative correlation between the fortunes of oil companies and those of airlines. If we lend to both of them, we get a diversification effect. The credit risk manager simply evaluates each creditor on its own merits, evaluating each one by itself without asking what the overall distribution is or what the overall risk factor is.

Consider the value at risk systems being implemented in many companies. Companies never looked at all the issues before. They asked, "Do we hedge or do we not hedge?" The value at risk tool enabled them to ask more questions: What is the risk if we enter this kind of business? Is it worth it? What is the risk-adjusted return for a certain business? A paradigm shift is required to go from a yes-or-no mentality to a probability-weighted mentality. A similar shift is required where credit is concerned. We need to shift from a yes-or-no mentality to a probability-weighted approach.

However, traditionally, loans were held in accrual accounts and so local credit people have been used to measuring risk only at the maturity of the loan. We differentiate here between an accrual account and a mark-to-market account.

In an accrual account, so long as a loan hasn't defaulted, it's okay. In a mark-to-market account, on the other hand, we ask what the value of the loan is. Has it been downgraded? What is the impact of a downgrade? If the loan is in an accrual account, the downgrade doesn't mean anything because so far the client hasn't defaulted. Only when a loan becomes distressed do I require a loss provision for it. Only when the client actually stops paying do I take corrective action.

A BIT OF HISTORY

Credit derivatives arose not from the needs of investors, but from the needs of the investment banks. This is the opposite of how standard options came about. The reason for Deutsche mark–U.S. dollar option is that a company had some exposure and wanted to offset its exposure by buying that option. The motivation for that derivative is the end user.

In contrast, motivation for the development of the credit derivatives market came initially from Wall Street. In the beginning of the 1990s, Wall Street began developing and marketing over-the-counter derivative products. The structured note market mushroomed. Consider that in Hong Kong in 1995, there were 83,325 million derivative contracts traded, 55 times as many derivative contracts as traded in 1990.

The sheer volume of products swamping the markets meant that derivative houses could not rely on traditional methods such as taking collateral, making loss provisions, and actively managing the credit risk exposure. The market just became too large. In addition, many investors took on the market risk of structured notes and they were reluctant to take on credit risks. The dealers had to create subsidiaries in the form of special purpose vehicles (SPVs) to originate the structures. These were bankruptcy remote, AAA-rated SPVs that the dealers created. The SPV marketed the highly structured note. The issuer of the note was someone like a Goldman Sachs special purpose vehicle rated AAA, (e.g. Goldman Sachs Financial Products GSFP) because the investor did not want the credit risk on top of the market risk. The investor took a range floater note and wanted it rated AAA. At the end of the day, Goldman Sachs took the credit risk of whoever was the issuer. They took back-to-back deals, but they took on the credit risk. Because of the sheer volume of deals, investment houses wanted to offload some of the credit risk. That is actually how the CD market started developing.

In 1993 Bankers Trust started offering its clients swaps with a new twist. In return for above-average payments with several hundred basis points over the relevant index, the clients undertook to cover the bank for any losses it might incur from a basket of predetermined creditors going bankrupt. If any of the predetermined creditors went bankrupt, the client promised to reimburse the bank. These were done on Japanese names because when the real estate crisis broke up, Bankers Trust was uncomfortable with these risks. So Bankers Trust had bought protection against these creditors defaulting. This is what is known as a credit swap. At the time, this was a leading-edge structure.

Credit derivatives are a growing area of business in many parts of the world.

CHAPTER 2

The Structures

TYPICAL CREDIT SWAP

Figure 2-1 illustrates a typical credit swap (also known as a default swap).

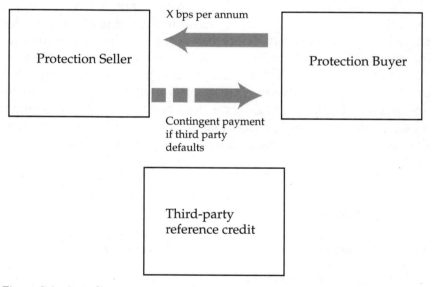

Figure 2-1. A credit swap.

The protection seller receives a periodic fee, say X basis points per year. In return, it makes a contingent payment to the protection buyer in case the third-party reference credit defaults. The precise definition of *default* varies from bank to bank and from trade to trade. It can mean:

- bankruptcy,
- insolvency, or
- failure to meet a payment obligation when due.

More details will be presented in Chapter 3. For now, let's just say that the third-party reference credit defaults. Some credit event occurs and then the protection buyer comes to the protection seller and says, "I lent $100 million, I can only collect $40 million of that, so you have to pay me the remaining $60 million." The contingent payment can be determined only if there is a default; the size of the contingent payment is the notional value of the loan minus the recovery value, or the amount that was actually lost.

Most trades include a materiality clause calling for significant price movements in the reference credit bond. The materiality clause demands that the market treat the credit event as "true." This prevents the swap from triggering unjustifiably if, for example, the reference credit omits a payment with one of its bankers because it disputes the legality of a contract.

A credit swap is similar to an insurance policy that compares the value of the car before the accident to the value of the car after the accident. However, there is a big difference. In the case of auto insurance, the protection buyer must have an insurable interest in the insured property. Not so with a default swap. The protection buyer is not required to own any position whatsoever in the referenced asset. The protection buyer does not actually have to suffer a loss in order to trigger a credit swap. Under an insurance policy, the insured party must suffer a loss to trigger the activation of the policy.

The Premium

The fee earned by the protection seller depends on:

- the maturity of the trade,
- the probability that the creditor will default,
- the credit rating of the swap counterparty,
- the relationship "correlation" between the reference credit and the swap counterparty, and
- the expected recovery value.

How much is the fee? How do we determine whether it is 50 basis points or 80 basis points? Without going into pricing models quite yet, we can mention a few things. The maturity of the trade makes a difference. The longer the term of the insurance, the more expensive the premium for it is. If you are writing a guarantee for two years, you might want to receive X basis points per annum for it. If you guarantee for ten years, a lot more can happen to the reference credit in that time frame, so you would probably want more than X basis points per year.

Another variable is the probability of the reference credit going into default. Is the reference credit rated AAA or rated B? Of course, there is a greater probability of the latter reference credit going into default.

We should also consider the credit rating of the protection provider. If I buy a credit guarantee from a protection provider, the price I will be willing to pay for it depends upon that provider's credit rating. Have I purchased the guarantee from a bankruptcy-remote, AAA-rated entity, or have I purchased a guarantee from a B-rated counterparty? The credit quality of whoever writes the deal also comes into play.

Much more important, however, is the default correlation between the reference credit and the swap counterparty, that is, the connection between them. You are not going to buy a credit guarantee from a protection provider if you know that the protection provider is a subsidiary of the reference credit, for example, if the reference credit is an airline and the protection provider is a subsidiary of that airline, or if the reference credit is an airline and the protection provider is also an airline. In general, it does not make much sense to buy credit default protection from a provider that is likely to default if the reference credit defaults or is exposed to the same types of risks. For example, you wouldn't want to buy credit protection on a Japanese company from a Japanese bank which belongs to the same conglomerate.

The problem is, how can a protection buyer assess the protection seller's exposure to the airline industry, or exposure to Korea? I may think that I am buying a credit derivative from a French bank that's not exposed in Korea. But maybe they are. They may have already written many default swaps on Korea. As these are off balance sheet instruments, how do I know what their exposure in Korea is? How can I measure that in a reasonable way? It's obvious that I am not going to buy a credit derivative on the Korean government from the Korean Development Bank. But if the protection seller is a French bank, how can I determine whether it has a lot of exposure in Korea or a little? The point is that it is difficult to assess the correlation without opening the books of that French bank. You ask what other deals they have on their books and the bank really doesn't want to reveal that. This causes a difficulty for the buyer of CDs.

Correlation

The correlation of default between the reference credit and the protection writer is important from the lender's point of view.

In Figure 2-2, the lender makes a loan of $100 million to the borrower and also takes a default swap from the protection seller. Now, for the lender to really lose that $100 million, two things have to happen: The borrower has to default and the protection seller also has to default. To determine the probability of joint default, we need to know:

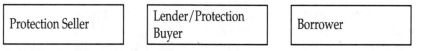

Figure 2-2. A loan with a credit swap.

- the default probability of the lender, and
- the default probability of the protection seller, and
- the correlation of defaults between the lender and the protection seller.

Let's assume, for example, that the lender is rated A and the protection provider is rated BBB. This situation is not as crazy as it might seem. If the lender and the protection buyer are totally uncorrelated with each other, then it might make sense to buy this protection because it will reduce the probability of joint default. If the correlation between them is low enough, the probability of both of them defaulting is substantially less than the probability of only one of them defaulting. Of course, if they are very highly correlated, then purchasing default protection from a low-rated protection provider doesn't help. Thus the correlation between these two is very important.

The problem here is how to measure correlation between defaults. Default is fortunately a rare event. Not everyone defaults all the time. How is the lender going to measure,the correlation between two very rare events? Assume that the borrower has never defaulted yet as a matter of fact, but is an actively running company. First the lender has to figure out the probability of the borrower defaulting, and that's hard enough. But let's assume that the lender can make some assessment of that. Then the lender has to estimate the probability of the protection writer defaulting. Finally, and this is the most complicated question, the lender has to assess the default correlation between the two. If the correlation is very high, then the probability of joint default is higher. If the correlation is very low, then the probability of joint default is also much lower.

The probability of a tube crash in London is very small. The probability of a subway crash in New York is also very small. What is the correlation that they both are going to happen on the same day? Very tiny indeed. But is it really impossible? How do you measure that?

Consider General Motors and Ford. Do they have a positive correlation or a negative correlation of default?

- On one hand, they are both car companies, so if Americans stop buying cars altogether they are both going to default. This seems to indicate a high default correlation.

- On the other hand, if people buy fewer General Motors products, they will tend to buy more Ford products. Some time ago there was a strike at General Motors. Ford sales climbed up dramatically. This would indicate a low default correlation.

What is the real default correlation between General Motors and Ford?

It's true that we can run some numbers on the computer. For example, we can compare the stocks of Ford and General Motors and try to infer the default correlation from the stock prices. But do you have any idea whether the default correlation should be positive or negative? We need an intuitive understanding to check the results generated by the computer.

The problem is further complicated by the fact that we are trying to measure the correlation under the extreme event of default. This is the main difference between physics and finance. Physics is concerned with the average result of the experiment.

What is the average time it takes the space ship to go to the moon? If it is off by a few seconds, it doesn't really matter because the moon is still there. So we are not really concerned with the "outliers," the extreme ends of the distribution. In finance, on the other hand, we are trying to measure what happens in an extreme event because it's at the extreme that we are most exposed to the loss. What happens in a market crash? What happens on a five-standard-deviation move, as occurred in Asia? That happens very rarely. What does that mean? It means that we don't have good statistics to measure that result.

A life insurance company has good statistics, because everyone dies. The default question is much harder, and determining default on a specific issue or a basket of specific issues is even harder.

Without going to models, I had a hard time determining the default correlation between Ford and General Motors on an intuitive basis. We can develop all kinds of theories and models, but how can we ascertain whether the result is correct?

The Contingent Leg

The contingent payment depends on the losses that would actually have been incurred by the protection buyer if it had held the bonds, in the case when the reference credit goes into default. It can be the fall in price of a benchmark floating rate bond a few months after the default event. How much below par did it fall? Credit swaps can be settled either in cash or in delivery of the underlying asset.

Physical settlement involves the protection buyer giving the protection seller the reference asset and receiving par in return. The protection buyer can put the bond at par to the protection seller.

In *cash settlement* the protection seller pays the difference between par and the recovery value of the underlying instrument. Cash settlement typically occurs two or three months after default to give the market time to estimate the recovery value. The term *recovery value* means the amount of the defaulted debt actually recovered.

Recovery Value

When the borrower defaults, is the recovery value 70 cents on the dollar or is it 20 cents? The lower the recovery value, the higher the contingent payment will be. In other words, the credit swap will be more expensive. Consider an airline. If it defaults, the lender has access to all its airplanes. We can sell them somewhere else. On the other hand, if the borrower is a high-tech software company whose only asset is some half-developed C code or C++ code, what is the recovery value there?

Recovery value has to do with the type of industry that you are talking about. That is why there are different curves, like an AA curve for financials and an AA curve for industrials. These two curves are different. The probability of default is the same but the recovery value is different, so the market charges different spreads for them.

When an actual default occurs, no one knows exactly what the recovery value is. A team of accountants goes and checks out the value of the airplanes, how many airplanes are owned, how many are rented, what the lease terms are, how many seats are in each airplane, how many tires are on each airplane, and so on. The accountants count everything and they say, "Based on the assets of the company, here's the recovery value, and here's how much each lender can expect to receive." Also, we have to take into account the type of debt: junior debt, subordinated debt, senior debt, etc. It usually takes two or three months to estimate the recovery value in case of default.

Secrecy Issues

As we mentioned, a credit derivative is an over-the-counter deal that is confidential. A borrower need not know that the lender has taken out a default guarantee. This approach provides a reasonable alternative to loan sale-downs. In some deals, the lender is prohibited from selling the loan in a secondary market. But an over-the-counter derivative is a separate deal that the borrower doesn't even need to know about, so it does not hurt the relationship.

However, there are other interesting secrecy questions. The protection buyer calls the protection seller and says, "The reference hasn't paid the coupon, so be ready to act on your credit swap." The reference credit hasn't officially defaulted yet, nor has the nonpayment been announced in the news yet, but now the protection seller knows. It has its own agenda in mind. It may want to start shorting some of the reference credit's bonds or shares. Is it then acting on inside information, or not? These issues must be addressed by market participants. Is the nonpayment considered inside information? Is the nonpayment a secret that the protection seller is not allowed to use, or is it allowed to pass the information on?

Legal Test and Market Test

In order for a credit swap to be activated, two tests have to be satisfied: a legal test and a market test. The legal test means specific events occuring, such as bankruptcy, insolvency, or failure to meet payment obligations when due.

But now there's a little distinction we have to make. In many instances, a borrower fails to pay a lender for legitimate reasons that have nothing to do with default:

- A delay occurred in the payment due to back-office problems. The coupon is going to be paid within a few days.
- There is a dispute over the legality of the trade. The borrower claims that it does not really owe the indicated amount.
- There are netting agreements in place. A subsidiary of the lender has not paid a subsidiary of the borrower, so they are netting out payments.
- The borrower thinks the trade was a mistake or there was a mistake on the term sheet, and the borrower is contesting part of the trade.

In order to prevent a credit swap from triggering in these instances, the confirmation typically also includes a market test. The market test usually has to do with the value of the bonds of the reference credit. Has the value of its bonds really declined? Has its spread really increased? Assume the spread on the borrower's bond has risen from 80 basis points to 800 basis points. Now the market is saying, "Yes, something is wrong." The borrower might not be able to meet all of its obligations. This is not a failure to pay because the borrower is contesting something; it is an actual failure to pay because the borrower does not have the money. It's a real default rather than a technical reason for not having paid.

Consider the following example. Several years ago the U.S. was very close to announcing a technical default due to the Gramm-Rudman laws. However, people did not immediately fear that their U.S. Treasury bonds would be worthless.

To summarize, there are two types of tests in a credit swap, the legal test and the market test. The market test is designed to prevent a credit swap from kicking in unfairly.

Moral Hazard

Theoretically, employees could buy a default swap on their employer. Consider a trader who takes a very risky bet with the bank's money. If the bet is successful, the trader earns a big bonus. If the bet is miscalculated and the bank defaults, the trader collects on the default swap. In either case the trader wins; there is a moral hazard. Key employees of a company can enter into a default swap and then gamble away the fortunes of the company.

Hedging

Consider a protection seller who has sold a default swap on IBM. If IBM were to default, the protection seller has to make a large payment to the protection buyer. How can the protection seller hedge its risk?

We examine several hedging techniques.

Consider a portfolio with a short position in IBM bonds and a short position in IBM stock. The value of IBM bonds and shares will drop to very low prices if IBM defaults. But since the portfolio is short, it is going to make a lot of money. Such a portfolio may *seem* to be a reasonable hedge. On the other hand, assume that IBM has not defaulted. Then, the value of IBM shares and stocks may simply go up. The short position will thus lose money while the default option's price will be mostly unchanged.

The default products have the characteristics of options. Consider the purchase of an at-the-money put option on the shares of IBM as a hedge. If IBM defaults, the shares will tumble in price, causing an increase in the price of the put. This solution is better, because the put has the characteristics of an option rather than a position in the spot. However, there are still problems with the put option: It is likely that the put option is quite expensive. Also, in the case of a default, the hedging instrument will need to pay out a lot. The put option will not provide an adequate cover.

The reason that the put option is so expensive is that the buyer of the put is paying a lot for protection against small moves in the price. For example, assume that the price of IBM shares drops from $100 (initial price) to $90 due to normal market movements. An at-the-money put would pay out $10. When we price the option, we consider the present value of the expected value of the cash flow. The $10 received in this case is multiplied by a high probability. Hence, low payouts on the put option are multiplied by high probabilities, and the probabilities make a considerable contribution to the price.

Another possibility is to purchase an out-of-the-money put option. Since it is out of the money, it will probably be much cheaper. Suppose one can estimate that in the case of a default, the share price of IBM would move from an initial price of $100 to a price of $50. It is theoretically possible to purchase an out-of-the-money put option that is stuck at $55. Such a put option would be much cheaper than the at-the-money put option. On the other hand, if IBM were to default and the stock move to $50, the out-of-the-money put would pay out only $5. This will not be a sufficient cover.

The difficulty is that the default products are binary events. Even a normal option is not *sharp* enough to hedge them. We consider a digital option. The digital put option pays a certain, predefined amount of money if the stock price at expiration ends below the strike. Theoretically, one can purchase an out-of-the-money digital option struck at $50.01 with a payout large enough to cover the losses due to a default. For example, assume that the recovery rate of IBM is $30. In case of default, the protection seller will have to pay out $70. The protection seller could purchase a digital option that paid out $70 if IBM stock were to end below $50.01. The digital option provides a payout that is binary in nature and is very similar to the risk profile being hedged.

In practice, however, there are several difficulties with an out-of-the-money digital put option. First, they are difficult to purchase in the market. It is rare to find a seller for such an option. Second, this hedging strategy relies strongly on the estimate of $50 as the final share price of IBM in case it defaults.

If IBM defaults and its share price drops to $55 instead of $50, the protection seller will still have to pay out on its obligation but will receive nothing from the digital option. This problem can be alleviated somewhat by purchasing a digital with a strike price *above* the default level. For example, one could purchase a digital put with a strike price of $60. The difference between $50, the assumed default stock price, and $60, the strike price of the option, is taken as a security measure. However, even then it could transpire that IBM defaults and that its stock price ends at $61. In addition the digital put stock struck at $60 is much more expensive than the one struck at $50.

An additional hedging strategy involves the use of "power options." These options have a payout formula that is linked to a power of the price of the underlying security. For example, a square option has a payout linked to S^2 where S is the price of the IBM stock. One could consider a square put option whose payout is $max(X-S^2,0)$.

For example, consider long position in a square put option whose payout is $max(3600-S^2,0)$ coupled with a short position in an option whose payout is a $max(2500-S^2,0)$.

If IBM were to default and its stock were to end at $50, the square option would pay out $3600 – $2500 = $1100.

The protection seller only needs $70, so it purchases a small amount of these options, say $70/$1100 or about 0.0636 of this combination of options for each default put sold.

The advantage of this approach is that in the case IBM defaults and the stock ends at $55, the square options would still have a payout of $36.59:

$$0.0636 * (max(3600-3025.0) - max(2500-3025.0)) = \$36.59$$

In addition, it is slightly easier to purchase and hedge out-of-the-money square options than it is to purchase digital options. The square option can be considered a smooth approximation of the digital.

What if the same default option had been written on a sovereign? The sovereign has no stock, so we cannot use stock options to hedge the exposure. On the other hand, the sovereign typically has a currency. If the country defaults, its currency value drops. Hence, it is possible to hedge default swaps on sovereigns with options on their currencies. Alternatively, hedge with options on the stock index of that country.

DOWNGRADE OPTIONS

There are also structures that pay out in case of a credit rating downgrade by a ratings agency. Some dealers have begun to offer "downgrade options." We have seen a few deals done on credit rating changes, but the protection sellers are nervous about offering them because their models do not handle the calculations. A credit rating may change based on a particular decision taken on a particular day by somebody at the ratings agency. An analyst at Moody's may have a bad day and decide to downgrade a credit rating. This is not subject to a normal or log normal distribution, so downgrades are very difficult to model.

From the point view of the dealers, it is hard for them to sell a derivative product whose underlying instrument is based on someone's arbitrary decision. They can sell a derivative that is based on the market price of a loan, because they can come up with a probability distribution.

Protection buyers, on the other hand, prefer downgrade options. They fear that by the time the reference credit actually defaults, so will the protection seller. This is due to non-trivial default correlation between the two. Purchasing "credit downgrade" options means that there is a higher chance that the protection seller will survive when the option is activated.

CREDIT INTERMEDIATION SWAPS

A credit intermediation swap is basically like a back-to-back deal. As illustrated in Figure 2-3, assume a U.S. investment bank wants to deal with a French company. The U.S. bank does not have the resources to establish the creditworthiness of the French company,

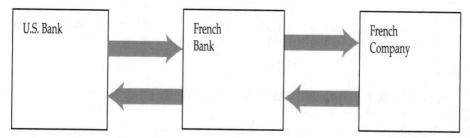

Figure 2-3. A back-to-back transaction.

so it enters into a credit intermediation. The U.S. bank does the deal with a French bank and the French bank in turn does the exact same deal with the French company. So long as the French company keeps performing, the French bank just passes all the payments from it to the U.S. bank and from the U.S. bank to the French company. However, should the French company default, the U.S. bank and the French bank will continue the deal on their own. The U.S. bank is not exposed to the credit risk of the French company. Instead, the U.S. bank is exposed to the credit risk of the French bank.

The U.S. bank may have six French banks that it deals with. These are the banks on its "approved list." It is easier for the U.S. bank to perform credit analysis on these six banks than on the hundreds of French companies it could deal with. The French banks are happy to do the extra legwork involved and perform the due diligence checks on the many different French companies, because they know how to do it. They are very familiar with the French market. The French bank may collect fees for intermediation. From the point of view of the U.S. bank, this structure has several advantages:

- The U.S. bank has to be comfortable only with the French bank, and not with the French company.
- The regulatory capital charge may be much lower for dealing with a French bank than for dealing with a French company.

Credit intermediation is very similar to an AAA-rated counterparty that stands in the middle between two counterparties that are back-to-back. The AAA counterparty might stand in the middle between X and Y. Say that X doesn't want to take on Y's credit risk, and vice versa. However, they both like the deal. They each individually contract with the AAA-rated credit intermediator. The intermediator essentially guarantees both to each other and takes spread fees from both of them.

DEFAULT SUBSTITUTION SWAPS

Figure 2-4 is an illustration of two banks, bank S and bank T, with their respective loan portfolios. Bank S has lent $10 million to a sugar processing plant and is overexposed to it. Bank T has lent $10 million to a tobacco growing company and is overexposed to it. In Figure 2-5 we illustrate a default substitution swap whereby bank T guarantees S against defaults of the sugar plant up to $5 million and bank S guarantees T against a default of the tobacco manufacturer, also up to $5 million. Essentially, they just trade guarantees on the part of each other's exposure, just a crossover. This trade may make sense for both of them. Assume that the sugar plant and tobacco plant have similar probabilities of default but there is low correlation between the two of them. This type of trade helps both banks to diversify their books. Bank T, because of

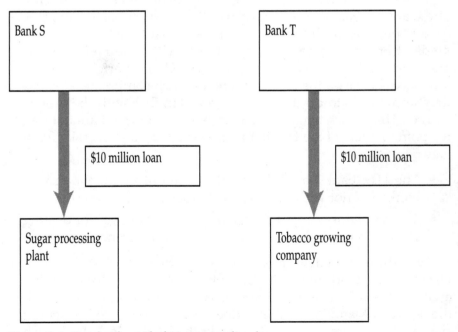

Figure 2-4. Two banks with their outstanding loans.

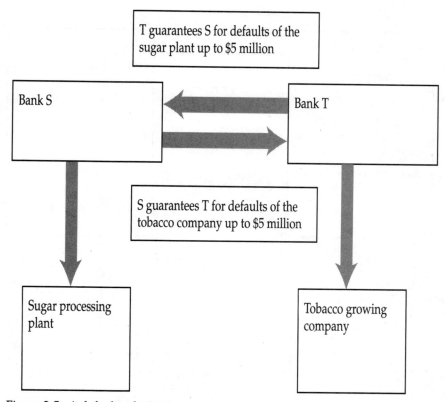

Figure 2-5. A default substitution swap.

its business, is very familiar with the tobacco manufacturer, so it's very easy for T to lend money to the tobacco manufacturer. Yet bank T does not want to be overexposured to one company, so it swaps with S and the diversification reduces both T's and S's exposures.

The default substitution swap involves the two banks writing credit swaps and exchanging them. The outcome of this trade is revenue-neutral diversification.

Total Return Swap

One of the most popular structures is the total return swap, also known as a total rate of return swap or simply TROR. As illustrated in Figure 2-6, one counterparty pays out the total return of an

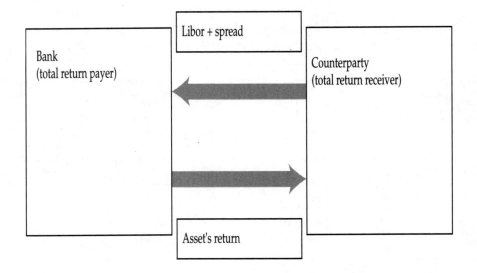

Figure 2-6. A total return swap.

asset, including any interest payment and capital appreciation, and in return receives a regular floating rate payment, such as Libor plus spread. The TROR is settled periodically, for example, every three months.

In a total return swap, the total return payer strips out all of the economic exposure and credit risk of the asset without having to sell it in the open market. In return, the total return payer receives Libor plus spread. The total return receiver, on the other hand, gains economic exposure to the asset without having to buy it in the open market. For example, the total return receiver may be able to get exposure to the underlying asset at a financing rate that will be much lower than the rate at which it can raise funds in the market, especially if the receiver's credit rating is not very high. So the spread the total return receiver pays may be less than the spread at which it can raise funds in the open market.

Consider a commercial bank and a hedge fund. The commercial bank makes a lot of real estate loans. The hedge fund can't make real estate loans. To make these loans, you have to borrow huge amounts of capital, market your services as a loan provider, manage and administer the loans, and deal with the back-office problems. An alternative for the hedge fund is to sort of rent the commercial bank's balance sheet. Rather than buy the loans from the bank, the hedge fund does a total return swap and gains exposure to the loans. There's tremendous growth in credit card backed securities and asset-backed securities. Traders in these assets securitize the loan or credit card payments and pass them on. In a total return swap, on the other hand, you don't buy the loan outright but you receive all the performance of the loan—all the fees and all the returns. Later we will see how, from a regulatory capital and economic capital point of view, these swap structures make sense.

Credit Risk in a TROR

The total return receiver pays Libor plus a spread, and the total return payer pays the total return of an asset. The total return means all the coupons, all the fees and, of course, any capital appreciation in the value of the asset when it is marked to market. This is very similar to an equity swap. With an equity swap you also pay Libor plus a spread and you get the return on the FTSE, for example. The difference between an equity swap and a TROR is that the TROR is not pegged to the return of the FTSE or another index. Instead, it pays the return of a specific reference asset, a specific bond, or a specific book of loans.

Consider an interest rate swap. The credit exposure for the interest rate swap is not very high. You basically exchange fixed for floating. You may give your counterparty Libor and it gives you 6%. If Libor is 5.50%, you receive 50 bps times the notional

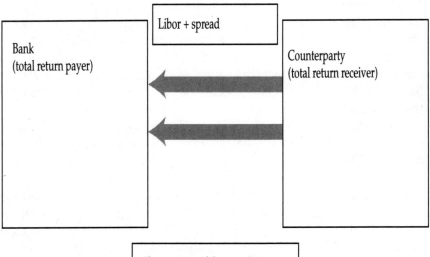

Figure 2-7. A total return swap, reference asset declines. There is a negative total return.

amount accrued for three months. If Libor is 6.50%, you owe 50 bps adjusted to the notional amount and accrued for three months. The amounts are netted out and the payments, in general, are not too big. Now, consider an equity swap. You pay your counterparty Libor and it gives you the return on FTSE. What if the FTSE declines during that three-month period? The total return on the FTSE is negative. Then the payment stream goes the other way. If the FTSE declines, not only do you have to pay Libor, you also have to pay the decline in the FTSE. That's an equity swap.

The same thing happens in a TROR. If the value of the loan declines, then both payments are directed to the same counterparty; see Figure 2-7. The total return of an asset might be negative. Why is this important? If you look at an interest rate swap, the exposure that the bank has to the client is not very great because the payments are netted out.

In a TROR, when the return on the reference asset is negative, two payments are due from the total return receiver:

1. An interest payment: Libor + spread.
2. A payment based on the decline in the reference asset.

If the reference asset has a negative return, the exposure is not only not netted out, it is doubled. In Figure 2-7, both arrows go the same way.

An interest rate swap and a TROR (or an equity swap) are quite different in terms of credit exposure. In the interest rate swap, payments are always netted out. In a TROR, not only are the payments not netted out, they could be doubled. They are both called swaps but they have quite different credit risk exposures from the point of view of the total return payer. If the underlying asset declines, the total return payer could be owed substantial sums of money.

Maturity

In practice, the maturity of the total swap rarely matches the maturity of the underlying asset. For example, one could do a TROR of two years on a thirty-year bond. In this fashion the total return receiver can receive the total exposure to that thirty-year bond but only has to finance its position for two years. Suppose an investor wants to buy a two-year bond from company X but company X only issues thirty-year bonds. A TROR could be an attractive vehicle in this instance.

The total return payer, on the other hand, gets rid of its entire exposure to the bond for the first two years including capital risk, interest rate risk and so on. The entire bond will be marked to market to determine the total return on that asset. Thus the total return payer does not have to sell its thirty-year bond and then buy it back again to realize the same market return.

Alternatively, the payer may not want to have any exposure to the bond during years 6 to 10, but would like the exposure to remain during the first 5 years and during years 11 to 30. The TROR can be structured to accommodate this need.

To summarize, the total return payer negotiates protection for a limited amount of time without having to liquidate the asset.

The receiver finances short and invests long:

- The total return receiver finances for two years (the duration of the swap).
- But it receives a total return tied to the performance of a thir-ty-year bond.

Exposure to a Credit Desired

Suppose a client wants six months of exposure to a long-term bond. Some alternatives open to that client are:

1. Buy the bond and sell in six months.
2. Buy a call and sell a put on the underlying.
3. Do a total return swap.

Alternatives 1 and 2 involve a combination of two trades. The client has to buy something and also sell something. Both involve two bid–ask spreads because each is two deals. Alternative 3, the TROR, involves only a single deal so it's two trades versus one trade. It's easier to manage the one trade. The client gets charged a bid–ask spread only once. And the client is not exposed to the vagueness of the market as to whether it can actually sell the bond later on.

Credit Spread Options

Credit spreads are options whose payout is tied to the spread between a risky bond and a risk-free government bond. The risky bond could be issued by a corporation, a state, or a province.

Consider a Canadian investor just before the famous Quebec referendum. In that referendum Quebec was to decide whether it would separate from Canada. The Canadian investor believes that if Quebec separates from Canada, spreads between the Quebec government bond and the Canadian government bond will widen by a lot. In this case, the investor would like to take a view on the spread between the ten-year Quebec bond and the benchmark ten-year Government of Canada (GoC) bond. Some possible strategies for our investor are:

- Go short one bond and long the other. This approach may result in a huge loss if the investor turns out to be wrong.

- Buy a put option on the Quebec bond. If the spread widens as predicted, the price of the Quebec bond will decline and the put will be in the money. But by purchasing a put, the investor is also taking a position on Canadian rates. Canadian rates could fall more than the spreads widen, which will result in a more expensive Quebec bond. Therefore, buying a put on the Quebec bond does not precisely focus on the investor's view.

- Purchase a spread option. The payout of such an option may be stated as follows: On expiration date the investor receives $K*Max(S-X,0)$ where S is the spread in basis points between the ten-year Quebec bond and the ten-year GoC bond, X is the stirke and K is a multiplication factor to translate the spread into dollars. For example, the option will pay based on what the credit spread is going to be in one year. If it's more than 50 basis points (the strike), then every basis point is worth $5,000 and that's what the option is going to pay.

Consider that if the European Union goes as planned, then Italian government bond yields and German government bond yields are likely to converge. If the European Union does not go as planned, spreads will widen right out. In this case we want to take a view not on interest rates, but on the spread between them. We are considering the spread between one index and another, in this case, one country's bond versus another's. We could also consider the spread between a risk-free asset and a risky asset.

There is much talk about the potential of spread options, but not much trading in them yet. It's a slow-growing market. It is tough to write such options because it is tough to hedge them. While the government bond might be liquid, the risky provincial bond is probably not as liquid. Think of the option writer's position: It has to hedge the risky debt by going short some of the risky bonds. These may not be so easy to borrow. For example, the borrowing rates on these bonds could be very high. Alternatively, the hedger could go short some of the risky issuer's stock (if it's a corporation), but then it runs into basis risks.

Another difficulty is that when spreads widen, they tend to widen by a lot. If the corporation gets into serious financial trouble, its spreads would widen right out. The option writer faces a nontrivial probability of having to pay huge sums on expiration. This is very different from a traditional option. Consider an option on an exchange rate, say the U.S. dollar versus the German mark. If the dealer sells a call option that is currently at the money, it might end in the money or out of the money. At worst, the option will end slightly in the money and the trader will have to make a small payout. It is highly unlikely that the option will expire deep in the money. On the other hand, when a dealer writes a credit spread option and there is a default, the payout will be quite large. If the option ends in the money, it will probably end up being deep in the money. It's a default and it's not as if the price of your bond is going to move from 100 to 99.50, which could occur in an interest rate option. The market just moved a little bit, so the bond ended slightly in the money, or the Deutsche mark–U.S. dollar exchange rate moved a few points, so the option is slightly in the money. The credit spread option is very unlikely to be only slightly in the money. So dealers perceive that spread options provide small premiums in comparison with the risks they involve.

An Example of a Credit Spread Put

At time T0, an investor sells a credit spread put on the ABC bond (see also Exhibit 6-1). The put expires one year after the settlement date, and the bond itself matures on a much later date.

Put credit spread on ABC bonds due December 31, 2023
Spread put buyer: Bank
Spread put seller: Investor

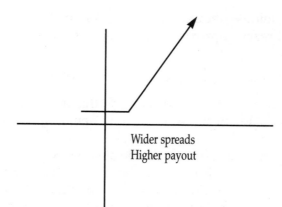

Wider spreads
Higher payout

Figure 2-8.

Notional principal amount: $10 million

Settlement date: Today

Exercise date: One year from today

Underlying index: ABC bonds due Dec. 31, 2023

Reference U.S. Treasury: The offer yield of the U.S. Treasury 6.25% due August 2023

Index credit spread: The yield to maturity of the underlying index using the Flat Bid Price (bid price net of accrued interest and any nonpaid coupons) of the underlying index minus the offer yield of the reference U.S. Treasury at 12:00 PM New York EST two days before the exercise date.

Current spread: 1.95%

Spread put strike: 2.05% (at the money forward strike)

Put option payment: *Notional * max (DUR*(Index Credit Spread–2.05%),0)*

DUR (duration): 8

Option premium: 1.25% of the notional principal amount payable by the bank to the investor on the settlement date

The payout diagram of this option is illustrated in Figure 2-8.

This looks very much like the payout diagram of a call option, yet it is a credit spread put option. The option allows the bank to put the bond to the investor at a yield of 250 bps above the relevant Treasury.

Note the use of the duration (DUR) term in the confirmation sheet. Duration typically measures how bond prices react to changes in yield. Without considering convexity, if yields change, bond prices react approximately according to the following formula:

Change in price = Change in yield * Duration * Original Price

The bank's purpose in purchasing this note is to be protected in case the spreads of the ABC bond widen. If spreads widen, the change in the price of the bond will be approximately proportional to the duration of the bond. To be absolutely precise, we would have to consider the duration at the time of the expiration of the option. However, duration is also a function of interest rates. Because the purpose of this option is to protect against a change in spreads, the confirmation includes an approximate duration number that is fixed at the initiation of the option.

Note the interesting use of bid and offer prices on the term sheet. It uses the bid price method for the index and the offer price method for the U.S. Treasury.

- The offer price is higher than the bid price. Therefore, the offer yield is low.
- On the other hand, because the bid price is low, the bid yield is high.

When we subtract

(the bid yield of the underlying index)
minus
(the offer yield of the reference U.S. treasury)

we obtain a high value for the index credit spread. This increases the potential payout at expiration from the investor to the bank.

Credit Spread Forwards

By combining a call option and a put option, we obtain a credit spread forward. This is similar to a normal forward, except that the underlying is the spread. For example, at time T0, an investor contracts to purchase a floating rate bond at a price of $100 on a later date, say T1. The bond itself matures on an even later date, T2.

```
T0----------------------------- T1 -----------------------------------------------T2
Transaction              Forward date              Bond matures
```

Obviously, a forward on a floating rate bond is a credit spread deal. If the credit spread of the issuer improves, the bond will increase in price to above par and the forward deal will show a profit. Alternatively, if the issuer's credit spread declines, the price of the bond will decline, for example to $95, but the investor will still have to purchase it for par. Note that since the bond itself has a floating rate coupon, the investor is not taking a view on interest rates.

Forward deals of this type can also be done on fixed rate bonds. Assume that the investor contracts to purchase a fixed rate bond at a price of $100 on T1. The main exposure in this deal is to interest rates. If interest rates decline, the price of the bond is likely to increase and the forward deal will show a profit.

To isolate the credit component, the investor transacts to purchase the reference fixed rate bond at a certain spread over U.S. Treasuries. For example, on January 15, 1999 the investor transacts to purchase the XYZ ten-year bond on January 15, 2000 at a spread of 80 bps to the U.S. ten-year Treasury bond. This is the yield at which the investor will buy the XYZ bond. On June 15, 2000 the parties to the transaction will examine the yield on the benchmark U.S. Treasury ten-year bond. They will add 80 bps to the Treasury yield to get the corporate yield. They then convert the yield to a corresponding price, and that is the price at which the investor will purchase the bond.

Usually, forward deals are cash settled. On date T1, at expiration of the forward, the seller of the forward would pay the buyer:

$$\text{(Spread in forward agreement − Spread on date T1)} * \text{Duration} * \text{Notional}$$

If this amount is negative, the buyer pays the seller.

In our example, if the corporate spread of the XYZ bond tightens to 60 bps over U.S. Treasuries, and its duration is 6.5, then the seller of the forward must pay the buyer:

$$(0.80 − 0.60) * 6.5 * \$10,000,000 = \$13,000,000$$

What happens if the XYZ company, the issuer of the bond, actually defaults between January 15, 1999 and January 15, 2000? For example, on June 1, 1999 the issuer defaults.

If the issuer defaults before the closing date of the forward deal, there is no credit spread forward because the bond is gone. The deal is simply cancelled out. Thus the default risk of the reference bond is borne by the seller of the forward.

On the other hand, if the issuer has not defaulted but has simply been downgraded, the original agreement holds. By January 15, 2000 the yield is at U.S. Treasuries plus 200 bps. The investor still has to buy at U.S. Treasuries plus 80 bps. So the default risk is borne by the seller, but the downgrade risk is borne by the buyer.

In the period between T0 and T1, default risk is borne by the seller of the forward. In the period between T1 and T2, the risk is borne by the purchaser.

This could lead to a bizarre situation. A buyer of a forward on a bond with deteriorating quality could actually want the issuer to default.

Volatility

Typically, the volatility of credit spreads is tremendously high. A client starting to get into this business is typically used to quotes on the volatility of interest rates. Interest rate volatility might be in the area of 5 to 15%. Equity volatility may be higher, at 30 to 60%. In comparison, credit spread volatility may be in the range of 80 to 200%.

Clients who hear such volatility quotes may get nervous. The reason volatility is very high is that the credit spreads themselves are tiny. They are measured in basis points. Remember that volatility is the change divided by the actual price. If the actual prices are small, every tiny movement results in high volatility numbers.

Consider the volatility of interest rates in Japan. The volatility of interest rates there may be in the range of 80 to 120%. Volatility is high because the interest rates are so low. Every tiny movement is a big change on a proportional basis, and results in high volatility numbers.

The same is true of spreads. When there is movement of 10 basis points, we are not measuring the volatility of interest rates in the U.S. where rates are about 5% or 500 basis points. We are measuring the change with comparison the credit spreads, which may be 50 basis points. The resulting volatility will be much higher. For example, on one day in 1994, one could have measured the volatility of the RJR bond 8.30% of 1999. The yield volatility was 22% and the credit spread volatility was 48%.

STANDARDIZATION

It is quite difficult to standardize a credit derivative. For example, we may be able to agree on a price but we have not decided what exactly constitutes a default. Is it insolvency, bankruptcy, or merely a failure to pay? What type of market test do we want? Do spreads have to rise above 200 bps or above 300 bps? Maybe we have not agreed on the precise term. Each deal is different. In particular, each deal is structured on a specific underlying credit or a basket of credits. A credit derivative based on company X is a totally different deal from the same derivative based on company Y.

Compare this situation with interest rate options. They are usually quoted on the Libor rate, which is the standard. The interest rate derivatives sales team says: "Almost everybody needs a Libor cap at 6%. Let's call all our clients and sell as many as we can." The downside of this is that the interest rate cap has become a commodity. Price competition is quite severe. In the U.S., interest rate cap deals are won or lost based on 0.1 bps price differences. In London, the price differences are somewhat higher, at 0.25 bps. Even if you make a sale, how much money have you earned? A similar situation exists with equity options that are created on a standard index such as the S&P or the FTSE.

Lee Wakeman of CIBC said: "The trouble with credit is that it is extremely name-specific; there's very little homogeneity out there."

"Credit swaps are highly structured deals tailored to specific end-user requirements," said Blythe Masters of J.P. Morgan.

With credit, each client has a very specific exposure. There is very little standardization. Each credit swap is designed for a particular investor's needs. The banks like this situation because they hope that credit derivatives will not become commodity instruments on which banks will have to compete on differences of 0.1 basis points. It's the hope of the banks that products will remain specially structured and expensively priced.

Banks are trying to apply a set of principles and create a large variety of structures that fit their clients' needs. It's almost a Lego™ block approach: Banks use the same principles, over and over to create different structures.

SPECIAL REQUESTS

Here are two examples of special requests that have been made. These examples illustrate the specialization and individualization of credit derivative structures.

One provider was asked to supply credit protection against a large U.K. bank for a 25-year term, but the protection kicked in year 16 and then decreased each year. For 16 years the client didn't need any protection; in year 16 they needed large protection, in year 17 a little less, in year 18 less, and so on. This is a very unusual type of credit derivative. We may assume that the investor had exposure to the U.K. bank with zero coupon bonds or bonds that have been stripped that mature in years 16 onward. Thus the client had declining exposure.

An Eastern European bank is rumored to have used a total return swap to unwind an exposure to its domestic equity market. The Eastern European bank owns 25% of the domestic equity market and is too much exposed to that market. The bank can't sell its stocks in the open market because its exposure is so large. If it tried to dump 25% of the equity market, prices would crash. The bank wanted to do a total return swap. Now, think of the position of the hedger. Somebody already owns 25% of that equity market. How are you going to hedge 25% notional of the total underlying market? It's not as if you have to hedge a tiny amount in a very liquid market. The entire market is not very liquid and somebody already owns a quarter of it. For the hedger to try to hedge in this situation is not a simple task by any means.

USE OF TOTAL RETURN SWAPS
BY CORPORATIONS

Assume that you manage the United Airlines Pilot Retirement Fund. Because you manage that fund, you have a lot of United Airlines stocks and bonds in the fund, maybe a bit too much for your liking. If you sell these United Airlines bonds—in effect, the pilots sell their own company's bond—that doesn't look very good from a political point of view. Alternatively, the fund can use a total return swap to offload some of the risk in the market. That's reasonable. It does not have to be well publicized because it is an off-balance-sheet instrument.

A corporate treasurer can use a total return swap. Let's assume that the corporation has a lot of cash and it wants to buy its own bonds back. The government and the regulators are very much against corporations buying their own bonds back, especially when interest rates are high and the bonds are cheap. Depending upon the tax restrictions and amounts that are purchased back at a premium or discount, there could be very expensive tax consequences for that transaction. Rather than purchase the bonds directly, the corporation can enter into a total return swap.

"The capital structure of many U.S. corporations is extremely complicated," says Phillip Borg, global head of Credit Derivatives at Bankers Trust in New York. "It is not uncommon for one level of debt within the structure to trade extremely cheap or dear relative to others. Using credit derivatives, the corporation can arbitrage out the pricing anomaly or retire the debt altogether."

CREDIT-LINKED NOTES

We've already mentioned that in a total return swap, the total return payer (typically the dealer) takes on a huge credit risk. If the reference asset declines, the total return receiver owes two payments. One payment is *Libor + the spread* and the other payment is based on the decline in the index. Should the total return receiver (the client) default now, the total return payer (the bank) will lose a lot of money. The total return swap is not a suitable product for the retail market. The bank does not want to have to "chase" counterparties down to claim their debts.

A credit-linked note (CLN) overcomes this problem. With a credit-linked note the bank avoids the credit exposure altogether.

Consider the whole class of institutional investors that are forbidden by their mandate to buy derivatives. If they buy a bond or a note, that's fine. In the early 1990s an entire structured note market was developed to cater to those clients. The client purchased a note or a bond that paid a coupon and had principal. The coupon and maybe the principal payments were tied to some underlying market price or event.

It is possible to create a structured note on top of a credit derivative. Typically the investor receives a coupon and principal redemption at maturity, unless there is a credit event. In the case of

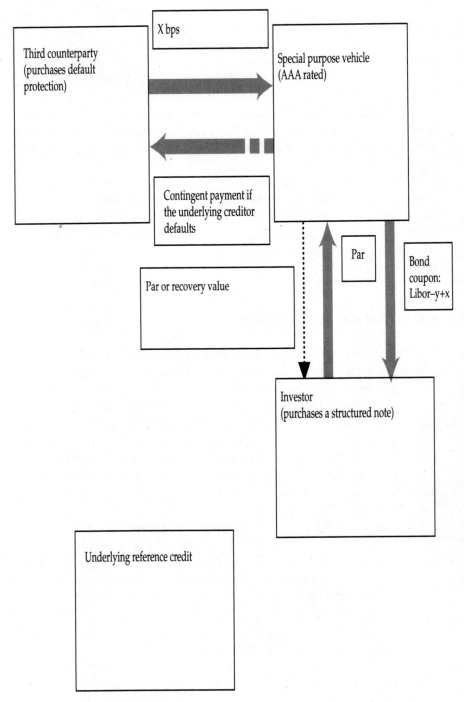

Figure 2-9. A credit-linked note.

a credit event, the investor might forfeit the coupon and possibly the principal.

In Figure 2-9, the issuer sets up an AAA-rated, bankruptcy remote vehicle. The vehicle sells a credit swap to a third counterparty. The third counterparty is, in fact, a protection buyer who pays a premium of X basis points per annum in return for the protection.

On the horizontal axis of the figure we have a normal credit swap.

The investor purchases a structured note for $100 (par). The note pays a large coupon so long as no credit event occurs. The coupon is set at Libor–y+x. This is compared to a normal floating rate bond issued by an AAA-rated SPV. Such a bond might pay Libor–y basis points (e.g. Libor–10 bps). The coupon of Libor–y+x is enhanced, so it's a very nice coupon to receive.

The investor receives the coupon until the bond matures, and then the investor gets back par. This is a normal bond with an enhanced coupon unless a credit event occurs. If a credit event occurs, the special purpose vehicle has to pay a contingent payment to the protection buyer. The contingent payment may be 100 minus the recovery value of the reference asset. In addition, as soon as a credit event occurs, the SPV will stop paying the investor coupons on the bond and will return to the investor an amount equal to par minus the contingent payment. Thus the SPV will pay the investor an amount equal to the recovery value of the reference asset.

Consider this from the point of view of an SPV.

- At maturity of the bond, if no default occurred, the SPV pays back par to the investor.

- If a default occurred during the life of the bond, then the SPV pays a contingent payment to the protection buyer, and par minus the contingent payment to the investor.

In either case, the SPV has paid back par.

Look at the example in Figure 2-10. Suppose there is a default in the underlying reference credit and the recovery value is 75. So, the SPV will pay 25 to the protection buyer and 75 to the investor.

How do we determine the coupon on the credit-linked note? Libor–y+x? Libor–y is just the financing rate of the AAA-rated vehicle. Assume that the SPV can finance at Libor–10 bps. Then we

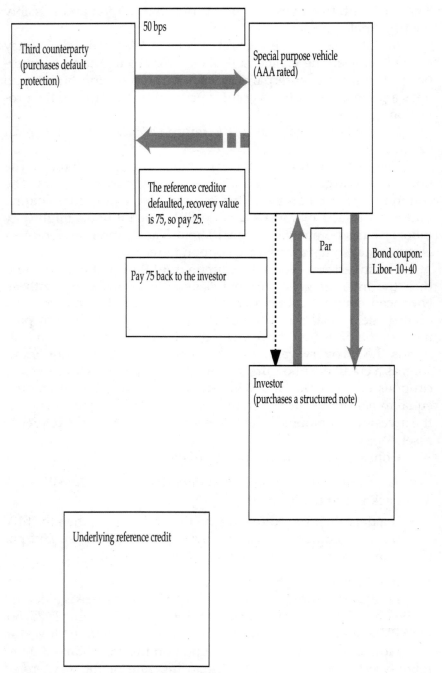

Figure 2-10. An example of a structured note.

take the X basis points that the SPV receives in lieu of the default swap. Assume that they sold it for 50 basis points per annum ($X=50$). The SPV can pay Libor–10+40 ($x=40$) and keep the 10 bps. The special purpose vehicle keeps a little bit of a spread in between. The "big" X received by the SPV doesn't have to be the same as the "small" x paid out, but they are somehow related.

Notice that the SPV doesn't have the credit risk of the investor, because the investor already paid the SPV $100 to begin with. Even if the reference creditor defaults, the SPV will simply pay the investor less than $100.

Banks don't like to purchase credit swaps from retail investors. The retail investor might pay or might not pay. The bank will have to start running after the retail investors, and the bank does not want to do that. In a credit-linked note, the bank will simply pay them less than $100. The bank is already done. The bank did not have to take on the credit risk of the investor because the investor has already paid the $100. The bank already owns it. So we can understand why this structure came into being. If there is a default the investor compensates the bank by receiving less than par.

Now consider the underlying reference credit. It just floats there in hyperspace. The reference credit doesn't even have to know that this whole structure has ever been created.

The Investor in a CLN

Consider the investor in a credit-linked note. The investor might be an investment management fund. According to the indenture of the fund, it may only be allowed to purchase AAA-rated bonds. The fund is allowed to purchase a CLN because the issuer is an AAA-rated SPV. If all goes well and the reference credit does not default, the fund will have earned a high coupon (Libor+x–y) as opposed to Libor–y which it could have earned by purchasing a straight bond.

An important distinction has to be made for structured notes in general that also applies to CLNs in particular. The AAA rating given to the issuer does not mean that the investor will receive the coupon and the principal. The AAA rating refers to the issuer's "ability to pay," not to its "obligation to pay." With structured notes, the investor was exposed to various market risks.

With a CLN the investor, in fact, is taking the default risk of the reference credit which, on its own, could be rated much lower than AAA. The investor may even be prohibited from buying the reference bond directly if it is of poor credit quality.

Another possible investor in a CLN is an investor who wants to buy exposure to the reference creditor. Assume that the reference issuer only issues a thirty-year bond but the investor wants to buy a five-year bond. With the CLN, the investor can buy something that resembles a five-year note. There are also regulatory capital considerations here. There are different capital requirements for five-year bonds as opposed to thirty-year bonds. The investor has to finance a bond for five years, which may be much easier than financing for thirty years.

In addition, maybe the investor is a fund. The indenture of the fund says it is not allowed to buy thirty-year instruments. The fund may only buy five-year instruments. With a CLN, it can buy a five-year instrument with an enhanced coupon.

The credit-linked note market is one of the fastest growing areas in credit derivatives.

The J.P. Morgan—Wal-Mart CLNs

Toward the end of 1996, J.P. Morgan issued two credit-linked notes worth more than $1 billion. The first of the two was issued in September, a $594 million ten-year note tied to Wal-Mart, the AA-rated U.S. retailer. Another deal of a similar size was transacted on December 18, 1996 on a second reference credit.

The Wal-Mart note was originally priced at 65 bps over comparable U.S. Treasuries. A comparable Wal-Mart note was trading at 40 to 45 bps over the U.S. Treasuries.

It is easy to find clients to purchase a credit-linked note. Consider the clients. They may buy the Wal-Mart bond at 45 bps over Treasuries or the CLN at 65 over. The CLN is cheaper. The main risk with the CLN is illiquidity risk. An investor can always sell a Wal-Mart bond because there is an active secondary market in corporate bonds. The CLN is much more difficult to sell in the secondary market. However, for clients who are planning to "buy and hold" and are not concerned with liquidity, the CLN may be an attractive alternative.

What may be more difficult is to find a counterparty who is willing to pay for credit protection, a protection buyer. At the time,

J.P. Morgan did not reveal its motives for arranging the deal. It may have wanted to reduce its own exposure to Wal-Mart. Alternatively, J.P. Morgan may have been approached by Wall Street banks wanting to reduce their exposure to Wal-Mart.

The deal includes a market test. Wal-Mart spreads, which were about 40 to 45 bps at the time of issue, must widen to at least 150 bps above the U.S. Treasury in order for a credit event to be announced. If Wal-Mart doesn't make a payment of one of its coupons because of a dispute, that does not constitute a credit event. The market is not going to widen out like that. But if Wal-Mart is in trouble, then the spread will widen. There is also an elaborate discovery mechanism for determining the recovery value in case of a default. J.P. Morgan will conduct a poll of five leading market makers every two weeks for three months to find the price of the defaulted debt.

In case of default, investors have two options:

- They can go for an early redemption based on a poll conducted immediately after default.
- They can wait for a later redemption based on the true recovery value of Wal-Mart's debt.

If no such value becomes apparent, J.P. Morgan will conduct another poll after an 18-month cooling down period

We can see that when the credit option expires, it's different from a U.S. dollar–Deutsche mark foreign exchange option. When the foreign exchange option expires, we know what the fixing rate is exactly. With the CLN, it could take quite a while to figure out the fixing rate.

In case of default, investors can ask for their money now or they can wait. It's up to the investors. The investors will only wait for the 18-month cooling down period if they think the recovery value they are being offered is too low and their expectation of the recovery value is much higher.

Sovereign

In which currency are credit spread options settled? As much business is written against sovereign debt as it is against corporate names.

In the mid 1990s many plays were done on the high-yielding Italian sovereign paper (BTPs). The Italians had antiquated tax laws. The BTPs traded at a deep discount over other OECD sovereign papers. It was a perfect credit arbitrage:

1. You bought a BTP.
2. You added a default swap to create an AAA-rated vehicle.
3. You swapped that vehicle into floating rate Italian lira paper.
4. Then, you swapped into U.S. Libor via a currency swap.

Investors in such structures were able to earn Libor+25 to Libor+30 bps on AAA-rated U.S. dollar. But the real money was in selling the credit protection. The insurer would write insurance that kicked in only if the reference credit traded below 50 cents on the dollar after default. The added value came from the fact that these structures were settled in Italian lira.

If the Italian government were to default, the Italian lira would also become much cheaper. From the point of view of the insurers, they received the premium in expensive lira. If they had to pay out, they would pay out in cheap lira. So the insurance writers hedged themselves pretty cheaply.

Today, most structures are payable in U.S. dollars or Euros.

CONVERTIBILITY RISK PRODUCTS

Several financial products are concerned with the feasibility of transferring money received in the local currency of a particular country to the outside world. They are known as convertibility risk products.

Consider a corporation doing business in Indonesia. All it wants is to be able to take its money out of Indonesia. The corporation is worried about possible changes in the law that governs the exchange of local currency to U.S. dollars and then transferring the U.S. dollars out of the country.

Some dealers offer protection against this type of risk. The risk can be broken down even further into its components:

- Can one move Indonesian currency from one account to another?
- Can one convert from Indonesian rupia into U.S. dollars?
- Can one take USD out of the country (expatriation risk)?

Protection can be sold to different clients who have differing needs. For example, if a client has liabilities to settle within the country, it does not have to purchase protection against expatriation risk.

Some dealers define the convertibility structures as foreign exchange rate options; others define them as credit derivatives.

At the beginning of 1998, investors had a strong appetite for exposure to the Russian ruble. At that time the Toyota Motor Credit Corporation (TMCC), rated AAA issued a $50 million ruble-linked bond. To create it, TMCC had to work around a few issues:

1. The risk that at redemption date, the ruble would not be freely convertible for political or other reasons.
2. The impossibility of clearing a ruble-denominated issue through either of the major Eurobond clearers, Euroclear and Cedel.
3. The difficulty of finding a counterparty who would be willing to swap the coupons into Libor, which TMCC required.

The result was a zero coupon note, structured by Merrill Lynch, that matured in 1999. The issue price was 75.55% of par. At maturity, payment will be based on the product of the principal amount and the percentage change in the dollar–ruble exchange rate between the issue and the maturity of the note.

To address the convertibility issue, TMCC added a two-year window after the note matures. The investor can still get paid if the ruble becomes convertible during that window. The maturity date was deliberately set to 1999 so as to avoid the political risk from Russian elections expected to take place after that date. The swap part of the transaction was made more appealing by capping the potential payout of the note to an exchange rate of 100 rubles to the U.S. dollar. Jean Liao of TMCC said the structure resulted in sub-Libor funding and access to a new investor base.

AN EXAMPLE OF A TRADE

In February 1998, Global Finance reported on the following trade: CIBC had secured a comandate with Ceskoslvenska Obchodni Banka (CSOB) to arrange a $500 million loan to Czech state-owned aircraft manufacturer Aero Vodochody for the design and manufacture of a government commissioned training plane for fighter pilots. However, before the government approval process was completed, the company had to make payment on supply contracts with Boeing and AlliedSignal. CIBC agreed to provide Aero Vodochody with a $100 million bridge loan to make the payments "if we could reduce our risk by 50%," said Shaun Rai, managing director of financial products at CIBC World Markets in New York.

The usual approach would have been a loan syndication, but the timing was too tight. Also, there was a danger that the ensuing $500 million syndicated loan would have been undercut in the marketplace. Instead, CIBC entered into two credit default swaps for a total of $50 million that were completed in a week, as opposed to 30 days for a conventional syndication.

The reference credit for the swap was a $250 million five-year Eurobond issued by the Czech Export Bank. If Aero Vodochody defaulted, CIBC could sell this bond at par to its two swap counterparties.

Note that CIBC has the right to sell a bond issued by the Czech Export Bank. This is not the same issuer as Aero Vodochody. However, they are both government agencies. If Aero Vodochody is in default, chances are so is the Czech Export Bank. In that case, the Eurobond issue would drop in price.

SUMMARY OF PRODUCTS

There are three main types of credit derivatives. Like any derivative products, there are forwards, swaps, and options. More complicated deals are transacted using these basic three building blocks. This is similar to the situation in interest rates.

- Forwards: FRA, interest rate forward.
- Swaps: Interest rate swap, convert a fixed rate to floating.
- Options: Interest rate option, such as a call option on a bond.

We have seen examples of the three different types of credit derivatives. They are products that allow us to separate credit risk from interest rate risk or market risk and to separate maturity from duration. We can buy a two-year structure on a thirty-year note, for example. We can achieve specific risk–return profiles, tailored to specific needs, with small administrative costs; and we gain value by taking risks on scenarios thought to be particularly unlikely. In general, these products allow the transfer and hedging of credit risks.

Legal and Regulatory Aspects

By Claude Brown

of Clifford Chance

It is probably axiomatic that a lawyer would hold out documentation as one of the key elements of a credit derivative (just as it is probably axiomatic that a lawyer would qualify any assertion with the word *probably*). However, in the case of credit derivatives, the turmoil in the financial markets has, during the course of 1998, demonstrated that much of the risk in using credit derivatives lies in the detailed wording of the documents evidencing these financial instruments. In some respects, this is hardly surprising; credit quality is not a tangible thing and, in many cases, it is itself evidenced by written instruments. For example, insolvency regimes are contained in laws or regulations, and events of default and financial covenants are found in the text of loan and bond documents. It is against these document-based credit events that credit derivatives seek to operate. In essence, the purpose of a credit derivative is to try to hedge the provisions in one document with those in another document. In doing so the possibility of "documentary basis" risk is created in the same way that a hedger of Eurobonds who uses a government bond based futures contract to hedge is exposed to the possibility of basis risk between the two instruments. Some of this risk can be minimized by tailoring the documentation to fit the underlying financial instrument. The better the fit, the less the risk. However, this is not without its drawbacks. Throughout the credit derivative market there is a continuing demand for standardized documentation to facilitate the rapid trading and transfer of risk. There is also a demand for deals to be completed quickly after their execution to avoid the other risks that can be inherent in having documentation outstanding for long periods of time. These requirements argue for uniformity in credit derivative documentation to enable dealers to transact on common terms and ensure a standard credit trading platform. In some respects this "one size fits all" approach is attractive for those who "trade credit." That said, the credit market is not homogeneous and although uniform trading platforms can appear attractive from one participant's perspective, they raise the risk of definitional imprecision for another. As participants have extended the use of credit derivatives into the emerging markets and sovereign loan arenas, so the standardized definitions found in industry documentation have become increasingly stretched. It is not easy to reconcile these conflicting demands on documentation for credit derivatives. It may be that, over time, a standardized trading set of core documents is used in interdealer transactions, while more bespoke documents are used by portfolio managers and risk controllers to hedge specific positions. Of course, this outcome would itself raise further questions. For example, how would a dealer sell a bespoke-tailored document to an end-user and hedge its own exposure in a market that requires the dealer to use standardized documentation? In extreme, the use of highly tailored products could of itself create some form of liquidity risk in that the particular risks transferred through the credit derivative may not be hedgeable in the interdealer market. That said, this issue has not yet developed sufficiently within the market to present two distinct groups of documents.

TYPES OF CREDIT DERIVATIVE INSTRUMENTS

Although some variations in the forms of credit derivative products appear from time to time, the credit derivative market appears to have coalesced into four or five generic categories of credit derivative products. While there are also some hybrids, the main categories appear to be:

- Credit spread products,
- Total rate of return swaps,
- Credit-linked notes,
- Convertibility products, and
- Credit default products.

CREDIT SPREAD PRODUCTS

It may well be that credit spread products produce particular difficulties for product structurers, but from a legal perspective, their documentation is relatively straightforward. The chief difficulty is keeping track of the plethora of variations used because credit spread products can take many forms. They can be structured as options, forwards, forward forwards, swaps, or even securities. Their common theme, however, is that of the credit spread. In simple terms, this involves taking the yields of two or more financial instruments and comparing the difference or "spread" between them. The real skill lies in identifying which elements of spread represent true differences in credit between the two instruments and which elements need to be excluded both in the structuring of the product and its documentation because they represent something other than credit, for example, illiquidity, convexity, or currency constraints. Thereafter the function of documentation is to write out these extraneous elements. The concept of credit spread can be found in the precedent confirmation published for a credit default swap transaction, published by the International Swaps and Derivatives Association Inc. (ISDA) in the definitions of "Materiality." The spread provisions in those definitions provide a useful starting point for the documentation of credit spread products.

TOTAL RATE OF RETURN SWAPS

The concept behind total rate of return swaps is not new. The instrument uses similar concepts to those found in equity swaps in that the economic risk of an asset or basket of assets is transferred from one party (the **TRORs Payer**) to the other party (the **TRORs Receiver**). In the case of a total rate of return swap, this economic transfer is expressed under two limbs (see Figure 3-1). The first is one under which the TRORs Payer gives the TRORs Receiver the economic benefit of any upside in the value of the underlying Reference Obligation. In turn this comprises two components: the appreciation in value of the Reference Obligation that may occur during the term of the contract, and any income that may be paid or received on the underlying assets. Under the second limb of the total rate of return swap, the TRORs Receiver will pay the TRORs Payer for any depreciation on the Reference Objects during the

Figure 3-1

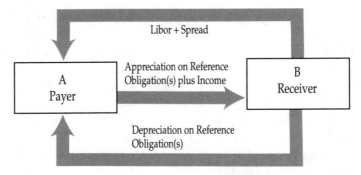

term of the contract. Consequently, the TRORs Receiver will benefit from any gain and suffer any loss on the Reference Obligation.
In addition, the TRORs Receiver will usually pay some form of
financing rate to the TRORs Payer. One way of analyzing a total
rate of return swap is to consider it to be a form of synthetic financing in that it is equivalent to the TRORs Receiver borrowing an
amount of money on which it pays the financing rate. It could then
use the money borrowed to acquire a portfolio of the Reference
Obligations from which it would gain the economic benefit of any
appreciation on those Reference Obligations during the term of the
financing (and the benefit of any income they may generate) while
being at risk to the loss of any depreciation. At the end of the
financing it could then sell the Reference Obligations, repay its
loan, and pocket any profits or realize any losses. In comparison,
the total rate of return swap offers a number of advantages. First,
it does not require that the TRORs Receiver enter into any financing arrangements. It also avoids the complications of acquiring
and holding the assets comprised in the Reference Obligations or
any unpleasantries if the disposal proceeds of the Reference
Obligations were such that it was left with insufficient funds to
repay the financing. In addition, a total rate of return swap can
allow the TRORs Receiver to be economically exposed to assets
that it would not normally be able to hold (for example, because of
restrictions on certain types of entity holding a particular asset).
From the TRORs Payer point of view, the credit derivative is also
attractive in that it allows it to pass to the TRORs Receiver the economic characteristics of the underlying Reference Obligations
without having to dispose of those assets. This could be particularly attractive to financial institutions that value their lender–borrower relationships but wish to control their credit exposure to

those borrowers. Another advantage for the TRORs Payer is that it can short the Reference Obligations synthetically by entering into a total rate of return swap without holding the underlying Reference Obligations.

Documenting total rate of return swaps is not particularly problematic provided a few points are noted to avoid difficulties. First, the obligation to pay over "income" to the TRORs Receiver must be drafted properly. While defining income on Reference Obligations such as bonds is not difficult, in that the wording only has to capture the concept of coupon payments, it can be more difficult when dealing with loan-based Reference Obligations which may provide for payments not only of interest but also of commitment fees, standby fees, drawdown fees, etc., in the income that they generate and which therefore need to be included in the definition. The wording must also seek to avoid imposing an obligation on the TRORs Payer to pay income in circumstances when the underlying asset does not pay. Similarly, if the TRORs Payer is using the total rate of return swap to short the Reference Obligations, then the wording needs to reflect the fact that it will not be the TRORs Payer who is receiving the income but some hypothetical holder of the Reference Obligations. It is generally true that loan-based Reference Obligations require more detailed drafting than securities-based ones. For example, if a borrower under a loan gets into financial difficulties, it is possible that it may wish to reach some agreement with its bank or banks under which it makes a single payment in respect of sums that it owes, even though those sums represent principal, unpaid interest, default interest, fees, and adviser's fees. In these circumstances, it could be unclear as to which elements of that payment are properly allocable to income (in which case they are paid over the TRORs Receiver in any event) and which bits are allocable to principal, in which case they would be used to determine whether there has been any appreciation or depreciation on the Reference Obligations for the relevant period of measurement. Whether securities-based or loan-based, one important distinction between the total rate of return swap and a financing trade is that in the case of the latter the TRORs Receiver acquires the assets. Therefore, in addition to any economic exposure it acquires, it also acquires the ancillary rights and obligations that may come with those assets. For example, there may be rights of the holder of the Reference Obligation to attend creditors' meetings or to vote on events that are important to the financial profile of the Reference Obligations. In using a total rate of return swap contract to replicate economic rights, the parties must also address how such other rights are to be distributed. It may be a source of some irritation to a TRORs Receiver to discover, having entered into the contract on the basis that it is acquiring economic exposure to a high coupon, short maturity bond, that because the Reference Entity was having financial difficulties, the TRORs Payer attended the creditors' meeting and voted for conversion of the Reference Obligation into a low coupon, long maturity financial instrument without consulting the TRORs Receiver. While this can be addressed by building in provisions about the way such rights are to be exercised and the duty to consult, it can still be problematic in cases when the TRORs Payer has entered into several total rate of return swaps with different counterparties in respect of a single portfolio of assets and the TRORs Receivers under the various total rate of return swaps express divergent views as to the way a single set of voting rights may be exercised.

Total rate of return swaps may also raise some tax issues because of the metamorphosis of the income payments on the Reference Obligations. Interest or dividends paid on the Reference Obligations by the issuer or borrower in most cases should fit into some form of definition of income under the tax legislation applicable to the issuer or borrower of the Recipient and the recipient of that income. However, strictly speaking, the payments made by the TRORs Payer under the total rate of return swap to the TRORs Receiver in respect of that income are not "income" but "payments in respect of such income." To put it another way, they should be described as "sums equal to such income," in other words, "synthetic income." This characterization may result in these synthetic income payments being subjected to a different tax regime than that which applies to payments of "true" income by the issuer or borrower. For example, it may be possible to reclaim any tax withheld on the payments by the issuer or borrower in the form of tax credits or tax rebates while it may not be possible to do so for synthetic income paid under the total rate of return swap. Alternatively, a double tax treaty may operate between the jurisdiction of the TRORs Payer and that of the TRORs Receiver that addresses payments of income but the wording of which is such that these synthetic payments under the total rate of return swap do not fit into the income article. It will therefore be necessary to find another article (for example "business profits" or "other income") in the tax treaty into which the synthetic payments can be slotted if they are to receive the benefit of the double tax treaty.

CONVERTIBILITY PRODUCTS

In the lexicon of credit derivatives, it is not finally settled that convertibility products can be said to be credit derivatives. In many respects, they can be viewed as variations on foreign exchange contracts or perhaps more accurately a hybrid of foreign exchange and credit derivative products. In essence, convertibility products address the ability of payments to be expatriated or remitted from one jurisdiction, either in the indigenous currency of that jurisdiction or in an exogenous currency. However, their terms also address events that may prevent, preclude, or inhibit the free conversion of the indigenous currency into the exogenous currency. This may be because of internal controls imposed by the authorities or because of a restriction imposed on the expatriation of funds. They are therefore contingent in their nature. An example of such a product would be a deliverable foreign exchange forward that converts to a nondeliverable forward foreign exchange contract upon the occurrence of certain prespecified events (such as the imposition of convertibility or expatriation controls). Some might say that these contingent events are not, strictly speaking, credit events but are better viewed as political events. Others would argue that whatever their classification, the consequence for the recipient of those funds is equivalent to the occurrence of a credit event in respect of the Reference Entity or, in the case of a Sovereign authority, such actions are properly viewed as "sovereign credit events." Whatever their classification, these convertibility products represent an evolution in contingent financial instruments in that they seek to break out various components of that generic risk that used to be classified as sovereign credit risk into its constituent elements. In doing so a distinction can be made between those events that impact on the creditworthiness of the sovereign (for example, a default on its borrowings) and those events that are within its control that can impact not only on its own indebtedness but also on that of entities incorporated within its jurisdiction.

CREDIT DEFAULT PRODUCTS

Not only are credit default products the most popular and prevalent of credit derivatives found in the markets today, they are also the category that raise the most issues when it comes to drafting their documentation. Credit default products have a distinct characteristic in that their pay-out profile is based on a contingency, the occurrence of which will be determined by the existence of one or more credit-related events. These credit-related events can range from the most severe, such as failure to pay or bankruptcy, to those that may or should probably be regarded as an "amber light" as to an imminent change in creditworthiness of the Reference Entity, for example, restructuring indebtedness and credit downgrades. Settlement can be either "cash" or "physical." These options are discussed further in a later section. The names given to these products can be confusing. Some are described as "credit default options" whereas others are described as "credit default swaps." To the uninitiated, both types of products can appear to have elements of optionality in them in that there is some sort of election to be made by one or both of the parties following the occurrence of a triggering credit event. However, in general terms, transactions in which only one party has the right (but not the obligation) to call a credit event (most commonly this right is given to the buyer of protection) are described as "credit default options" whereas those in which both parties have the right to call a credit event are called "credit default swaps." That said, this distinction is by no means universally applied. Apart from the benefits in marketing default products and the differences in their economic profile, the categorization of such products as "swaps" or "options" can also have tax and accounting consequences for the products (for example if option premia are accounted for in the profit and loss account upon receipt but swap payments are accounted for on an accrual basis).

Since its introduction in 1997, the ISDA precedent confirmation for credit swap transactions has become one of the most popular platforms on which to base the documentation of such default products. As the market has evolved and experience of the triggering of these products increases, so various modifications have been perceived to be necessary. The consequence of this is that the ISDA confirmation is currently under review, in particular the wording of some of the credit events such as Restructuring. It is envisaged that eventually a sovereign precedent confirmation will be added to the current nonsovereign confirmation and that both will be brought within a credit derivatives definitional booklet. The principal benefit of such a booklet is that the extensive definitions used in the current confirmation can be moved into the body of such a book that can then be incorporated by reference into the confirmation. This technique will hopefully reduce the lengthy document (currently some 18 pages) to something more manageable.

PAYOUT PROFILE

Under a credit swap, the payout profile varies according to whether certain conditions (the **Conditions to Payment** or more accurately the "conditions to settlement") are met (see Figure 3-2). However, until they occur, the Buyer under the transaction will pay a series of payments, either fixed or floating, during the life of the transaction. Alternatively, the parties may agree that the Buyer will pay the Seller a single premium on commencement of the transaction or at specified points during its term. The terms "Buyer" and "Seller" are best thought of in the context of the "Buyer of protection" and the "Seller of protection." However, care must be taken to differentiate this terminology from that frequently found in the market where participants also talk in terms of "buying risk" (i.e., "selling protection") and "selling risk" (i.e., "buying protection"). This chapter uses the terms "Buyer" and "Seller" in the context of a "Buyer of protection" and a "Seller of protection." If the Conditions to Payment are not met, then the Buyer will continue to make such payments as it is obliged to make under the terms of the credit swap transaction during its term and receive the benefit of the contingent protection afforded by the contract. However, if the Conditions to Payment are satisfied, then the parties will comply with their respective obligations under the Settlement Terms set out in the contract.

A frequent mistake that is made is assuming that there is a single Condition to Payment. Typically there is a menu of up to eight choices from which the CTPs can be selected, so there may be several conditions that must be satisfied before the Conditions to

Figure 3-2. Buyers' payments under a credit default swap.

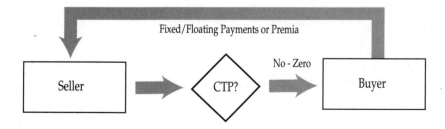

Payment are met. At a very minimum, the Conditions to Payment must include the occurrence or existence of a credit event, otherwise it will be hard for the product to satisfy the description of being a "credit derivative" (see Figure 3-3). Although some might say that failure to pay is the only salient credit event with which a Buyer of protection should be concerned, few would disagree that the imposition of bankruptcy or other form of insolvency regime on the Reference Entity is also a fairly good indicator of its imminent demise and ultimate failure to pay on any future obligations. The definition of a bankruptcy credit event that is most widely used in the market is based on the "Event of Default" found in Section 5(b)(vii) of the 1992 ISDA Multi-Currency-Cross-Border Master Agreement with the references to the "parties" and "Affiliates" in the Master Agreement replaced by references to the "Reference Entity" in the default swap confirmation. The definition has proved robust in a number of extreme credit situations (such as the demise of Barings and Peregrine). Indeed, in a corporate context there have been few criticisms of it. That said, work has been undertaken to produce some complementary wording for Japanese financial sector Reference Entities to reflect the new Japanese restructuring programs for such institutions under the package of reforms introduced during 1998. Further adaptation of this credit event is also required if the Reference Entity is a sovereign. In general terms, it is difficult for a sovereign entity to become bankrupt and therefore alternative triggering events that are analogous to a corporate

Figure 3-3. Conditions to payment—credit events.

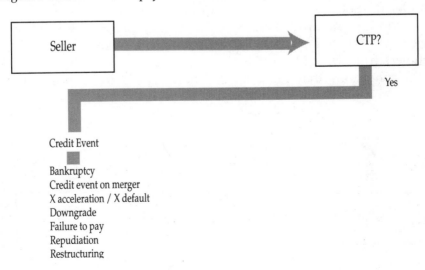

bankruptcy need to be introduced. The increased use of credit derivatives in emerging markets has also highlighted other unusual regimes that need to be addressed. For example, some jurisdictions (such as Russia) have a concept of intervention whereby the Central Bank or finance industry may intervene in the affairs of a financial institution and take over its day-to-day operations. Significantly, this is carried out under the applicable banking laws rather than the bankruptcy laws. Another form of unusual regime for financial institutions found in some jurisdictions (such as Brazil) is that of extrajudicial winding-up, whereby the financial authorities may simply close down a troubled financial institution without going through a court winding-up process. As its name suggests, an extrajudicial winding-up does not require the involvement of the courts and therefore provisions relating to presentations of petitions and so on are not applicable. Users of credit derivatives in emerging market jurisdictions therefore frequently find it necessary to conduct a form of legal due diligence before finalizing the documentation in order to ensure these sort of things do not prevent the product being triggered when it is supposed to be.

Credit Event upon Merger

Like the bankruptcy credit event, the Credit Event upon Merger is based upon the 1992 ISDA Master Agreement definition, in this case therein Section 5(b)(iv) of the Termination Events. This provision triggers a credit event if the Reference Entity merges with another entity, with the consequence that the resulting entity is materially weaker than the Reference Entity was before the occurrence of the merger. Again, while this proves to be a durable definition in the context of corporate credit events, its use for sovereign entities needs consideration. For example, few would consider that the invasion of one country by another would not be a triggering event, even when the country being invaded is weaker than the invader so that the creditworthiness of the resulting entity improves.

Cross Acceleration and Cross Default

On their face, these two credit events look remarkably similar. Before examining their differences, it may be worth highlighting a misunderstanding that frequently occurs in relation to credit derivative terminology. The term "Reference Obligation" is used to define certain obligations of the Reference Entity. The definition of Reference Obligations defines the particular obligations that are to constitute the Reference Obligations. Typically, these will be some form of financial instrument that the Buyer wishes to hedge or to which it wishes to gain exposure (i.e., by entering into a credit derivative without a corresponding underlying position). The definition of the Reference Obligation usually only appears in the mechanics of the determination of Materiality as a Condition to Payment or in the context of the Settlement Terms, either as a device by which the Cash Settlement Amount is calculated or as the Portfolio of underlying assets to be delivered once the Conditions to Payment have been met. However, Reference Obligations are **not** necessarily the triggering obligations against which a credit event may be determined. These "triggering obligations" are defined as "Obligations." Although the Reference Obligations may be defined as being the Obligations or a subset of them, this is not always the case. Obligations can be defined broadly as obligations in respect of borrowed money of the Reference Entity. Alternatively, they may be defined as all payment obligations that the Reference Entity has incurred or may incur. Obligations could also be specified as being solely the Reference Obligations or some other particular form of indebtedness of the Reference Entity. The important point to note is that, depending on the selection made for the definition of Obligations, the credit events need not necessarily occur in respect of the Reference Obligations. A clear distinction has to be made between Obligations that are triggered for the various credit events and the term Reference Obligations which, although it may be used in the context of triggers, need not be.

To return to Cross Default and Cross Acceleration credit events, both address the occurrence of events of default in respect of Obligations that **are not** payment defaults. The reason for this exclusion is that such payment defaults would be addressed under the Failure to Pay credit event. Consequently, Cross Acceleration and Cross Default focus exclusively on non-payment-related events of default. The difference between the two is that Cross Acceleration requires the relevant Obligations not only to exceed a Default Requirement (this is a dollar sum written into the terms of the agreement) but also that such Obligations are accelerated— they become due and payable before they would have otherwise been. An example of this is a four-year loan that is accelerated in year one because the borrower defaults on the covenants for its financial ratios. In contrast, a Cross Acceleration credit event is triggered when the relevant Obligations become *capable of* being accelerated, regardless of whether they are accelerate or not. An example of this is a syndicated loan, the terms of which provide that, following an event of default, the agent may declare the loan accelerated if so instructed by a majority of the lenders. If the borrower had breached a financial covenant, then such a loan could be capable of acceleration, but for a variety of reasons, the requisite majority of the borrowers may not instruct the agent to accelerate the loan. In these circumstances, it is likely that the Cross Acceleration credit event may be triggered whereas Cross Default may not. It also follows that the two are mutually exclusive (if Cross Acceleration is selected, there is little point in including Cross Default).

Downgrade

The downgrade credit event requires the parties to agree to a Specified Rating below which a specified Downgrade Obligation must not decline. The parties may also select the applicable Rating Agencies. The Downgrade Obligation may or may not be one of the Obligations defined and, as discussed earlier, may or may not be the Reference Obligation. Care should be taken to ensure that the Downgrade credit event integrates fully with any ability to substitute Obligations or Reference Obligations that may be given by either one or both of the parties or the calculation agent under the contract. The parties may also wish to consider the fact that an obligation that is redeemed or matured can also cease to have a credit rating by virtue of the fact that a rating is no longer necessary for a matured instrument. It would be an incongruous result for a Reference Entity to perform on the Downgrade Obligation and repay its debt only to find it has triggered a credit event by virtue of the fact that the Downgrade Obligation is no longer rated.

    The turmoil in the financial markets during 1998 also highlighted another quirk of using the Downgrade credit event. Typically, the Downgrade credit event uses Specified Ratings that are usually based on the long-term ratings of the specified Rating Agencies. In some Asian jurisdictions during the financial turmoil the downgrade sequence invoked by some rating agencies focused initially on the ratings given to deposits made with financial institutions in those jurisdictions, then the short-term debt ratings of the institutions and the sovereign debt ratings, before finally downgrading the long-term credit ratings of the relevant Reference Entities. This meant that there was a delay between the time that it became apparent that the creditworthiness of these institutions had deteriorated significantly and the applicable Downgrade credit event being triggered. One consequence of this is that protection Buyers are now more inclined to look at short-term ratings provided by the rating agencies in preference to the long-term ones.

Failure to Pay

Arguably, Failure to Pay is the key credit event. Some might argue that, regardless of the occurrence of any other credit event, provided that the Reference Entity continues to pay on its debt obligations, the Protection Buyer should not be able to claim under the credit derivative. A counterargument to this is that some of the other credit events are so clearly indications that the Reference Entity will not pay or will not be in a position to pay on the next scheduled payment date for that obligation that it is impractical to wait until that payment is due in order to see whether or not the Reference Entity will pay. The Failure to Pay credit event uses the concept of a Payment Requirement, which is a dollar sum used as a threshold to exclude de minimis failures from triggering the credit derivative. When selecting the period of protection to be provided by the Protection Seller under the credit derivative it is important to note that the Failure to Pay credit event takes into account any grace period that may apply to the delinquent Obligation. Therefore, if the Protection Buyer is not careful, it may find that a scheduled payment date has passed but because the grace period is still running, the protection afforded by the credit derivative has expired. Additionally, the Failure to Pay provision wording does not necessarily take into account any dispute with the Reference Entity that may exist as to the validity of such payment. Indeed, the precedent ISDA confirmation specifically excludes legal disputes with Reference Entity creditors from being a reason for holding that the credit event has not occurred. This can produce odd results. For example, if the amount payable under the relevant Obligation was subject to a calculation (for example, a bond, the redemption amount of which was calculated by reference to a basket of indices), a dispute may arise between the issuer and the noteholder as to the exact amount to be repaid.

If the issuer claimed that the amount payable was smaller than the amount that the holder considered due, the issuer may offer to pay the smaller sum. This smaller amount could be below the Payment Requirement. In these circumstances, the noteholder, if it had a credit derivative referenced against the disputed Obligation, may seek to recover from the protection Seller under the credit derivative. The protection Seller in these circumstances may find it very difficult to verify whether failure to pay the excess of the payment requirement had occurred. The protection Buyer would argue that it had because the Buyer as noteholder had not received the amount it was expecting (which was in excess of the Payment Requirement), whereas the Reference Entity (assuming it was even prepared to talk to the Protection Seller) would claim that its payment obligation had been performed and it had satisfied the obligation which was, in any event, below the Payment Requirement. Admittedly, such an example is structured to highlight a particular point and a great many Obligations would not ordinarily give rise to such disputes. That said, the example does serve to highlight the fact that consideration must be given to the individual credit events when seeking to tailor a credit default product to a specific Obligation or set of Obligations.

Restructuring

Restructuring is another credit event for which a distinction needs to be made between a sovereign and a nonsovereign reference entity. Indeed, events in Russia during 1998 gave rise to a review of this provision and agreement on some amendments to it that, at the time of writing, have yet to be implemented. However, it is expected that these amendments will address a number of perceived issues in relation to this credit event when used in the context of emerging market nonsovereign Reference Entities and sovereign Reference Entities generally.

Repudiation

Unsurprisingly, the repudiation or rejection or disclaimer of a contract by a Reference Entity is also capable of being categorized as a credit event. Indeed, it would be hard to envisage a situation under which a Reference Entity repudiated a contract but continued to perform its payment obligations in respect thereof.

Publicly Available Information (PAI)

Publicly Available Information or PAI is a CTP that was introduced into credit derivative documentation to avoid disputes as to whether a particular credit event had occurred or not (see Figure 3-4) by requiring the party triggering a credit derivative to adduce evidence of the fact that is in the public domain. PAI introduced a degree of objectivity into the Conditions to Payment. Of course, the parties need to consider the integrity of such evidence. Some sources of PAI are perceived by the credit derivative market to have a higher degree of integrity than others. In addition to providing a degree of objectivity when determining whether the CTPs have been satisfied, the use of Publicly Available Information may also be useful in addressing any confidentiality constraints to which the triggering party may be subject, as well as being helpful in avoiding breaching any insider dealing laws that use unpublished prices and sensitive information as a test of whether the offense of insider dealing has been committed or not. One point to note in using PAI is that the definition will generally exclude the introduction of such information into the public domain by one of the parties to the credit derivative. This can be particularly difficult for bilateral obligations of the Reference Entity when, for example, the protection Buyer is a party to the Obligation and is using the credit derivative as a hedge. If its own introduction of the relevant credit event into the public domain is excluded from constituting

Figure 3-4. Conditions to payment—PAI.

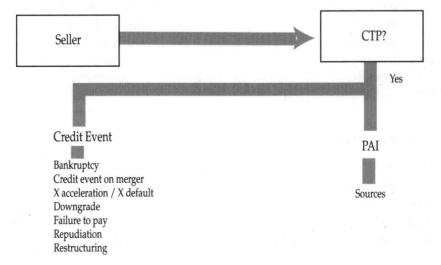

Publicly Available Information, it is improbable that the Reference Entity would willingly introduce it into the public domain in order that the PAI provision may be satisfied. Therefore, PAI is not necessarily helpful in all circumstances and does not always appear as a Condition to Payment. It should also be noted that Publicly Available Information needs to record the occurrence or existence of a credit event but does not need to satisfy any additional limbs of the relevant credit event such as materiality or thresholds. That degree of proof still rests with the party claiming that the credit event has occurred. Under the terms of Publicly Available Information the parties may need to specify the Sources of such Publicly Available Information to confine them to sources of repute or to exclude extraneous speculative reports. Experiences in 1998 indicated that, in some cases, evidence of Publicly Available Information was not carried by some of the more popular selected Sources so that credit events occurred that, even though they were in the public domain, did not appear in the relevant Sources, resulting in the PAI Condition to Payment remaining unsatisfied.

Notices

The structure of most default products renders it necessary for at least one party to deliver notice of the occurrence of a credit event in order for the Conditions to Payment to be satisfied. This notice would normally contain details of the occurrence or existence of a credit event but there may also be a requirement to deliver a Notice of Publicly Available Information (see Figure 3-5). Of course, it may be that the two notices could be telescoped so that a Notice of Publicly Available Information could also constitute a notice of the occurrence of a credit event. However, this is not always the case, particularly when there may be different timing requirements between the two notices. In the ISDA precedent confirmation, the triggering credit event must always occur by a prescribed time (sometimes described as the Scheduled Termination Date, which is a "hard" date written into the terms of the agreement). However, there is generally more flexibility in the approach taken to the timing of delivery of a credit event notice or a notice of Publicly Available Information. These could both have to be delivered either before the Scheduled Termination Date (i.e., all the protection expires on that date), or within a time window falling after the Scheduled Termination Date, during which one or both of the notices may be delivered (notwithstanding the fact that the

Figure 3-5. Conditions to payment—notices.

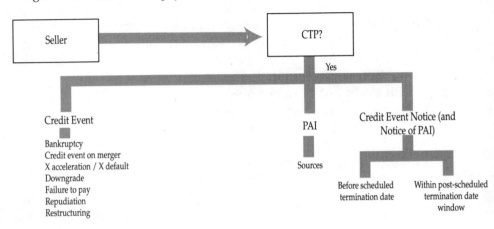

credit event must have occurred before the Scheduled Termination Date). The other point that has already been touched upon in relation to notices is the issue of which party has the right to deliver credit event notices and notices of PAI. If it is one party (usually the Buyer), then the product looks more like an option, whereas the ability of both parties to deliver notice is sometimes ascribed the characteristics of a default swap. It may appear odd that the seller of protection has a right to deliver a credit event notice or a notice of Publicly Available Information, given that it will have to pay out or deliver under the Settlement Terms to its detriment. Part of the reason for including such a provision may lie in the fact that the timing of the Settlement Terms may be important. For example, if a credit event were to occur on day one of a transaction, the Buyer may be inclined to wait to see if another credit event of greater severity occurred or if the payment it was likely to receive increased in any way during the balance of the term, since the contingency of the occurrence of one credit event may already have occurred. (Some credit derivatives do not distinguish between credit events that have occurred and are continuing and those that have occurred but have subsequently been cured, exacerbating the situation.) To address this and to introduce a degree of certainty into the occurrence of the event, some Sellers of protection require that they also have the right to deliver a credit event notice to control the timing of when the Conditions to Payment are satisfied. It is usually helpful if both parties have the ability to deliver notices to provide that only one such notice shall be delivered in respect of any one transaction.

Materiality

The concept of Materiality was introduced to desensitize the negotiations of the wording to be used in the various credit events. The reasoning was that, if there was an additional test as to whether there had been a material change in the value of the Reference Obligations, there could be greater flexibility in the definition of a credit event. At the very least, the exactitude with which the Payment Requirement and Default Requirement needed to be selected could be relaxed. That said, Materiality was by no means universally accepted and some dealers remain relatively hostile to its use, particularly when Materiality needs to be determined over a protracted period, because it also extends the uncertainty as to whether the Conditions to Payment will or will not be satisfied. Broadly, the Materiality provisions divide into two categories, those relating to Price Materiality and those relating to Spread Materiality (see Figure 3-6). Price Materiality further subdivides into provisions that apply to floating rate Reference Obligations (which in general terms assume that the mark-to-market value of a floating rate obligation reflects a change in its creditworthiness when measured against an original benchmark established at the outset of the transaction) and fixed rate obligations, for which the calculation is more complex because of the need to strip out the impact of any interest rate influence on the change in price that may occur after the credit event has happened. This is achieved by referencing the Reference Obligation against a risk-free, high-quality swap curve to neutralize the interest rate impact. Spread Materiality side-

Figure 3-6. Conditions to payment—maturity.

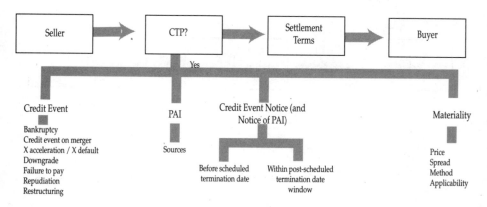

steps the complexities of producing a yield curve immune price Materiality test with respect to fixed interest obligations by merely measuring the yield of the Reference Obligation and then comparing it against an interpolated swap rate. From this the Final Spread is derived, which is then compared against the initial prescribed Materiality to determine whether the Materiality test has been satisfied.

SETTLEMENT TERMS

Once the Conditions to Payment have been met, both parties are obliged to comply with the Settlement Terms. The two primary means of settlement are physical or cash (see Figure 3-7). Typically, the type of settlement is selected at the time the parties enter into the contract. However, it is possible to make the election as to whether cash or physical settlement is to apply once the Conditions to Payment have been satisfied. This election may be given to the Buyer or to the Seller only, or alternatively either party may make the election. If the latter approach is taken, then it is necessary to ensure that the other party will not be in a position to override it and, in any event, a fallback should be specified.

Figure 3-7. Settlement terms—cash/physical election.

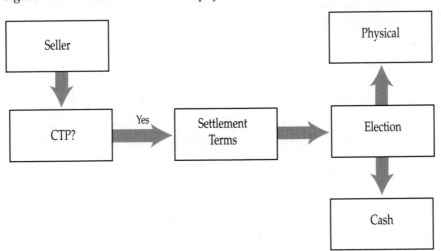

Physical Settlement

In general terms, Physical Settlement operates so that once the Conditions to Payment are met, the Buyer of protection delivers to the Seller a Portfolio of obligations of the Reference Entity and the Seller pays to the Buyer the Physical Settlement Amount (see Figure 3-8). The economic purpose behind this structure is to ensure that the Buyer is returned to the position it was in before the credit event occurred. Consequently, the Physical Settlement Amount or PSA is normally expressed as a dollar sum, in some instances adjusted by a Reference Price to reflect the fact that there may be a lengthy period between the trade date and the effective date of the credit derivative, during which time the Reference Price of the Reference Obligation may change. Delivery in the context of the Portfolio to be received by the Seller is widely defined and encompasses such means of transfer as would be expected for a Portfolio that may contain securities, loans, or derivative contracts. Typically, the Portfolio is expressed to comprise Deliverable Obligations. The nature of Deliverable Obligations can vary between credit derivatives. Historically, the most popular Deliverable Obligations were the Reference Obligations themselves and it is perhaps in this context that the mechanic is easiest to understand. The Buyer of protection would be concerned about the creditworthiness of its Reference Obligation (for example, a bond) and would therefore acquire protection against the possibility of default by the issuer (i.e., Reference Entity) by entering into a Physically Settled credit derivative under which it bought protection from the Seller. If a credit event occurred, then the face value

Figure 3-8. Settlement terms—physical settlement.

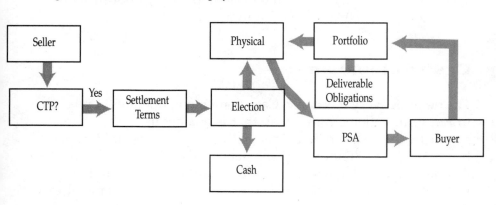

of the bond held by the Buyer would be specified as the Physical Settlement Amount and the Buyer would receive that sum against delivery of the defaulted or impaired Reference Obligations. Over time, however, the universe of Deliverable Obligations has broadened. Of course, it can still be solely the Reference Obligations, but nowadays it could as well be any other *pari passu* obligations of the Reference Entity. The reason for this is that the difficulties associated with Cash Settlement make it easier in some instances to deliver a generic package of obligations of the Reference Entity equal to the PSA, selected from a broad universe of such obligations. The other reason for the increase in popularity of this method of settlement is that it allows parties more flexibility as to the choice of deliverables, which is particularly attractive if the credit default contract is used by the Buyer to short the creditworthiness of the Reference Entity. It can do this by entering into a credit default transaction without any underlying credit exposure to the Reference Entity. Following a credit event, the value of the Deliverable Obligations of the Reference Entity should (in theory) decline so that it is possible for the Buyer to acquire them more cheaply than the pre-credit-event value at which the Buyer shorted them. Since the Physical Settlement Amount will be a dollar sum, the Buyer can then deliver a Portfolio containing Deliverable Obligations with (in the case of securities) an outstanding principal balance or (in the case of a loan) a commitment amount, equal to the Calculation Amount acquired at a lower price. However, the Buyer does not have completely free rein as to what it may select as the Deliverable Obligations. In addition to the requirement that they must be obligations of the Reference Entity (either as debtor or as guarantor) and they must rank *pari passu* with the Reference Obligations, there will also be constraints on the currency of their issue and the manner in which they are repaid (e.g., not structured notes, convertibles) and their duration.

Cash Settlement

The other delivery mechanic, Cash Settlement, operates in relation to Physical Settlement in a way that is analogous to the relationship between cash-settled exchange traded products and physically-settled ones. Following satisfaction of the Conditions to Payment, the Seller will pay a Cash Settlement Amount to the Buyer (see Figure 3-9). However, unlike Physical Settlement, the

Figure 3-9. Settlement terms—cash settlement.

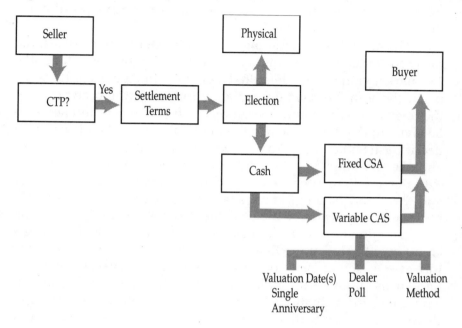

Buyer does not deliver a Portfolio of Deliverable Obligations. The Cash Settlement Amount will reflect the difference between the pre-credit-event value of the Reference Obligations and the post-credit-event value, or Final Price. Typically this Final Price is determined by some form of polling mechanic in which various dealers are asked to provide quotes. The best or average (depending on the terms of the deal) of the dealers' quotes are considered to be the Final Price which, when subtracted from the Initial Price and the resulting difference multiplied by the Calculation Amount, produces a dollar sum that is payable to the Buyer by the Seller. In theory, it should produce an analogous economic result to Physical Settlement. For example, if the Initial Price and Reference Price is considered to be 100 and following the occurrence of a credit event and satisfaction of any other Conditions to Payment the value of the Reference Obligation is determined by dealer poll to be 40, then under Physical Settlement while the Buyer will receive 100 from the Seller, the Seller receives an impaired asset with a value of 40. If, following delivery by the Buyer, the Seller were to sell it into the market, its net loss would be 60. Alternatively, if Cash Settlement were selected as the applicable Settlement Terms, then the post-credit-event Final Price of 40 subtracted from the Initial

Price of 100 would produce a Cash Settlement Amount of 60 with the Buyer retaining the asset, resulting in an aggregate position for the Buyer of 60 plus 40, or 100.

The means of determining the Final Price in order to calculate the cash settlement amount is not always straightforward. Firstly, the market value of the defaulted asset may fluctuate significantly, particularly in the days immediately following the occurrence of the relevant credit event. Therefore, careful consideration needs to be given to the date on which the Reference Obligation is first valued if Cash Settlement is to be used. Too soon after the credit event and the marking down of the asset by the market may be too extreme; too long after the Conditions to Payment have been met and there may be a market squeeze or some other non-credit factor that produces an unrealistic value. Not only is the timing of the first valuation important. To get a more objective view of the post-credit-event value of the Reference Obligation it may be necessary for several valuations to occur at prescribed intervals (commonly known as anniversary polling). While this may be helpful in smoothing the valuations used to determine the Final Price and therefore the Cash Settlement Amount, some dealers dislike it as a technique because it extends the period of risk and the time for which they have to hedge the contingent position pending determination of the outcome. This waiting period can be exacerbated if the Materiality Condition to Payment is also selected and the Materiality test requires an observation to be made on each anniversary Valuation Date. Another issue that arises is that the market may become illiquid (for example, illiquidity in some of the emerging markets during 1998 made it very difficult to obtain quotes at all, let alone accurate ones). While various fallbacks can be prescribed, ultimately a Cash Settlement mechanic will have a backstop of a calculation agent or one party's good faith determination. It was partly for this reason and for other difficulties associated with dealer polls (i.e., confidentiality) that the broad basket of Deliverable Obligations was introduced into the Physical Settlement mechanic in order to avoid the need for Cash Settlement.

Another technique to avoid the need to get valuations in a difficult or turbulent market or particularly for illiquid Reference Obligations is for the parties to pre-agree the likely diminution in value in the Reference Obligations at the outset of the contract. If the Conditions to Payment are met, then the pre-agreed amount is paid over without the need for valuation. These "binary" or "digital" credit default products are themselves not without problems. If the Buyer is using a digital Cash Settled credit default product as a hedge on an underlying position, it is at risk that the fixed Cash Settlement Amount is less than the difference between the pre- and post-credit-event values of the Reference Obligations. Of course, the converse is also true in that it may overestimate the diminution in value and obtain a windfall. However, in either event, the risk is clearly with the Buyer, who may not receive either full accounting or full regulatory capital relief for such a product. The product also may contain a moral hazard for the Protection Seller in that it could be at risk of paying out more to the Buyer than the Buyer needs in order to compensate it for the relevant credit event. For example, the Reference Obligation may be a revolving credit facility that is undrawn at the time a credit event occurs and the Conditions to Payment are met. However, because the Conditions to Payment are met, the obligation of the Protection Seller to pay the Protection Buyer the fixed Cash Settlement Amount will crystallize, even though the Buyer had no exposure to the credit facility. However, because it is entitled to receive the Cash Settlement Amount, the Buyer could nonetheless deliver a credit event notice and claim the windfall profit represented by the binary amount received. Clearly, one option for the Seller would be to require some evidence as to the loss of the Buyer before making a payment on such a product, but to do so would raise the specter of the risk of the contract being recharacterized as one of insurance and may therefore not be a practical option for such a structure.

When using Cash Settlement, it is also necessary to consider the valuation method (i.e., whether it is to be bid, mid, or offer prices quoted by the dealers in the poll). Logically, it should be bid in that one is trying to value the price at which the Reference Obligation can be sold following the occurrence of a credit event, but this is not universally applied. One other issue to bear in mind, which is as relevant for Physical Settlement as it is for Cash Settlement, is the treatment of accrued income and, if the Reference Obligation has defaulted, the treatment of due but unpaid income. A broad range of market conventions are used for dealing with the right to accrued income on obligations, and no universal rule can be discerned. For example, some bond markets typically quote bond prices clean of accrued interest but they require an amount to be added to the consideration paid for such securities to the purchase price to reflect the accrued interest that is delivered with the bond. Conversely, other products (some traded loans, for example) deal with accrued interest differently and the convention may be not to give recognition for accrued interest to the acquirer in all circumstances (e.g., after a record date). While the ISDA precedent confirmation gives general principles as to how to treat accrued interest, it is always wise to ask how it is to be dealt with under a default product before drafting the documents to avoid any confusion arising at the time of the valuation or settlement.

SUMMARY

Great strides have been made in a relatively short period to standardize credit derivative documentation, particularly that of the credit default products. Common vocabulary has now been established that allows dealers to use it as a "shorthand" to enable them to focus on the important economic issues. That said, the documentation, like the market it serves, continues to evolve and reflect the experiences of the participants. Whatever damage that the turbulence in Southeast Asia and Russia in 1997 and 1998 caused the derivative and other financial markets, one consequence for credit derivatives was that it provided a slew of credit events against which the efficacy of the documentation of credit derivatives could be benchmarked. While it is regrettable that the documentation did not always stand up to such stress testing, it at least gave the market and its participants an opportunity to avoid future losses by learning from past mistakes.

REGULATORY CAPITAL TREATMENT OF CREDIT DERIVATIVES

If anyone required evidence that credit derivatives represented a new class of derivatives they need look no further than the problems they have caused the regulators of the world's financial markets when setting regulatory capital standards for their use. The regulators have not focused exclusively on regulatory capital as a means of supervising this growing market, but perhaps inevitably, the opportunities for obtaining regulatory capital relief by the use of credit derivatives has achieved much attention from portfolio managers and financial institutions generally. In several instances, the financial regulators have been hampered by the fact that the framework of rules in which they are required to operate did not

Figure 3-10. The history of credit derivative regulation.

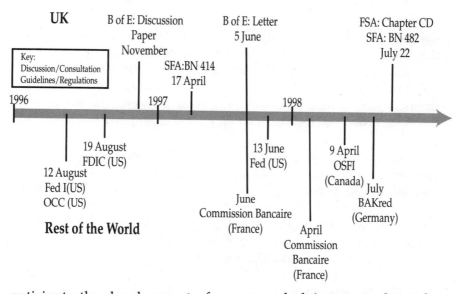

anticipate the development of a new underlying asset class of a derivative instrument, and they have been forced to produce new rules on their treatment (see Figure 3-10). Though it is true to say that credit protection products are not new, the older products (for example, guarantees, standby credit facilities, etc.) did not generally result in the volume trading of credit as an asset class that credit derivatives now generate, nor did they constitute as liquid a market as credit derivatives have proved to be. In seeking to devise regulatory capital rules for credit derivatives, the regulators have been constrained by two international frameworks. The first is that of the Basle Committee of the Bank for International Settlements (BIS), whose membership consists of the G10 countries plus some others (including Luxembourg). The initial set of capital rules was introduced by the Basle Committee in Capital Accord of 1988, predating most credit derivative products. Since the Basle Committee takes more of a club-like approach than a formal agreement, in the implementation of commonly agreed policies it has more flexibility to address new products than more formalistic arrangements. The national banking regulators, being members of this club, can agree on new rules and implement those in their domestic markets as the need arises. However, in doing this they do not have a completely free hand. One eye must always be kept on maintaining a level playing field between banks and securities houses. Also, the absence of a structured framework in which to operate means that some disparity in the treatment of common products by different regulators can arise. Taken to extreme, such anomalies can create noticeable competitive advantages or disadvantages for financial institutions regulated in different jurisdictions. The regulators are also constrained in part by their own countries' legislative and political agendas. However, generally speaking, the Basle Committee framework has enabled those financial regulators who are part of it a degree of freedom to devise a common regulatory capital treatment for credit derivatives in a relatively short period of time.

That said, a significant majority of the banking regulators are located in jurisdictions which are members of the Basle Committee and are also Member States within the EU. While the EU legislation and the Basle Committee rules on regulatory capital broadly try to keep pace with each other, the EU regulatory capital treatment of credit derivatives has to operate within the legislative process of the European Union. From time to time this can generate asynchronicity between the EU regime and that applicable to the other jurisdictions of the Basle Committee (principally, the United States of America, Switzerland, Japan, and Canada). In addition, the requirement to work within a multinational legal framework means that changes to the legislation that drives the regulatory capital treatment in the EU can take some time to implement, again causing the regulators difficulties in reacting quickly enough to market developments in innovative financial markets. For securities firms, the distinction is even more pronounced. As yet, there is no coherent body of regulatory rules that is universally applicable to the regulatory capital treatment of securities houses in the same way that the Basle Committee rules applies to banks. However, within the EU, the Solvency Ratio Directive of 1989 (SRD), which deals with the banking books of the financial institutions, applies to both credit institutions (i.e., banks) and investment firms (i.e., securities houses), as does the Capital Adequacy Directive of 1993 (CAD), which contains additional provisions dealing with the regulatory capital treatment for the trading books of both types of institution.

THE UNITED KINGDOM

In addition to the potential for asynchronicity between the EU legislative framework and that of the Basle Accords, the U.K. currently faces an additional issue in setting down its regulatory capital treatment of credit derivatives. Since June 1997, the regulation of the U.K.'s financial institutions has been undergoing a fundamental change. The several regulators that used to have responsibility for the various market sectors are being replaced by a single regulator, the Financial Services Authority or FSA. To date, the role of the Bank of England in supervision and surveillance of banking institutions has been taken over by the Financial Services Authority as has that of the Securities and Investments Board. Although the Securities and Futures Authority (or SFA), as the regulator responsible for supervising securities houses in the U.K., has not yet been brought fully within the auspices of FSA, this is currently scheduled to happen by the year 2000. However, this major reorganization has not ostensibly altered the general thrust of the regulatory capital treatment of credit derivatives in the U.K. The Bank of England first issued a discussion paper on the regulatory capital treatment of credit derivatives for banks in November 1996. Among other things, it set its face against allowing default-based credit derivatives in the trading book. Following representations from market participants, this policy was modified in June 1997 when certain credit default products were allowed into the trading books in limited circumstances. After a number of discussions with market participants in a practitioners' forum, the Bank and subsequently the FSA revised the proposed rules set out in the discussion paper and the FSA published them in the new Chapter CD of its Banking Supervisory Policy Guidelines in July 1998. At the same time, it issued a written report on the results of the consultation exercise in the practitioners' forum, explaining why some of the practitioners' proposals had not been adopted. It is important to note that Chapter CD is the regulation. The report of consultation, although interesting reading, is not law.

At the same time that the FSA, in its capacity as successor regulator to the Bank of England, issued Chapter CD of its Banking Supervisory Policy Guidelines in July 1998, the Securities and Futures Authority issued its Board Notice 482. The SFA had attended the market practitioners' consultations with the Bank of England and appears to have tried when possible to keep its policy on credit derivatives in line with that of the Bank of England and subsequently with the policy of the FSA. To a large extent, it has been successful in achieving this objective although there are still some anomalies between the FSA's regulatory capital treatment for credit derivatives for banks when compared against that of the SFA's policy for regulatory capital charges for securities houses.

The other primary difference is that, unlike the FSA's Chapter CD, which replaces the previous policy set out in the discussion paper, the SFA has adopted an additive approach. Consequently, Board Notice 482 does not completely replace the SFA's initial announcements on credit derivatives set out in Board Notice 414 issued on April 17, 1997, and the two Board Notices must be read together in order to ascertain the SFA's stated policy on credit derivatives.

THE FSA'S CHAPTER CD

In Chapter CD of its Banking Supervisory Policy Guidelines, the FSA sets out its criteria for admissibility of credit derivatives to the trading book. These follow its policy on other instruments in that the activity must meet the dual test of being a trading book instrument (within the FSA's definition) and also satisfy the FSA's trading intent criteria. In addition, the credit derivative positions must be marked to market daily to the FSA's standard requirements for marking financial instruments in the trading book to market. Finally, the inclusion of these credit derivatives must be consistent with the regulated institution's Trading Book Policy Statement filed and agreed with the FSA. Subject to these requirements, Chapter CD allows credit derivatives based on relatively illiquid Reference Obligations, such as loans, into the trading book. This marks a noteworthy concession because loan assets of themselves are not allowed within the trading book under the CAD rules because they do not ordinarily fit the trading instrument criteria, even though they may well meet the trading intent criteria if held as part of a loan trading portfolio. However, the FSA has also prescribed a liquidity criteria for credit derivatives referenced to relatively illiquid Reference Obligations. If an institution wishes to bring these types of derivatives into the trading book, an additional regulatory capital charge is required to act as a cushion for valuation uncertainty. As yet, the FSA has not officially pronounced on the size or form of this cushion. However, the liquidity criteria are not reserved exclusively for use with loan-based credit derivatives. They also extend to non-loan-based credit derivatives and illiquid financial instruments generally. The FSA also allows credit-linked notes (CLNs) to be "issued off the trading book" provided they meet the risk transfer requirements set out in Section 9 of Chapter CD. This enables regulatory institutions to issue CLNs under which they acquire protection from the note-holder, and use that protection to hedge their trading book position in the underlying asset. Credit spread options have separate rules applicable to them whether they are held in the trading book or banking book.

In contrast to the FSA, the SFA requires both the trading book and non-trading-book positions of a firm regulated by it to be marked to market on a close-out basis (although it is true to say that most SFA-regulated firms do not have banking books of the same size as those of firms regulated by the FSA). Further, the SFA does not require a capital charge to be held against valuation uncertainty but uses the bid–offer spread as a means of creating regulatory capital charges for illiquidity in that short positions have to be marked to market against the offer side of the market while long positions need to be marked to market against the bid side. That said, the SFA still follows a CAD-driven test for trading intent and trading book instruments similar to that used by the FSA.

FSA BANKING BOOK TREATMENT FOR CREDIT DERIVATIVES

The FSA sets out a number of factors that need to be considered when determining the regulatory capital charge for use of credit derivatives in the banking book (see Figure 3-11). The applicability of these factors will depend upon whether the regulated institution is buying protection under the relevant credit derivative or selling it. Generally, the Buyer of protection (Protection Buyer) is subject to all six of the factors whereas the Seller of protection (Protection Seller) is subject to only three.

Figure 3-11. FSA banking book—factors for credit derivatives.

	Funded / Unfunded	Payout Structure	Asset Mismatch	Currency Mismatch	Maturity Mismatch	Baskets
Buyer	●	●	●	●	●	●
Seller	●	●				●

Funded or Unfunded

The first factor is whether the credit derivative is funded or unfunded. In general terms, an unfunded credit derivative is one by which the Protection Buyer does not have monetary or collateral assurance that the Protection Seller will perform its obligations prior to those obligations crystallizing. A credit default swap is an example of such an instrument. In contrast, a funded credit derivative is one whereby the Seller has provided some assurance of its performance either by means of collateral or by some form of prepayment. An example of a funded credit derivative would be a credit-linked note through which the issuer of the note receives the issue price as funding and will be required to return it as redemption proceeds if the Conditions to Payment (CTPs) are not met. If the CTPs are satisfied, the issuer will retain an amount equivalent to the Cash Settlement Amount under an unfunded credit default product. Similarly, a credit default product that has some form of collateralization (for example, under a credit support annex appended to the ISDA Master Agreement used to document the default product) is considered to constitute a funded credit derivative.

From the Protection Buyer's perspective under a funded credit derivative will have the protection gained by entering into the funded credit derivative recognized to the amount of the funding. Therefore, if the issuer of a credit-linked note receives 100% of the issue price on the date of issue, the Protection Buyer would receive 100% recognition for such a product, whereas if it took only partial payment of, say, 25%, the recognition would be limited to 25% accordingly. To the extent that the credit derivative is unfunded, the Protection Buyer may replace the risk weighting depending upon the protection bought where the risk weighting of the asset referenced under the credit derivative is lower than that of the Protection Seller, the risk weighting of the Protection Buyer will be that of its counterparty, not the underlying asset. For example, if the protection Buyer holds a loan to a corporation in its banking book, this would be risk weighted at 100% because of the corporate nature of the borrower. However, if the bank were to acquire protection under a credit derivative from a protection Seller that was an OECD bank, then the risk weighting of the Reference Obligation would be reduced to that of the OECD bank, or 20%. Finally, it should be noted that unfunded credit positions are accorded a guarantee treatment so the basis that it is the most analogous parallel to be found within the Capital Adequacy Directive.

The funded or unfunded factor is also applicable to the Protection Seller. Mirroring the treatment of the Protection Buyer, an unfunded credit derivative constitutes a Direct Credit Substitute for the protection Seller in that it is considered to be in the same position as if it had acquired the underlying Reference Obligation. Another way of looking at it is the credit derivative is treated as if the Seller had guaranteed the loan. Accordingly, following the example previously used, it would acquire 100% risk weighting in respect of the corporate loan, in the same way as if it had made the loan itself. For a funded credit derivative, the Seller's amount to be risk weighted is equal to the amount of the funding provided (either by way of collateral or as the issue price of a CLN). The risk weighting, however, is the higher of that of the Reference Entity and that of the Protection Buyer. In some ways this can be equated to placing a bet in a casino. The risk of the Protection Seller is analogous to that of the customer at the casino. The customer could lose money either because the bet made does not pay off (i.e., the risk weighting of the Reference Entity) or because the casino does not pay on the bet (i.e., the risk weighting of the Protection Buyer). Therefore, the rationale is that the protection Seller should assume the worst-case scenario—that it will not get its money back because of the greater risk that either the Reference Entity may trigger the credit derivative or that even if it did not, the Buyer may not return the funding or collateral to the Seller if the Conditions to Payment were not satisfied.

Payout Structure

The next relevant factor under the FSA rules is the payout structure. Again, this applies to both the Protection Seller and the Protection Buyer. If the payout structure is Cash Settlement or Physical Delivery, then the protection Buyer will receive regulatory capital relief to the full value of the maximum amount of the payout. Conversely, if it enters into a digital or binary credit derivative with a fixed Cash Settlement Amount, it will only receive protection to the limit of that payout. The regulatory capital consequences of that payout structure for the Protection Seller mirror those of the Buyer. Consequently, on a digital payout, the risk weighting charge incurred by the Seller of protection is that of the Reference Entity to the limit of the fixed Cash Settlement Amount. For Cash Settlement and Physical Delivery, the risk weighting is that of the Reference Entity to the possible maximum of the payout.

Asset Mismatch

The third factor that the FSA takes into account when determining the regulatory capital treatment of credit derivatives held in the banking book is whether there is an asset mismatch between the underlying asset to be hedged and the Reference Obligation contained in the terms of the credit derivative. This factor applies to the Protection Buyer only. If there is an exact match between the Reference Obligation and the underlying asset (i.e., they are the same obligation of the Reference Entity) the Buyer will receive full regulatory capital recognition. Similarly, it will receive full recognition if there is a "close match" between the Reference Obligation and the underlying asset. However, if there is not a close or exact match, then the regulatory capital consequence of holding the credit derivative in the banking book is ignored. A similar result will ensue if the credit derivative is held as a "naked short," in other words, if the Protection Buyer has bought the credit derivative without an offsetting position in the underlying asset in the banking book. If there is not an exact match between the Reference Obligation and the underlying asset to be hedged by the credit derivative, it is necessary to consider whether there is a sufficiently close match between the two for the Protection Buyer to obtain regulatory capital relief. In order for a close match to be recognized, the Reference Obligation and the underlying asset must have a common obligor, (i.e., the borrower-issuer of the underlying must be the same as the Reference Entity in respect of the Reference Obligations under the credit derivative); and the Reference Obligation must rank *pari passu* or be junior to the underlying asset in the event of a liquidation of the Reference Entity and, in the FSA's own words, there should be "cross default clauses" between the Reference Obligation and the underlying. What is meant by this latter requirement is not entirely clear. It would be curious if there were a requirement that the Reference Obligation be triggered upon a default on the underlying or vice versa. A better view of the interpretation of this clause would be that the credit derivative and the underlying have common triggers so that, should the underlying asset fail to perform, the credit derivative will be triggered. However, this has to be read into the FSA's current rule on the subject.

Currency Mismatch

The FSA will also allow the Protection Buyer some recognition of the benefit of holding the credit derivative in its banking book even if there is a currency mismatch between the underlying and the credit derivative. The FSA's concern appears to be that, if an asset held in the banking book were denominated in one currency but the credit derivative paid out in another currency, it would be possible as a result of currency fluctuations for the amount of protection derived from the credit derivative to be less than the losses suffered on the underlying. Accordingly, while a currency mismatch is allowed, the Protection Buyer is required to conduct a daily revaluation (presumably of both assets) to gain regulatory capital relief. The Protection Buyer only receives regulatory capital relief for the protection afforded by the credit derivative to the maximum of the revaluation of that instrument. Further, the revaluation amount counts as a forward foreign exchange exposure for the foreign exchange exposure calculations. For a funded credit derivative, this foreign exchange position is the amount of the funding received by the Buyer of protection. For unfunded credit derivatives, it is the higher of 8% of the maximum payout upon the occurrence of a credit event or the bank's own estimate of the contingent foreign exchange exposure. The rationale behind this ruling appears to be that the foreign exchange mismatch is not omnipresent in that it needs the occurrence of a credit event under the credit derivative to be crystallized. Accordingly, the FSA is prepared to recognize the credit event—the contingent nature of the foreign exchange exposure based on the regulated institution's own calculations—subject to a floor of 8%.

Maturity Mismatch

Another FSA banking book factor that applies only to the Protection Buyer is the maturity mismatch factor (see Figure 3-12). Unlike the asset mismatch test, which focuses on the nature of the Reference Obligation and the underlying asset, the maturity mismatch factor focuses on the maturity of the underlying asset and the term of the credit derivative. If they are the same, then full

Figure 3-12. FSA banking book—factors for credit derivatives.

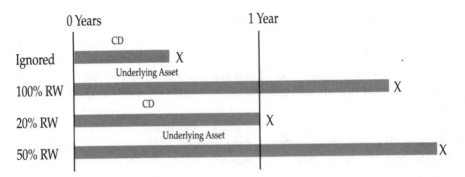

recognition is given for the credit protection generated by the credit derivative. Although Chapter CD is silent on the matter, it also appears that if the credit derivative has a term that is longer than the maturity of the underlying asset, full recognition will be given. However, if the term of the credit derivative is shorter than the maturity of the underlying asset, it is necessary to consider whether the residual (not the original) term of the credit derivative is one year or more, or less than one year. If it is the former, then the protection afforded by the credit derivative is recognized. However, there is a 50% "credit conversion factor" applied to the risk weight of the obligation of the underlying asset to allow for the forward exposure that arises from the fact that, once the credit derivative expires, the underlying asset will have no protection. While it is open to the Protection Buyer to acquire further protection to cover the residual maturity, the FSA in applying this rule appears to be seeking to prevent situations in which deterioration in the credit quality of the Reference Entity at the time of expiry of the credit derivative is such that the credit protection for the underlying is either unobtainable or prohibitively expensive. In some ways, this can be viewed as analogous to a concern that a regulator would have about using short floating-term borrowings to fund fixed long-term assets. If the credit derivative has a residual term of less than one year, then no recognition of the protection is afforded under the FSA's rules.

Basket Products

The final factor that needs to be considered when calculating the regulatory capital charge imposed by the FSA on banking book credit derivatives is whether the product is a basket structure (i.e., there is more than one Reference Entity referenced in the credit derivative). Chapter CD distinguishes between "first to default" (also known as "first past the post" structures) and "green bottle structures" in which default on one Reference Entity leaves part of the credit derivative structure in place as protection for the others. (This description is based on a traditional English song entitled "Ten Green Bottles" that has the refrain, "If one green bottle should accidentally fall, there will be nine green bottles standing on the wall.") In the first past the post structure, when the occurrence of a credit event in respect of one Reference Obligation causes the credit derivative to pay out and then collapse, the Protection Buyer chooses which of the underlying assets it wants to match against the credit derivative. It can only choose one asset for the credit derivative to hedge even though the credit derivative may have many more Reference Obligations in its terms. For a green bottle structure, the protection is prorated between the underlying assets held by the Buyer. In both cases, the risk transfer requirements applicable to basket products set out in Section 9 of Chapter CD must also be met. For the Protection Seller, the first past the post structures result in a heavy capital charge that is calculated as being the aggregate of all the Reference Entities comprised in the basket. Therefore, although the Protection Buyer receives regulatory capital relief for the use of a first past the post structure in respect of only one underlying asset, the Protection Seller is burdened with a regulatory capital charge for each of the Reference Entities. For the Protection Seller under a green bottle structure, the regulatory capital charges are prorated between the Reference Entities.

FSA TRADING BOOK TREATMENT

The Chapter CD contemplates the use of models for the calculation of regulatory capital charges for credit derivatives held in the trading book. Implicitly the recognition of models for the trading books means that any acceptable model would have to model specific risk and be acceptable to the FSA. While the FSA will recognize models (as will the SFA) it also sets out the regulatory capital treatment under its standard (i.e., non-model-based) approach. Those institutions whose models do not achieve recognition or that do not have a suitable model for modeling the risks inherent in credit derivatives when held in the trading book have to use the standard approach.

Under the standard approach, the FSA considers there to be three capital charges relevant to credit derivatives. The first is general market risk, being the tendency of financial instruments such as interest rate products to move up and down as the yield curve flexes. The second charge is that for specific risk, or the risk inherent in a particular financial instrument. It is somewhat simplistic to regard this as purely the credit risk of the issuer or borrower of the relevant financial instrument. Specific risk is also intended to address other risks such as illiquidity risk. The third charge is a counterparty risk charge. The counterparty risk charge also applies to credit derivatives held in the banking books when the credit derivative is held in OTC derivative form, unless an acceptable funded structure or credit enhancement technique is employed.

The FSA's guidelines for trading book treatment of credit derivatives also recognizes three product categories. The first is total rate of return swaps (both funded and unfunded), the second is credit default products (again both funded and unfunded), and the third is credit-linked notes (which, by definition, must be funded).

General Market Risk

Generally, credit default products incur no regulatory capital charge for market risk when held in the trading books. Credit-linked notes incur a general market risk in respect of any coupons that may be paid on them. The issuer of the credit-linked note is considered to be short the coupon (because it is paying it away to the noteholder) and the holder of the credit-linked note is considered to be long the coupon. However, there is no general market risk on the Reference Obligations incurred by the holder of note. Total rate of return swaps are considered to generate a long or short notional position in a Zone A Government Bond in respect of the financing leg of the total rate of return swap paid by the TRORs Receiver to the TRORs Payer. This notional position will be in respect of a fixed coupon bond or FRN, depending on whether the financing leg is fixed or floating. In addition, the TRORs Receiver will be considered to be short the Reference Obligation (because it transfers the economic risk and therefore the general market risk of the Reference Obligation to the TRORs Receiver). Conversely, the TRORs Receiver is considered to be long the Reference Obligation. General market risk positions can be offset (i.e., a long position in general market risk can be offset by a corresponding short position). Therefore, if a TRORs Payer held an underlying position in an asset that is also the Reference Obligation of the total rate of return swap, it can use the short position generated by the total rate of return swap to offset the general market risk charge incurred by its physical holding in the underlying asset.

Specific Risk

The second regulatory capital charge applied to credit derivatives in the trading book is that for specific risk. For total rate of return swaps and unfunded credit default products, the TRORs Payer (in the case of a total rate of return swap) and the Protection Buyer (in the case of an unfunded credit default product) are considered to be short of the specific risk of the Reference Obligation. Conversely, the TRORs Receiver and the Protection Seller are long the specific risk of the Reference Obligation. Credit-linked notes and credit default products, being comparable, generate similar long or short specific positions for the parties to them. However, the Protection Seller (i.e., the noteholder in the case of a CLN and the Seller in the case of a funded credit default product) is also considered to be long the specific risk of the Protection Buyer (i.e., the issuer in the case of CLN, and the Protection Seller in the case of a funded credit default product) because of the possibility that the funding or issue price may not be returned to it at the end of the transaction should the Conditions to Payment not be met. It is interesting to note that unlike the banking book, an additive approach is used in that these funded structures generate two specific risk charges for the Protection Seller. To return to an example used previously, the consequence of applying this rule is akin to requiring the Protection Seller to incur a specific risk charge for both the bet and the casino in which it places such a bet even though the maximum loss it can suffer is limited to the bet.

When the credit derivative has multiple Reference Obligations, such as a basket product, for a total rate of return swap, the TRORs Receiver is considered to be long the prorated specific risk of each Reference Obligation and the TRORs Payer is deemed to hold a corresponding short position. For unfunded credit default products that work on a first-past-the-post basis, the

Protection Buyer chooses which Reference Obligation in the basket it wishes to be short the specific risk of and the Protection Seller is considered to be long the specific risk of each Reference Obligation. For funded credit default products, in addition to the treatment for unfunded credit default products, the Protection Seller is also considered to be long the specific risk of the Protection Buyer. Credit-linked notes, however, are treated differently in certain circumstances from funded credit default products. If the credit-linked note is not a Qualifying Debt Item, then the noteholder (being the Protection Seller) will be considered to be long the specific risk of all the Reference Obligations as well as being long the specific risk of the issuer of the CLN. However, if the credit-linked note meets the requirements for being a Qualifying Debt Item or QDI (among the universe of eligibility requirements that can make it a QDI is that the note is a listed product), then the noteholder will only be treated as being long the specific risk of the issuer of the credit-linked note.

Specific Risk Offset

As has already been discussed, long and short positions in general market risk can, subject to some limitations, be offset by a regulated institution under the FSA rules. As a result of the FSA's rules being derived from the EU's Capital Adequacy Directive, the same flexibility is not available for the offsetting of specific risk. Strictly applied, the Capital Adequacy Directive's rules on specific risk offset are onerous. Unless the instruments are identical (i.e., same obligors, same maturity, same currency, etc.), the Capital Adequacy Directive does not allow for the recognition of any offset between long and short specific risk positions for each instrument. Indeed, the CAD is even more onerous, requiring the long and short specific risk positions to be added together to produce a gross specific risk charge. This burdensome requirement is sometimes referred to as the "double whammy." That said, the FSA will allow specific risk offset for credit derivatives under certain limited circumstances. Provided that the underlying asset and the Reference Obligation of the credit derivative have the same obligor and the FSA's matching criteria for specific risk offset and the risk transfer requirements set out in Section 9 of Chapter CD are met, then some recognition of offset will be allowed. In determining whether specific risk offset is available between a credit derivative and an underlying position held in the trading book, it is also necessary to consider whether there is a maturity mismatch between the two instruments. A maturity mismatch has no impact on a total rate of return swap but, in the case of a credit default product or a credit-linked note, if either instrument has a shorter maturity than the underlying then although offset will be allowed, a specific risk forward position is also created. The overall effect of this is to create a single long specific risk position in the underlying, which avoids the impact of the double whammy being imposed on both long and short specific risk positions on an additive basis, but creates no saving from the use of a credit derivative to hedge. Chapter CD is silent on the consequences of the credit default product or CLN having a longer maturity than the underlying asset.

Counterparty Risk

Since credit-linked notes are securities, there is no counterparty risk charge incurred (although a credit-linked note may be subject to settlement risk if settlement does not occur within the prescribed time set out in the FSA's Guidelines). Because total rate of return swaps involve two-way cash flows both in respect of the Reference Obligation limbs and the funding limb, both parties incur counterparty risk charges.

Unfunded credit default products create a counterparty risk charge for the Protection Buyer because it will have the risk that the Protection Seller will not comply with the Settlement Terms, should the Conditions to Payment be met. Conversely, the Protection Seller will only incur a counterparty risk charge in respect of the Protection Buyer if the Buyer is required to make continuing premium or interest rate payments during the term of the product. The methodology used to determine the counterparty risk charge is common to both books. In essence, the technique requires the calculation of a Credit Equivalent Amount (this can be regarded as a device by which off-balance-sheet derivatives are brought on-balance-sheet for the purposes of calculating the regulatory capital charge). The Credit Equivalent Amount is equal to the calculating party's positive mark-to-market value for the relevant derivative position, adjusted by the risk weighting of its counterparty and the registered institution's risk asset ratio as prescribed by FSA. In addition, there is an add-on representing the potential future credit exposure or PFCE that may arise as a result of entering into the derivative contract. This PFCE add-on is applied to the notional amount of the credit derivative, regardless of whether the mark-to-market is positive or negative for that party. The effect of this is to create a "standing charge" to protect against the risk of future fluctuations in the mark-to-market value. The appropriate PFCE add-on to be used in respect of credit derivatives is a question that has vexed the financial regulators in several jurisdictions for some time. Under both Basle and the Capital Adequacy Directive, there are four categories of PFCE add-ons, those for interest rate products, equity products, foreign exchange products and commodity products. The general principle is that a product that cannot be readily slotted into one of these four categories should attract the highest PFCE add-on charges, in other words, those for commodity positions. Perhaps unsurprisingly, market participants argue that these are inappropriate for credit derivatives and that there would appear to be very little parallel between the volatility properties of a credit derivative and those of a commodity derivative. Chapter CD prescribes that, if the Reference Obligation is a Qualifying Debt Instrument, then interest rate add-ons may be used; but if the Reference Obligation is not a Qualifying Debt Instrument, equity add-ons will apply.

RISK TRANSFER REQUIREMENTS

As already mentioned, Section 9 of Chapter CD sets out some further risk transfer requirements of the FSA. These appear to borrow heavily from the FSA's rules on securitizations and participations. Section 9.2 sets out the general requirements that are applicable to all credit derivatives. These provide that the credit derivative must comply with the terms of the Reference Obligation and all relevant consents for the use of the credit derivative must be obtained (including presumably, when applicable, the consent of the Reference Entity). The credit events must cover the credit events of the underlying asset so that if the underlying asset experiences a credit event, the corresponding credit event in respect of the credit derivative will also be triggered and so that there can be no recourse by the Seller to the Buyer for any losses incurred as a result of the Protection Seller being obliged to comply with the settlement terms. Section 9.3 contains particular provisions for single-name and first-past-the-post basket credit derivatives, and Section 9.4 applies to funded packaged credit derivatives, such as those that are found in some of the popular loan portfolio securitization structures that are currently found in the markets.

REGULATORY CAPITAL TREATMENT OF CREDIT DERIVATIVES IN GERMANY

The responsibility for preparing the rules for the regulatory capital treatment of credit derivatives in Germany falls to the *Bundesaufsichtsamt für das Kreditwesen*, or as it is more commonly known, the BAKred. In July 1998, the BAKred published its draft circular on the treatment of credit derivatives (*Rundschreiben an der Behandlung von Krederivate*). Although various industry associations have commented extensively on the draft circular and a new version is expected imminently, a revised version has yet to appear. Accordingly, the following narrative sets out the BAKred's thinking as expressed in the draft circular, although it is expected that some parts of the circular will be substantially revised when it is published in final form.

Unlike the FSA, the BAKred will only admit credit default products and total rate of return swaps into the trading book if the underlying Reference Obligation is a security or a money market instrument. Accordingly, credit derivatives with loan-based Reference Obligations are not admitted into the trading book. A further restriction is that Protection Buyers are allowed to admit only credit default products and total rate of return swaps into their trading books; it is not possible to "issue CLNs" off the trading book in order to hedge trading book positions. Accordingly, CLNs are allowed into the trading book only for the Protection Seller, in other words, when the regulated institution has bought a credit-linked note. In contrast to the FSA rules, the BAKred sets out express documentation standards that must be met in both banking and trading books as to the use of master agreements, efficacy of documentation, and responsibility for its preparation.

BAKRED AND THE BANKING BOOK

The BAKred does not specifically consider the distinction between funded and unfunded credit derivatives except to provide that the proceeds of the issue of a credit-linked note have to be earmarked by the issuer for collateralization of the underlying asset to obtain for relief for the issuer of the credit-linked note. In respect of the OTC credit derivative products, they are accorded the guarantee treatment, provided that the underlying asset and Reference Obligation have a common obligor, are denominated in the same currency, and that (for credit default products and credit-linked notes) the maturities of the credit derivative and the underlying asset are matched. In keeping with the FSA's Chapter CD, credit default products and total rate of return swaps are treated as Direct Credit Substitutes in the hands of the Protection Seller, which is commensurate with the guarantee treatment, while credit-linked notes are risk weighted at the higher risk weighting of that of the Reference Entity and the issuer of the credit-linked note. In respect of maturity mismatches the BAKred adopts a different treatment from that of the FSA. Although maturity mismatches are allowed in the banking book for credit default products and credit-linked notes, the mismatch maturity is treated as a forward purchase of the Reference Obligation, resulting in 100% of the risk weighting for the underlying asset while the credit derivative's risk weighting is ignored, effectively generating no capital relief in using a credit derivative. Like the FSA, maturity mismatches are not considered by the BAKred to be relevant for total rate of return swaps. In the trading book, credit default products incur no general risk charge while a TRORs Payer is treated as being short the Reference Obligation and also long a notional floating rate note (presumably equivalent to the funding limb of the total rate of return swap) while the converse is true for the TRORs Receiver. The BAKred requires equity add-ons for the PFCE and does not allow a lower add-on for credit-linked notes that constitute qualifying debt instruments.

REGULATORY CAPITAL TREATMENT OF CREDIT DERIVATIVES IN FRANCE

Following up on its discussion paper published in June 1997, the French Commission Bancaire published its paper, *Traitment Prudential de Instruments Dérivés de Credit*, in April 1998. In its paper, the Commission Bancaire sets out the criteria for admissibility of credit derivatives in the trading book. In common with the Capital Adequacy Directive and the other EU regulators, the Commission Bancaire requires the instrument to be held with an intention to trade. Further, the instrument must be tradeable. The Commission Bancaire sets out various indicia of tradeability. These include marking the instrument to market, quotes being available from market makers, the Reference Entity having at least one rated security in issue, and the Reference Obligation of the relevant credit derivative being liquid (although the liquidity test is not specified). Furthermore, the regulated dealer must be competent in the market for either the credit derivative or the Reference Obligation and must also have a reliable valuation model. In the banking book, the Protection Buyer will be accorded the guarantee treatment for its holding of a credit derivative provided that the guarantee is unconditional and not capable of challenge under its terms or any master agreement to which the credit derivative may be subject. Furthermore, the guarantee must exceed any materiality threshold applicable to the position. In keeping with both the BAKred and the FSA, the credit derivative must have the same obligor as the underlying asset and the credit derivative must be sufficiently senior to the underlying asset for the correct treatment to be recognized. There is an automatic deduction of 10% of the protection afforded by the instrument if the credit derivative and the underlying asset are in the same currency, but this increases to 20% if they are in different currencies. One significant distinction from the treatment of the credit derivatives by other regulators is that guarantee treatment will only be recognized if the protection Seller is a credit institution or investment firm, limiting the universal potential protection Sellers from which a regulated French institution may acquire its credit derivative. Although the Commission Bancaire follows the other regulators in providing that the impact of credit default products and total rate of return swaps on the protection Seller is that they are treated as Direct Credit Substitutes in its books, it will treat the deemed position of a protection Seller under a credit-linked note as additive unless it can demonstrate a high intra-basket correlation.

The Commission Bancaire will allow maturity mismatches between a credit derivative and an underlying position in the banking book subject to a residual maturity test. This test differs from that of the FSA in that if the residual maturity of the underlying asset is one year or less and the residual term of the credit derivative is equal to or greater than that of the underlying asset, then the guarantee treatment will be recognized for the Protection Buyer. However, if the residual maturity of the underlying asset is greater than one year and the residual maturity of the credit derivative is also in excess of one year but still less than the asset, then the guarantee treatment will be accorded to the credit derivative position but a 50% weighting of the underlying asset's risk will be added for the future exposure. It is interesting to note that the main determinant is the residual maturity of the underlying asset rather than the residual term of the credit derivative. In the trading book, the Commission Bancaire will only allow specific risk offsets if there is an exact match and imposes a double charge on specific risk mismatches, in other words, an additive charge for both the long and short specific risk positions. For counterparty risk, the Commission Bancaire applies asymmetrical PFCE add-ons. For the Protection Seller, the test is whether the issuer of the Reference Obligation (i.e., the Reference Entity) is an eligible issuer. If it is, then interest rate add-ons are applied, but if it is not an eligible issuer, then equity add-ons are required. However, the treatment is different for the Protection Buyer for which eligible issuer Reference Obligations generate equity add-ons while ineligible issuer Reference Obligations require commodity add-ons to be used.

SUMMARY

By examining the regulatory capital rules of Germany, France, and the U.K., it can be seen that even within the ostensibly standard requirements of the Capital Adequacy Directive, it is possible to produce differing regulatory capital rules for credit derivatives. In part, this is a result of the nature of Directives under EU legislation. In order to take effect under national laws, they require implementation (in contrast to EU Regulations, which take direct effect). Therefore, their implementation at national level has the potential to produce variations in their interpretation, particularly when the implementing regulators find it necessary to integrate their provisions with other non-EU national legislation. The other difficulty facing EU regulators seeking to implement rules for credit derivatives under the Capital Adequacy Directive is the absence of specific provisions in the Directive dealing with credit derivatives (and indeed a number of other new financial products). One challenge for the regulators within the EU will be to ensure that the hard coding of the Capital Adequacy Directive (which enshrines regulatory capital treatment as law) and CADII does not prevent flexible implementation of changes to the regulatory capital regime to track the overhaul of the system that is currently under consideration by the Basle Committee if EU institutions are not be placed at a competitive disadvantage vis à vis non-EU Basle-compliant jurisdictions. It also remains to be seen how other EU member states will implement the Capital Adequacy Directive in respect of credit derivatives. Whether the anomalies identified above between the German, French, and U.K. jurisdictions will be reflected in the rules of other EU member states and whether they are sufficiently significant to create arbitrage possibilities remains to be seen. However, what is apparent is that the novelty of credit derivatives was not something that was anticipated by the drafters of either the Basle Capital Adequacy Accord or the EU's Capital Adequacy Directive.

CONCLUSION

As credit derivatives evolve they are becoming increasingly mainstream in the context of the derivative products. Just as 10 to 15 years ago interest rates and cross currency caused lawyers to examine the legal and regulatory issues raised by their appearance, so lawyers and regulators have had to reassess the received wisdom of the financial markets in the context of these innovative products. In some respects they do not raise any different issues from those raised by other derivatives. They are still contracts or agreements, subject to the formalities and jurisprudential rules of their applicable law. Similarly, unless they are recharacterized, they are subject to the laws and regulations applicable to the marketing of financial instruments generally. However, in other respects, they raise new issues, primarily as a result of their increasing proximity in economic effect to other risk management products, such as guarantees and credit insurance. Given that these products are themselves responses of former generations of financial engineers to the perennial problem of credit risk, it is perhaps unsurprising that credit derivatives adopt comparable approaches to the problem.

CHAPTER 4

Analysis of Credit Spreads

In this chapter, we consider the credit spread curve and its properties. The credit spread of a bond ABC is the yield of the ABC bond minus the yield of the corresponding U.S. Treasury if it's in the U.S. or U.K. Gilt or German bund or the risk-free government bond. The corresponding U.S. Treasury is the U.S. benchmark bond with a similar maturity to the ABC bond. In some countries, like Switzerland, there is no liquid government bond market, so we have to take the swap curve, subtract the credit spread, and then transfer it to an equivalent risk-free curve. Then we compute the spread out of the implied risk-free curve.

AN EXAMPLE OF A SPREAD CURVE

Table 4-1 is an illustration of some typical credit spread curves. These credit spreads obviously change from day to day. For example, the AAA spread for two years is 15 basis points over the benchmark U.S. Treasury, for three years it's 20, for five years it's 25, and so on. We note that the credit spread curve (except for the last line) is upward sloping because the longer an investor holds a debt, the more uncertain it is and, the higher the probabil-

	2 years	3 years	5 years	7 years	10 years
AAA	15	20	25	27	30
AA	20	25	30	32	37
A	30	40	45	50	58
BBB	62	68	75	80	85
BB	200	225	250	300	300
B	300	350	375	400	400
CCC	1100	950	775	725	700

Table 4-1. An example of a credit spread curve. All numbers are in basis points.

ity of default. As the probability of default goes higher, the investor has to be compensated for it.

The exception is the CCC curve, which is downward sloping. A CCC-rated company is more likely to default in the near term. Each year that it survives whatever difficulties earned the CCC rating, it is less likely to default. If the CCC-rated company hasn't defaulted in the first couple of years, it is less likely to default later on.

Now suppose that the CCC ten-year bond yielded 1100 bps over Treasuries. Then, over a ten-year period, the investor would have earned 11000 bps. This would be overpaying because if the CCC survives the first few years, it is likely to continue to survive. Even if they were to default after a few years, the added coupon would more than make up for the amount lost after consideration of the recovery value.

The market is telling you that the first year is when you get the most value because that's when the probability of default is greatest. If the issuer survived the first year, the second year there is a lower probability of default, the third year even lower, and so on.

COMPUTATION OF THE FORWARD SPREAD

A key element of any derivative pricing discussion is the determination of the at-the-money forward price. It is well known, for example, that Libor futures are not good predictors of future Libor rates. However, these futures are still used as the basis for option pricing methods.

Similarly, forward spreads are not good predictors of future spot spreads. We can compute a forward spread, the expected spread on a five-year bond, two years from today. This theoretical forward spread is not necessarily a good predictor of what the actual future spot spread is going to be. However, we do not, in general, have a better predictor.

Suppose we knew how to calculate the forward price of a bond. If we could calculate the forward price of a bond, we could also compute the forward spread. We would simply follow these steps:

1. Compute the forward price of the corporate bond.

2. Convert the price to a forward corporate yield. Remember that the bond has a shorter maturity.

3. Compute the forward price of the U.S. Treasury bond.

4. Convert the price to a forward risk-free yield.

5. Subtract the two forward yields to obtain the desired answer: the forward spread.

Table 4-2 is an example of the computation of the forward price and yield of a corporate bond. In our example, we have a five-year maturity bond with a coupon of 6.00%; the bond yield to maturity is 6.50%. A five-year 6.00% coupon bond yielding 6.50% is priced at $97.89.

To compute the forward price of the bond we use a classical no-arbitrage argument. The expected forward price is such that the expected profit from a hypothetical two-year repo trade should be zero. This assumption is justified because if the expected profit from repo trades were greater than zero, the entire market would be transacting them continuously. Likewise, if the repo were expected to lose money, all market participants would engage in reverse repo trades. In practice, repo trades have short maturity times (e.g., a few weeks).

Assume that the repo rate for this bond is 6.30%. Also assume that an investor can repo that bond for two years (although usually repo trades are transacted for much shorter terms).

The assets of the investor are the coupons. These are 6% bonds, so the investor receives $3.00 every six months for two years. The first $3.00 coupon will arrive in six months (0.5 years), the next in one year, and so on.

The investor's liabilities are the borrowing costs of the bond. These are calculated at the repo rate of 6.30%. The price of the bond was $97.89. Hence, every six months the investor will have to pay $3.08. The liabilities here are $3.08 due in six months, another $3.08 due in one year, and so on.

Now, grow the assets as well as the liabilities at the Libor rate to the termination of the deal. In this example we assume that the repo rate is equal to the Libor rate. For example, a $3.00 coupon received in six months will be worth $3.29 in two years, assuming an interest rate of 6.30%, and so on.

The future value of the total assets is $12.58 and the future value of the liabilities is $12.93. The repo trader is expected to lose

Calculation of the forward price of a bond

Maturity	5 years
Bond price	97.89
Bond coupon	6.00% semiannual
Bond yield	6.50%
Repo rate	6.30%

Forward price for two years in the future

Time	Assets	FV at repo	Liabilities	FV at repo	*Assets:*
0.5	$3.00	$3.29	$3.08	$3.38	6.00% coupon paid
1	$3.00	$3.19	$3.08	$3.28	semiannually
1.5	$3.00	$3.09	$3.08	$3.18	*Liabilities:*
2	$3.00	$3.00	$3.08	$3.08	6.30% repo rate on
					finance
					This is equal to $3.08

			$12.58	$12.93 every six months
		Difference		$(0.35)
		Forward price in two years		
			$98.25	
		Forward yield in two years		
		6.653%	98.25	

Table 4-2. Computation of the forward price and yield of a bond.

$0.35 on the trade. Because we assumed that this is a zero-profit trade, the price of the bond must increase by the same amount. The forward price of the bond is therefore $98.25.

To convert this price to an equivalent yield, remember that in two years, the five-year bond will be a three-year bond. The price-to-yield computation must be adjusted accordingly.

We now repeat the same process for the U.S. Treasury and then subtract the two forward yields from each other. This gives us the expected at-the-money forward spread.

ESTIMATION OF VOLATILITY

How do we estimate the credit spread volatility between the corporate bond and the U.S. Treasury bond? Assume we have a corporate bond that is liquid in the market. One could take the historical daily prices of the corporate bond and the historical daily prices of the U.S. Treasury bond, and then convert the prices to yields and compute the historical spreads. From the historical spread series, one could obtain the volatility of the spread.

But there's a problem. Let's take a two-year historical data set of spreads. The same bond that was a five-year bond at the beginning of the historical series is a three-year bond at the end of the series. What is the spread whose volatility this algorithm is computing for? The five-year spread? The three-year spread? Or somewhere in the middle? The problem arises because of the aging of the bonds.

What one would like to do is to create a constant maturity series. This is simple to do for the U.S. Treasury because there are a lot of outstanding bonds. If the risky debt is also a large issuer, such as the Province of Quebec or Province of Ontario, a constant maturity series can also be created. But what if the issuer is not so large? What if it only has a single outstanding bond?

In this case, we need to create a hypothetical constant maturity series. The issuer doesn't have many bonds, but perhaps we can find another issuer in the same industry who issues bonds at the same interest rate and the same credit rating and the same general type of spread as our original issuer. Or, perhaps we can find several issuers similar to our original issuers and treat them as one generic issuer. Using this technique, we have a chance of creating a constant maturity series that mimics our issuer's debt. That is, if our original issuer were to issue five-year bonds at regular intervals, it would be priced similarly to the other bonds in our index.

Note that the aging problem does not occur when computing the U.S. dollar–Deutsche mark exchange rate volatility. We can look at the historical U.S. dollar–Deutsche mark exchange rates without adjustment because the U.S. dollar–Deutsche mark spot rate has the same financial interpretation today as it had two years ago. It's just a rate and we can figure out the volatility of that rate. But the bond that was a five-year bond two years ago is not the same bond today, because today it is a three-year bond. It is not the same instrument it was.

PROBABILITY OF DEFAULT, RECOVERY VALUE, AND CREDIT SPREADS

Consider the three terms:

- probability of default,

- recovery value, and
- credit spreads.

Corporate spreads observed in the market are a function of several variables. These include liquidity, convexity, flows, bid–ask spreads, special situations, and so on. For example, an eight-and-a-half-year corporate bond would be compared to the ten-year U.S. Treasury. So we need the credit spread but we can only observe the corporate spread. However, if we assume that corporate spreads are mostly a reflection of the market perception of how risky an investment is, then we can create a relationship between these three terms.

In general, we can observe the spread in the market. The recovery value can be estimated from historical findings. Table 4-3 is an illustration of imputing the probability of default from the credit spread and the recovery value. We consider a one-year zero coupon bond that yields 8.00%. The recovery rate is estimated at 40 cents on the dollar. The yield on the risk-free one-year Treasury strip is 6.00%.

Take two portfolio managers, T and C.

- Portfolio manager T buys $100 worth of U.S. Treasury strips.
- Portfolio manager C buys $100 worth of corporate zero coupon bonds, each with a face value of $1. Thus C buys 100 separate bonds.

Under the risk-neutrality assumption, both portfolio managers should end up with equally valued portfolios after one year. If the market predicted that T will always outperform C, no one would invest in corporate bonds. Likewise, if the market predicted that C will consistently outperform T, no one would buy Treasury bonds.

How many corporate bonds are going to default? If none of them (0%) were to default, they would be worth $108. If all of them were to default, they would be worth $43.20 (which is the recovery value of 40% multiplied by $108).

In general, if P percent of the corporate bonds were to default, the value of the portfolio would be:

$$V = P*(1+Y)*R+(1-P)*(1+Y)$$

Here P is the percentage of bonds that defaulted, Y is the corporate coupon, and R is the recovery value.

Probability of default for a one-year zero coupon bond.

Y	**8.00%** yield of the corporate zero	
R	**40.00%** recovery value	
F	**6.00%** yield of the Treasury strip	
P	3.09%	

Own 100 Tsy bonds	106	
Owns 100 Corp bonds	106	$P*(1+Y)*R+(1-P)*(1+Y)$

Table 4-3. Probability of default.

Probability of default for a one-year zero coupon bond.

Y	**8.00%** yield of the corporate zero	
R	**0.00%** recovery value	
F	**6.00%** yield of the Treasury strip	
P	1.85%	

Own 100 Tsy bonds	106	
Owns 100 Corp bonds	106	$P*(1+Y)*R+(1-P)*(1+Y)$

Table 4-4. Probability of default is close to the credit spread when the recovery rate is zero.

The probability of default implied by the market is that P which would result in the value of V being equal to $106, the value achieved by the Treasury strips. In our case, $P = 3.09\%$

A rule of thumb is that if the recovery rate is zero, then the credit spread roughly measures the probability of default. In Table 4-4, the recovery rate is set to zero. The credit spread is 200 basis points or 2.00%. The probability of default is 1.85%, close to 2.00%.

CHAPTER 5

Revenue-Neutral Diversification

Portfolio theories are increasingly being applied to the management of credit portfolios. Significant progress has been made in the analytical frameworks for quantifying credit risk concentrations. In this chapter, we discuss several trade ideas involving credit derivatives.

CREDIT RISK MEASUREMENT

Before considering the use of credit derivatives, the bank's credit risk measurement system must be up to par. The bank must be able to measure its exposures. This involves a certain maturity in managing that credit risk, or at least measuring it. There are two parts to this problem:

1. Measuring the credit risk—A large bank has many deals on its books. The bank may have made loans to many different counterparties: individuals, corporations, small businesses, etc. Some loans have been made through the central office, and other loans have been made by the individual branches. In addition, the bank has dealings involving derivative transactions, loan portfolios, etc.

2. Analyzing the credit risk—After the current credit exposure has been identified, the bank can then proceed to implement credit risk measurement systems such as CreditMetrics and CreditRisk+. These are covered in Chapters 11 and 12 respectively.

Step 1 involves collecting the data, which is an information technology (IT) challenge. Each branch and each department may keep records in different formats and on different computer systems. Step 2 involves using analytical systems on the data collected and asking what-if questions. A sample what-if question is: Is it worth paying a certain premium for a credit swap, in order to reduce risk? The answer depends on a lot of factors, some of which are difficult to measure. For example, default and financial data obtained from some emerging markets is opaque or even unobtainable.

Now assume that the bank can pay nothing, increase its diversification and reduce its risk. Revenue-neutral diversification is rapidly gaining a lot of interest.

BACKGROUND

Revenue-neutral diversification involves the use of credit swaps in order to reduce risk without reducing expected returns.

Consider a bank that has 20% of its total loan portfolio committed to a U.S. tobacco company (see Figure 5-1). That's a clear concentration of risk. The bank has no exposure to Asian steel companies. Asian steel companies are determined to have a low default correlation with the existing portfolio. This is the background behind the trade.

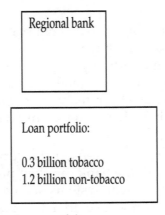

Figure 5-1. A bank with a loan portfolio.

THE TRADE

As illustrated in Figure 5-2, this bank could improve its risk–reward profile by simultaneously:

- Buying a credit swap to hedge a portion of its U.S. tobacco exposure.
- Selling a credit swap on an Asian steel company in an equal amount that generates revenues equal to the cost of the tobacco risk hedge.

We assume that the credit risk of the Asian steel company is roughly equivalent to the credit risk of the original U.S. tobacco position. In Figure 5-2, both trades are done with the same credit derivatives desk. This need not be the case. Each deal is separate and can be transacted with different counterparties.

The first credit swap virtually eliminates the credit exposure on a $50 million loan to a specific tobacco company. However, by itself this transaction reduces portfolio revenues by the amount of the premium, $250,000 per year. That is the premium being paid for the protection.

Without a sophisticated risk analysis system, a credit portfolio manager cannot be certain that hedging alone improves the risk return profile of the portfolio. While it clearly reduces risk, it also reduces return. The bank doesn't want to reduce return. The point is to reduce the risk without reducing return.

The bank purchased a credit swap at a cost of $250,000 per year. Now it needs to increase its return by exactly the same amount. It increases return with the sold credit swap. Selling the credit swap on the Asian steel company increases the return by an amount that precisely offsets the reduction of $250,000 per year.

In Figure 5-2, the bank is on the left and the credit derivatives desk is on the right. The bank buys U.S. tobacco protection at 50 basis points per annum. The bank also sells steel protection at 55 basis points per annum. The tobacco credit swap notional was $50 million. The reference asset is the loan with a maturity of four years denominated in U.S. dollars. The Asian steel credit swap has a notional amount of $45.45 million. The reference asset is a loan with a maturity of four years.

If the bank had only purchased a credit default swap on the U.S. tobacco company, it would have reduced its risk. However,

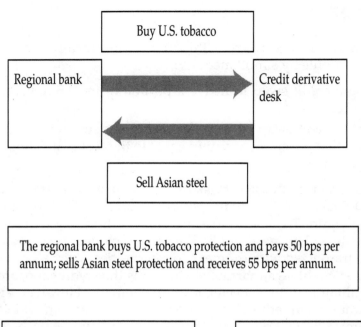

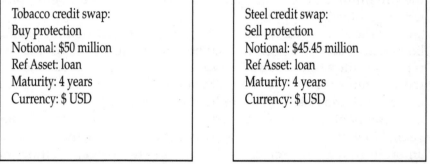

Figure 5-2. Revenue-neutral diversification.

the bank would have to pay a premium of 50 bps per annum, which would erode earnings. So it decided to sell a credit default swap on an issuer that was judged to have a similar probability of default. It is difficult to find another credit default swap for exactly four years whose price will be exactly 50 bps. Therefore, the bank finds a close match, a credit default swap on the Asian steel company that costs 55 bps. The notional amounts are adjusted so the cash amounts paid and received for the protection will match out precisely.

50 bps per annum * $50 million = $250,000 per year
55 bps per annum * $45.45 million = $250,000 per year

The bank might be concerned about selling protection against a creditor it is totally unfamiliar with. That is a valid concern. However, currently the bank has 20% of its risk in a single industry, the tobacco industry. It is obvious that it needs to hedge that risk or diversify it away.

EQUIVALENT POSITION

Credit derivatives present us with two solution strategies:

1. Insure (hedge) against the risk by purchasing a credit swap on the tobacco company.

2. Diversify the risk by also selling a default swap on the Asian steel company.

After the two trades are completed, the risk of the revised portfolio is less than that of the original portfolio. The position of the bank is equivalent to having loaned $50 million less to the U.S. tobacco company and $45.45 million to the Asian steel company, see Figure 5-3.

Now it is obvious that for this trade to work, the default correlation between the Asian steel company and the original U.S. tobacco company must be low. Assume that the default correlation

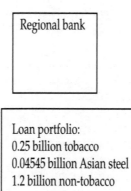

Figure 5-3. The equivalent position.

between them is high and that they will default together. Now the difference between Figures 5-3 and 5-1 is not so striking any more.

The objectives of this trade are twofold: to diversify away from the tobacco risk without reducing returns. In fact, the bank is not trying to increase overall return here.

There's one caveat to this kind of trade. You want roughly the same notional amounts and approximately the same credit rating. Revenue-neutral diversification works best if the credits exchanged are approximately equal. This limits the degree to which large differences in notional amounts might distort the distribution of risk in the portfolio.

The bank does not want large differences in the notional amounts. This forces them to swap risks on issuers with very similar spreads. Similar spreads mean similar credit ratings. The credit risk associated with the Asian steel company is roughly similar to that associated with the U.S. tobacco company.

The acceptance of this trade is a matter of culture. Some banks feel more comfortable holding the entire tobacco debt since they are familiar with the tobacco industry. They would not want to enter the trade as they feel they know nothing about the Asian steel companies.

We have just reviewed a credit derivative solution to a common problem: overexposure to a particular creditor. With revenue-neutral diversification, a bank can effectively diversify its portfolio without losing income.

CHAPTER 6

Examination of Term Sheets

In this chapter, we look at actual term sheets of trades that have been transacted in the markets. We analyze each trade and understand the motivation for the trade from the buyer's point of view as well as the seller's. Actual terms sheets are difficult to obtain because they are considered somewhat proprietary. For that reason we have erased some of the actual names and replaced them with ABC or XYZ, for example.

PUT CREDIT SPREAD

Exhibit 6-1 shows an example of a put credit spread. In this example, the bank is purchasing a put on the credit spread of ABC bonds.

On the expiration date, we examine the spread between the ABC bond and the U.S. Treasury bond. If the spread is wider than 2.05% (or 205 basis points) the investor will have to compensate the bank. For example, if the credit spread on the expiration date is 3.00% (or 300 basis points) the payout will be computed as:

$$\$10 \text{ million}*8*(3.00\%-2.05\%) = \$760,000$$

Note that this is termed a put option even though the payment formula looks more like a call option.

The term

$$\max (\text{Index Credit Spread}-2.05\%,0)$$

looks very much like

$$\max(S-X,0)$$

or the payout formula for a call option.

E x h i b i t   6 - 1
P U T   C R E D I T   S P R E A D

**Put Credit Spread on ABC Bonds Due Dec 31, 2023
(as of 11/14/1994)**

Spread put buyer:	Bank
Spread put seller:	Investor
Notional principal amount:	$10 million
Settlement date:	Today
Exercise date:	One year from today
Underlying index:	ABC bonds due Dec. 31, 2023
Reference U.S. Treasury:	The offer yield of the U.S. Treasury 6.25% due August 2023
Index credit spread:	The yield to maturity of the underlying index using the Flat Bid Price (bid price net of accrued interest and any nonpaid coupons) of the underlying index minus the offer yield of the reference U.S. Treasury at 12:00 PM New York EST two days before the exercise date.
Current spread:	1.95%
Spread put strike:	2.05% (at-the-money forward strike)
Put option payment:	Notional * max (DUR*(Index Credit Spread-2.05%),0)
DUR (duration):	8
Option premium:	1.25% of the notional principal amount payable by the bank to the investor on the settlement date

---

Note that the investor has to reimburse the bank in case the spread increases. If the spread increases, the bond value drops. So the bank has a put option on the ABC bond. Had this been a regular put option, the bank would have been allowed to put the bond to the investor for a specific dollar amount, e.g. par. This option is a credit derivative because its payout formula has to do with the credit spread of the bond to the U.S. Treasury. Essentially the bank is allowed to put the bond at a prespecified spread to the U.S. Treasury.

What is the relevance of term *DUR* in the payout function? Duration measures the relative change in the price of a bond as its yield changes. Thus we can expect the price of a bond with a duration of 8 to move by about 8 percent for every 1 percent move in yields. In this case, we are not concerned about changes in the risk-free rates. Rather, we are concerned about changes in credit spreads. Duration is used to relate the change in the bond price of ABC to the change in spreads. There are two caveats:

1. A formula that only uses duration is an approximation to the price–yield relationship. A better approximation would include the effects of convexity. The approximation works well if the change in spread is relatively small and the convexity effect is marginal. In this case, this works to the bank's advantage. The ABC bond has a positive convexity. Hence its price drop as yields increase is not as large as would have been predicted by approximating with duration alone.

2. To really capture the price–yield relationship on the expiration date, we would have to consider the duration of the ABC bond as of *that date.* So rather than using a fixed number, such as 8, for the DUR term, the term sheet could have used: "DUR: The duration of bond ABC on expiration date." Because duration is also a function of interest rates, this would have exposed the bank and the investor to further interest rate risks. Instead, they chose to approximate the duration on expiration date with a fixed number. The number 8 is probably close to the duration of the bond at the date of the term sheet.

Note the interesting use of bid and offer yields in the term sheet. Obviously, for every bond the bid price is lower than the offer price. Hence, the bid yield is higher than the offer yield. The payout formula indicates a spread consisting of a bid yield minus an offer yield. The bid yield is high and the offer yield is low. This means that the spread is wide and the payout that the bank may expect from the client is large. It is larger than if we would have used bid to bid, offer to offer on mid-market to mid-market yields.

Of course, the bid and offer yields on U.S. Treasuries are quite similar to each other because there is a very liquid market for the Treasury bonds. But there is probably a large difference between the bid and offer yields on the ABC corporate bond, because it may not be as liquid a bond.

The investor is obviously taking a view that the credit rating of ABC bond will improve and that the option will expire out of the money.

DIGITAL SPREAD OPTIONS

Exhibit 6-2 shows an example of a structured note with embedded digital spread options. In this example, the client is expressing a view that the spread on the Brazil par bond will remain stable.

Exhibit 6-2
DIGITAL SPREAD OPTIONS

One-Year Note Linked to the Brazilian Par Bond
(as of 11/14/1994)

Issuer:	To be determined, AA or better
Principal amount:	$50 million
Settlement date:	Two weeks from today
Maturity date:	One year from settlement date
Price:	Par
Underlying index:	Brazil Par Brady bonds due 4/15/2024
Reference U.S. Treasury:	The U.S. Treasury 7.125% due 2/2023
Index credit spread:	The yield to maturity of the underlying index using the Flat Bid Price (bid price net of accrued interest and any nonpaid coupons) of the underlying index minus the offer yield of the reference U.S. Treasury at 12:00 PM New York EST two days before the exercise date.
Coupon:	0%
Principal redemption value:	■ If index credit spread is >=4.00% and <=6.00%
	111.00% of par
	■ Otherwise
	102.00% of par

Current index credit spread: 5.35%

In this note, the investor will get tremendous performance if the credit spread of the Brady bond is between 400 and 600 basis points one year from the issue date.

Note that these are digital, "all or nothing" options. If the credit spread is in the allotted slot, (e.g., 5.99%) the investor will receive $111.00 at maturity. On the other hand, if it is outside of the allotted slot (e.g. 6.01%), the investor will only receive $102.00.

The investor is paying for the option by forgoing the interest on the bonds. A typical AA-rated issuer probably has to pay a much higher coupon, for example, 6.00%. The buyer of the note is forgoing a large part of the coupon. In essence, the buyer paid $4.00 for the option. In return, it will get paid $9.00 if the credit spread is in the allotted slot.

In this structure, the client is essentially long a digital option that pays $9.00 on expiration if the credit spread is above 4.00%. The client is also short a similar option with a strike of 6.00%. Obviously, the 4.00% strike is in the money, and the 6.00% strike is out of the money. Hence, the client has to pay for these options. The client pays for these options by forgoing a part of the interest on the bond. Figure 6-1 illustrates the payout of the two digital options embedded in the bond. A term used to describe these two digital options is the "step." They look like the stair step used in aerobic fitness classes.

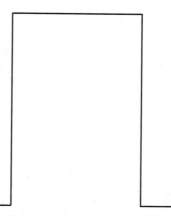

Figure 6-1. Payout of two digital options—the "step" function.

ASSET SWAP PUT CREDIT SPREAD

In this example, which is illustrated in Exhibit 6-3, the bank purchases a put credit spread option whose underlying is an asset swap.

The structure in Exhibit 6-3 works as follows:

At initiation of the trade, the bank pays the investor 40 basis points times the notional amount. In our case, the notional is $10,000,000 so the payment is $40,000.

E x h i b i t   6 - 3
A S S E T   S W A P   P U T   O P T I O N

**One-Year XYZ Bonds 6.75% Due 12/1/2005 Asset
Swap Put Credit Spread Option
(as of 11/14/1994)**

Swap details:

Underlying issue:	XYZ 6.75% bonds due 12/1/2005
Notional principal amount:	$10 million
Contingent asset swap settlement date:	One year from today
Asset swap maturity date:	12/1/2005—bond maturity date
Asset swap price:	$100
Asset swap coupon:	3-Month Libor + 0.60%, quarterly, ACT/360
Current asset swap level:	3-Month Libor + 0.55%

Credit spread option details:

Put option buyer:	Bank
Put option seller:	Investor
Put credit spread option:	The bank has the right but not the obligation to sell the investor the asset swap on the determination date.
Option payment by the bank:	0.40% of the notional principal amount
Determination date:	Five days prior to the contingent asset swap settlement date
Cash settlement provision:	The investor may choose to cash settle the option on the determination date. If selected, this settlement would be the present value of the difference between the asset swap coupon and the then-current trading level of the underlying issue.

One year later, the bank has the right to begin an asset swap. If the bank initiates the asset swap, then the following occur (see Figure 6-2):

- The bank sells the asset to the investor for par.
- The investor passes a 6.75% coupon to the bank.
- The bank pays the investor Libor + 0.60%.

Initiation of Swap

Bank ——— asset → Investor
      ← 100

Lifetime of Swap

Bank —— Libor + 0.60%   → Investor
   ← 6.75% coupon from bond

Figure 6-2. Asset swap details.

If the bank exercises the option, the asset swap goes into effect. The investor buys the bond for a price of par.

Throughout the life of the swap, the bank pays the investor Libor+0.60% and the investor pays the bank the 6.75% coupon on the bond, even if it defaults. Note that at maturity of the bond, the investor gets to keep the principal of the bond if it doesn't default.

The bank would like to sell the bond at par to the investor if the yield on the bond is high. There are two possible causes for an increase in the bond yield:

1. An increase in interest rates.
2. A higher possibility of default that leads to widening spreads. These spreads cause the bond yield to become higher.

Now, the bank pays the investor Libor+0.60% against receiving a fixed rate so the first case is canceled out. That is, if interest rates increase, it is advantageous to the bank to sell the bond to the investor for par. But it is not to its advantage to give the investor a floating rate against receiving a fixed rate (an interest rate swap). In fact, both of these effects exactly cancel each other out. For example, Libor is at 14%, interest rates are very high. The bond is below par so the bank wants to activate the asset swap and get $100 for the bond, which is trading below par. But on the other hand, the bank has to pay high interest on the floating side and receive a low fixed rate, so this negates the bank's gain. If Libor stays low but the spread increases, the price of the bond decreases as before. But in this case, the interest rate swap is not detrimental to the bank and the bank will choose to exercise the option.

The bank will only exercise the option when the spread widens. Therefore, this structure is a credit derivative.

What happens if the bond defaults during the lifetime of the swap? It's an asset swap. The bank gives the investor Libor plus 60 basis points and the investor gives the bank a fixed coupon of 6.75%. The fact that there is a bond there has nothing to do with that. Once the asset swap starts, the investor is exposed to the bond. The asset swap is totally separate from the bond. If the bond defaults, the investor still has to make coupon payments. Also, the investor has paid $100 for a bond that has defaulted. Even if the bond doesn't pay any coupons to the investor, the investor still has to pay 6.75% interest to the bank.

Why would an investor sell this option? What is the view that the investor is expressing? The investor receives 40 basis points. The investor is saying that this spread is not widening, that it is happy to receive Libor plus 60 because current asset swap levels are Libor plus 55. For the investor to receive Libor plus 60 the spread has to widen. If the spread stays the same or narrows, the bank won't exercise the option. So the investor is expressing a view that the spread will stay more or less the same or even contract. The investor is actually taking a view on these XYZ bonds and it receives cash for taking that view, 40 basis points. Note that the investor is taking the view on the credit spread and not on the interest rate.

What about the default risk of the bond? If the bond defaults during the first year, there is no swap because there is no bond. So if the bond defaults during the first year, the bank faces a loss. On the other hand, if the bond defaults once the swap starts, that's the investor's problem because the investor owns the bond. However, if the issuer doesn't default but only deteriorates, the bond's credit spread goes up and the bank is very happy because it activates the asset swap. So we need to make a distinction between default and the spread widening.

ZERO-PREMIUM COLLARS

A dealer can combine a call and a put and create a collar. Of particular interest are collars in which the client is long one option and short the other and the premiums of both options exactly offset each other. These are known as zero-cost collars. Of course, they are not really zero-cost, they are merely zero-premium. The term *zero-cost* is a misnomer because as a client, you may end up having to pay for the structure. This can happen if the option you are short expires in the money. So we prefer to call them zero-premium. (Note, however, that the fact that you don't have to pay a premium today does not mean that you will not pay later on.)

There are a lot of reasons why companies prefer zero-premium structures. If you are a company and you pay an option premium it is a cost that is deducted from you. It is visible on the balance sheet. When an option you purchased expires in the money and pays out, it just goes into the general ledger, and is regarded as a taxable income. For many reasons, companies like structures in which they don't have to pay a premium up front even though they might not receive the same payout later on. There are some tax, regulatory, and accounting advantages to zero-premium structures. They are very popular.

A question arises as to why a company would pay for options that many times expire out of the money. Management might consider this and put pressure on the finance department to find a way to reduce the cost (especially if a competing firm did not use options and now has money to spend on a better advertising campaign). There is real resistance in the corporation to paying option premiums. On the other hand, corporations realize that they need hedging tools.

For example, suppose you are a gold mine in South Africa and did not use options. Now that gold is so low, you are out of business. The gold mine may have been in the family for many generations and you have to close it down. The gold mine closes because you did not buy put options to protect against the price decline in gold. In terms of using options, you are "damned if you do and damned if you don't."

As with all credit derivatives, the strikes may be based on price (for floating rate notes) or on credit spread (for fixed rate bonds). This is similar to the investor establishing a long position in the underlying bond but being buffered against losses because the put can be somewhat out of the money. In a normal collar on a fixed rate bond, the investor would also be exposed to interest rate movements. Here they are not. The investor (and the dealer) are only exposed to credit spread.

As illustrated in Figure 6-3, it is possible to create credit spread collars. The investor is long a credit spread call that is at the money and short a credit spread put that is somewhat out of the money. A term sheet is shown in Exhibit 6-4.

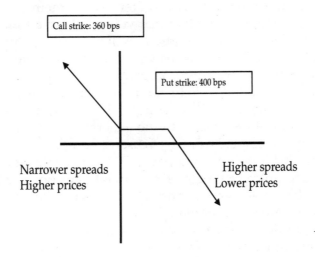

Figure 6-3. A credit spread collar.

Note that the investor purchases an at-the-money call on the credit spread and sells a 50 bps out-of-the-money put. Note also that the Duration (DUR) is fixed at trade date. It is not the duration of the underlying at the maturity date.

The investor buys a credit spread call from the bank and simultaneously sells a credit spread put to the bank. The bank is willing to trade for a notional of anywhere between $5 million and $25 million. The underlying index is the spread of the ABC Global bonds. The index spread at maturity is the yield to maturity of the ABC bonds using the flat bid price of the bond minus the offer yield to maturity of the U.S. Treasury. As we've observed before, such a definition of spread pushes the payout in the favor of the bank.

The call payment is determined by the notional times the maximum of 360 minus the index credit spread and zero. The put payment is determined by the maximum of the index credit spread minus 400 or zero. Again, this is a put option even though it looks like a call, $max(S-X,0)$.

Exhibit 6-4
ZERO-COST COLLAR

Zero-Cost Credit Spread Collar Linked to ABC Global Bond 10.95% Due 11/1/1999
(as of 11/14/1994)

Call spread buyer:	Investor
Call spread seller:	Bank
Put spread buyer:	Bank
Put spread seller:	Investor
Notional amount:	$5 million to $25 million
Settlement date:	Two weeks from today
Maturity date:	One year from settlement date
Underlying index:	ABC 10.95% Global bond due 11/1/1999
Index credit spread at maturity:	The yield to maturity of the ABC Global bond 10.95% due 11/1/1999 using the flat bid price of the bond minus the offer yield to maturity of the 7.875% U.S. Treasury Note due November, 1999.
Spread call payment:	Notional * max(0,DUR*(360-Index Credit Spread))
Spread put payment:	Notional * max(0,DUR*(Index Credit Spread-400))
Spread call strike:	360 basis points
Spread put strike:	400 basis points
DUR:	The modified duration of the underlying index as quoted on the Bloomberg screen DUR. Current duration is 3.60 years. The duration is fixed at trade execution.
Current spread:	350 basis points

Observe the duration number in the payout formula again. As already discussed, duration is the duration of the bond. It measures the change in the price of the bond as the yield changes. In this term sheet the actual modified duration of the bond as computed by Bloomberg is used. Note that the duration is fixed at trade date and not computed at expiration date. If you really wanted to hedge the price change with respect to yield change, you would compute the duration of the expiration of the option. If you were to recompute duration at expiration, you would also be exposed to interest rate risk, because rates can change before expiration. The term sheet views duration as an approximate number that is calculated today and kept as a constant.

Note that there is an uneven risk–reward relationship in this trade. The credit spread of the ABC Global bonds may improve some. It is difficult to imagine that the spread will become zero or even very close to zero. On the other hand, the spread could easily widen by many hundreds of basis points. Thus, the put writer (the investor) has more of a downside than the call writer (the bank).

COMBINING CREDIT AND FOREIGN EXCHANGE

Exhibit 6-5 illustrates a structured note with a credit spread component and a foreign exchange component.

The note is issued by an AA-rated issuer or better; the principal amount is $10 million. The note matures in six months and pays a coupon of Libor. In addition, the principal redemption is computed according to a very bizarre formula. The investor might get its principal back, or it might get something else. The investor might get more than par or might get less than par. The note is subject to a minimum principal redemption of zero. The issuer is not going to call the investor and ask for more money, but in fact the investor can lose the entire principal amount. Now, here is the challenge that faces portfolio managers: The dealer sends this term sheet by fax and the portfolio manager has to determine whether this is a good investment or a bad one. The portfolio manager is going to get a Libor coupon, but what is the expected outcome on the final principal? How much principal is the investor going to receive? The portfolio manager understands investors could get a lot below par, but also a lot more. What is the expected gain? What

Exhibit 6-5

STRUCTURED NOTE COMBINING CREDIT AND FOREIGN EXCHANGE

Mexican Peso Linked Brazil IDU Credit Spread Note
(as of 11/14/1994)

Issuer:	AA-rated issuer or better
Principal amount:	$10 million
Tenor of investment:	Six months
Price:	Par
Coupon:	Libor
Principal redemption:	Principal amount + Brazil IDU component + Mexican Peso component. Subject to minimal principal redemption of zero.
Brazil IDU component:	Principal amount * DUR * 5 * (7.03% – Credit spread).
Credit spread:	Brazil IDU yield – UST 6.875% due August 1999.
DUR:	3.0
Spot Credit spread:	7.03%
Mexican Peso component:	Principal amount * 5 * (3.5248 – Peso Spot)/Peso Spot.

Subject to a minimum level of zero. Locked at zero if peso spot trades 3.5248 at any time prior to the pricing date.

Peso spot:	The exchange rate of Mexican Pesos for U.S. Dollars, expressed in terms of peso per dollar, at which the bank can sell pesos for dollars on the pricing date for settlement on the second following Mexico City business day, net of any taxes on foreign exchange transactions that may be imposed by Mexico.
Today's Peso spot:	3.4400 Pesos per USD
Top of band:	3.5248 Pesos per USD
Pricing date:	The date that is two Mexico City trading days prior to maturity.

risk factors is this note exposed to and in what manner? The challenge that faces a portfolio manager is to try to decompose this note via reverse engineering to its component parts. The portfolio manager must decide: What are the components? What type of view am I taking by buying this note? What are the risk factors? What is the minimum I can get? What is the maximum? How does volatility affect it? What about correlation? The pricing question is only one piece of the puzzle.

This note is subject to some non-obvious terms. If the Mexican peso trades at a certain level at any time before maturity, the structure is knocked out. The payout has to do with the rate at which Mexican pesos can be converted to U.S. dollars, subject to taxes that may imposed by the Mexican government. The investor is also taking on some political and convertibility risks.

This structure is designed for an investor who believes in a combination of a tightening on the Brazil IDU credit spread and a Mexican peso strengthening over the next six months. This trade offers an efficient method of taking both views. The investor may achieve an annualized return of 88% in six months if IDU spreads tighten by 100 basis points and the Mexican peso strengthens to 3.35.

What happens if credit spreads widen? Let's assume spreads widen to 9.03%. Then, the investor receives a principal amount of:

$$\$10,000,000 - \$3,000,000 = \$7,000,000 \text{ U.S. dollars}$$

The Mexican peso component can only increase the principal redemption amount. The Brazil IDU component can also hurt it. Hence, the Mexican peso component is an option and the Brazil IDU component is like a forward.

The issuer is rated AA or better. That is the least of the investor's concerns. The investor should be much more concerned with the market risks arising from the Brazil IDU spreads and the Mexican peso exchange rates. However, many of these kinds of structures have been sold in the past to investors who were not able to completely understand the risks involved in the structure. The investors were happy purchasing a bond from a decently rated issuer and perhaps did not understand the precise risks embedded in that bond.

This is a very important point: The credit ratings imply the ability of the issuer to pay but they don't rate its necessity to pay. The actual principal and coupon payments of the note may be tied, like in this structured note, to some market event or to the performance of a specific loan. The note could be rated AA or even AAA and still not pay out at maturity. At some point, the credit rating agencies were contemplating rating bonds with AAA_r. The little r would signify that there are other risks in the marketplace.

VERY STRUCTURED PRODUCTS

Exhibit 6-6 shows a structure based on the yields of Argentine bonds. Obviously, comprehending this structure requires a lot of specific knowledge about Argentina and its different bonds. We only include it here to show how completely specialized these trades can become. What we are trying to demonstrate is not so much the details of this particular trade, but how highly structured these trades are and the fact that they are suited to a very particular view. What view is the investor taking in this trade? The investor would have to be an expert on this type of Argentine debt.

BINARY BONDS

The binary bonds basically include digital structures. Usually they consist of a coupon-enhanced bond. This bond typically pays a higher coupon than the reference underlying bond. The yield enhancement is typically 30 to 100 basis points. These bonds are typically issued by bankruptcy-remote special purpose vehicles.

These bonds carry more default risk than the reference underlying bonds. In the event of default or if the underlying credit trades to a default level, the coupon payment on the binary bond shall cease and it will redeem at zero. If you buy a regular bond and it defaults, you have a recovery value. If you buy the binary bond and the underlying credit defaults, you get zero. (See Figure 6-4.)

Regular Bond Coupon 6% Recovery value: 70

Binary Bond Coupon 7% Recovery value: Receive zero if the regular bond defaults.

Figure 6-4.

E x h i b i t   6 - 6
A R G E N T I N E   T R A D E

Forward Spread Note
Argentine BOCON's vs. Argentine Stripped Pars
(terms as of November 11, 1994)

Issuer:	To be determined, Single A or better
Principal amount:	$10 million to $50 million
Settlement date:	Two weeks from today
Maturity date:	April 1, 1997
Price:	Par
Coupon:	Libor flat floating rate, or equivalent fixed coupon
Principal redemption value:	Par + Index Value
Index value:	Index value shall be determined by the formula below, to be applied at the index determination date.
Formula:	5 * (Stripped Yield of Argentina Par Brady Bonds due 3/31/2023 + 4.25% – Swapped Yield of Argentina Bocon Previs Bond due 4/1/2001).

Principal redemption can never be below zero.

Current spread:	–1.60%
Index determination date:	April 1, 1997

Calculation of stripped yield for Argentina Par Brady bonds:

Offer side of Argentina Pars of Reuters TTOK—Bid side of UST Strip of 2/15/2023 on Bloomberg PXS5. Using this price and the coupon on the Argentina Par bonds, the semiannual yield to maturity is calculated assuming a principal redemption of zero.

Calculation of swapped yield for Argentina Bocon Previs bonds:

Determined as: (1) the bid side of the BOCONs on Reuters page RPZA; (2) the fixed coupons, on a monthly pay, Act/365 basis, obtained on the index determination date from swapping all future floating coupons of the BOCONs; and (3) applying the coupons to the notional equivalent of the BOCON (original face plus accrued interest on April 1, 1997, then amortizing at a rate of 2.08% of notional for 47 months and 2.24% for one final month, to May 1, 2001).

Which client would buy this? What view is the investor taking? This particular structure is actually applicable to somebody who is taking a view on the recovery rate. The investor is predicting a much lower recovery value than what the market is saying. According to the market the recovery value of the bond is 70. There is a certain probability of default and the bond trades at a corresponding yield to maturity. Assume the investor is thinking that in case of default, the actual recovery value will be closer to 20. In this case, the investor may be willing to forgo the recovery value in order to obtain a higher coupon. The binary bond achieves this investment objective.

These are very hard structures to sell because several investors don't understand them. There were a lot of lawsuits over trades like this, as well as several disputes. Some investors did not understand that they would get zero in case of default.

The binary bonds typically have a maturity range of about 3 to 7 years. The underlying reference bond may be a different currency denomination than the binary bond. The binary could pay a coupon in U.S. dollars so long as a German bond doesn't default. When the German bond defaults, all coupon payments on the binary bond stop and it redeems at zero. That is, no principal will be paid back to the investor. The underlying reference bond might be in a different currency or it might be in the same currency.

In Exhibit 6-7 we have a coupon-enhanced ABC linked note. This is a binary bond. The underlying bond issued by ABC has a coupon of 7.45%. The maturity date of the structured note is February 9, 1998, so it's the same maturity as the ABC bond, only a few days afterward. Why a few days? Because that gives the trust time so that it can receive the principal on the underlying bond in case it didn't default. In addition, the trust wants to actually be able to collect the proceeds of the coupons before passing them to the investor. They don't want to pay the investor a coupon and find out that ABC defaulted on the actual coupon payment date. It will take the trust a few days to deliver the coupon to the investor or to figure out that the underlying bond has defaulted. The binary bond gives the investor a 9.45% coupon, which is the current ABC yield plus 80 basis points. The principal redemption is par, unless the default provision is activated. What is a default provision? If at any time during the life of this note ABC fails to make a payment due on the ABC 7.45%, all interest payments will cease and the structure will be redeemed at zero. There is no market test here; ABC only has to miss a payment.

Exhibit 6-7
A BINARY BOND

Coupon-Enhanced ABC 7.45% 2/1/98 Linked Note
(as of 11/14/1994)

Issuer:	Bankruptcy-remote AAA-rated Special Purpose Vehicle
Underlying trust asset:	ABC 7.45% of 2/1/98
Principal amount:	$5 to $10 million
Settlement date:	Two weeks
Maturity date:	February 9, 1998
Price:	Par
Coupon:	9.45% (current ABC yield + 0.80%)
Coupon payment dates:	February 9 and August 9, short first coupon
Principal redemption:	Par, unless default provision is activated
Default provision:	If at any time during the life of this note, ABC Inc. fails to make a payment due on the ABC 7.45% of 2/1/98, interest payments will cease and the structured note will be redeemed at zero.
Current ABC yield:	UST 8.125% 2/98 + 1.22%

The binary bond may be suitable for investors who hold bonds to maturity and who are quite convinced that the underlying bond will not default. Even if it does default, the investor monetizes the recovery value because the investor thinks that the recovery value is much lower than the amount priced by the marketplace. One natural type of underlying security could be a subordinated issue of a high-quality issuer. Such a bond may have a low probability of default because the issuer is highly rated. In case of default, the subordinated debtholders stand behind the senior debtholders. Therefore, the recovery value of a subordinated debt might be very low. Because the underlying note is a subordinated debt, so many other debtholders stand in line in front of them that, if there is a default, by the time it is the subordinated debtholders' turn, there are not going to be any assets left. Who else would buy the binary notes? Consider a small Korean bank that buys this note and the asset is a bond issued by the Korean Development Bank or another large bank in Korea. If the Korean Development Bank goes into default, then the small Korean bank has much worse problems than whether it will receive the recovery value of this particular note. It is probably exposed to the large bank in a variety of deals. Taking this idea to the extreme, an institution might be tempted to buy binary bonds whose underlying reference asset is issued by the very same institution. Notice that here the dealer who sells the bonds doesn't even care whether there is a high correlation or low correlation, because the dealer has already received the $100. In this type of deal the dealer does not have to be concerned with the credit quality of the counterparty. If there is a default in this trade, the dealer simply doesn't return the $100. The binary bond is like a credit-linked note but has a lot more price variability because there is no recovery value.

Exhibit 6-8 is an example from a marketing material package. Where is the mistake in the argument illustrated?

The argument in Exhibit 6-8 is that the XYZ five-year bond has a 7% probability of default in five years. The recovery value for the XYZ bond is 40%. Now, compare that to purchasing a five-year binary bond with the same XYZ bond as the underlying security.

The holder of the binary will lose the recovery value of 40% if the XYZ defaults. There is a 7% chance of that. So the binary bond holder loses 2.80%.

E x h i b i t 6 - 8
I N F O R M A T I O N F R O M
M A R K E T I N G M A T E R I A L

Example: A Binary Note on the XYZ Five-Year Bond

Expected cumulative probability of default:	7.00%
Expected recovery value upon default:	40.00%
Expected value forgone:	7%*40% = 2.80%
Zero-one coupon enhancement per annum:	1.00%
Coupon enhancement present value:	4.20%

Conclusion: Purchase the zero-one bond because the present value of the coupon enhancement exceeds the expected forgone value.

On the other hand, the binary bond pays 1% extra per annum. Over five years, it pays 5% extra. Taking the present value of the additional cash flows, the binary bond pays 4.20% more than the straight XYZ bond.

It looks like the investor receives 420 basis points for giving up 280 basis points. Where is the mistake in this argument? There is no guarantee that the XYZ bond will default after five years. This argument is all very nice so long as XYZ defaults exactly after five years. What happens if XYZ defaults before five years? It could default after one year or after two years. For example, if XYZ defaults after one year, the investor only gets one enhanced coupon. Thus the investor only got 100 basis points and lost the entire recovery value. If we only consider the scenario in which XYZ defaults at the end of five years, we wrongly assume that the investor has already received all of the enhanced coupons. Think of a life insurance company that counts on receiving all the premiums if I die at 102. If I pay the premiums and I die at 102, the insurance company will be very happy and in this case, so will I. But if I die at 55, the insurance company will have collected only X years of premium against the insured payout.

Why is the price sensitivity of the binary bond much higher than that of a regular bond? Because if a regular bond doesn't default, its price is close to $100. If it does default, the price is its recovery value, say $60. What about the binary bond? If the underlying security doesn't default, the price is close to $100. If it does default the price is zero. Suppose the underlying starts deteriorating. As it hovers close to the default range, the underlying bond price will move to somewhere close to $60. The binary bond will move up and down in price in a way correlated with the underlying security but at a much higher price sensitivity. The binary bond might move to a price close to $0. That's kind of obvious. The volatility of price is much higher because the binary bond can go up or down much more severely.

BASKET CREDIT-LINKED NOTES

The basket credit-linked note (CLN) pays an enhanced coupon over the average yield of a basket of three or more underlying reference bonds. In Figure 6-5 we have three reference bonds. Let's call them ABC, DEF, and GHI. So we have a basket. Then we have

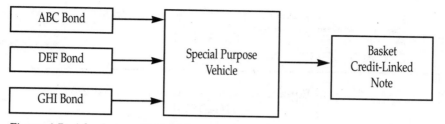

Figure 6-5. A basket credit-linked note.

a bankruptcy-remote special purpose vehicle that collects the coupons and then passes a coupon to the basket CLN. So far so good. Now the question is, what happens if one of these defaults?

The basket credit-linked notes were created for investors who were nervous about receiving absolutely nothing in the case of the binary bond. Investors wanted to get something even in the case of a default. The challenge was to design a security in which the investor can receive something in the case of default and, at the same time, still receive a higher coupon. The major advantage of a basket CLN is that the default event will not result in a complete loss of principal.

In Exhibit 6-9 we have an illustration of a basket credit-linked note. In case of default, the investor will be delivered an amount of the defaulted bond equal to 80% of the full-in face value of the basket CLN. It looks like the investor only relinquishes 20% of the expected recovery value upon default, but that's not exactly correct, as we will see later. The underlying bonds of a basket credit-linked note are typically reference bonds that are close in maturity, but not necessarily of the same country or industry or credit rating. The issuer itself may be a special purpose vehicle or, as in this case, a company. In this example the issuer is rated single A. The maturity of the structures is about three-and-a-half years. The price is par. The basket CLN pays the investor Libor plus 135 basis points. That's a very nice coupon for a single –A-rated issuer. What's the default provision? The investor gets principal redemption par, unless the default provision is activated. If, at any time during the life of the note, one of the bonds in the basket defaults in principal or interest payment due, the investor will receive 80% of the notional amount face value of the defaulted bond or any other bond in the basket and the issuer will have no further obligation to repay interest or principal. So long as there is no default and all of

Exhibit 6-9
A BASKET CREDIT-LINKED NOTE

Coupon-Enhanced Basket Credit-Linked Note
(as of 11/14/1994)

Issuer:	To be determined, single A or better
Principal amount:	$5 to $10 million
Settlement date:	Two weeks
Maturity date:	June 30, 1998
Price:	Par
Coupon:	6-month Libor + 1.35%, Act/360
Coupon payment dates:	June 30 and December 30, short first coupon
Principal redemption:	Par, unless default provision is activated
Default provision:	If, at any time during the life of the note, one of the bonds in the basket defaults on principal or interest payment due, the investor will receive 80% of the notional amount (face value) of the defaulted bond or any other bond in the basket, and the issuer will have no further obligation to repay principal or interest.

Basket:

Bonds	Maturity	Yield
Boise Cascade	12/1997	L+68
American Airlines	7/1998	L+98
U.S. Steel	7/1998	L+39
Korean Dev. Bank	6/1998	L+40
Bank of China	3/1999	L+58
Average yield:		L+61

them survive, that's fantastic for the investor. The investor keeps getting paid the high coupon of Libor plus 135 basis points. Then the investor receives par redemption. Now, consider the case in which one of them defaults. What happens to the investor in the basket CLN? Rather than paying par redemption, the issuer stops paying the coupon to the investor and pays 80% of the face value of the defaulted bond or any other bond. Of course the issuer is going to pay the investor the defaulted bond because, at that point, it is going to be the cheapest. The issuer is going to give the investor 80% of the face value of the defaulted bond. Let's say the defaulted bond trades at $50, because its recovery value equals 50. The issuer is paying 80% of the face value of a bond that costs $50. How much is that? $40. The face value is $100, but the price is $50. Because the investors only receive 80% of the face value of a bond whose price is only $50, they actually get only $40 worth of bonds. One can argue that is a little bit better than getting zero in the case of the binary structure. At least the investor is getting something back. In this note, the investor earns 6-month Libor+1.35% semi-annually, representing an enhancement of 0.74% over the current basket yield. The investor takes additional risk but only in the event that one of the bonds in the basket defaults.

Now consider the companies that are the underlying issuers of this structure: Boise Cascade, American Airlines, U.S. Steel, Korean Development Bank, and Bank of China. Presumably American Airlines and Bank of China have low correlation between them. Is that good for you or bad for you as an investor in one of these structures? Low correlation is bad for the investor. Usually we say that we want a highly diversified portfolio but in this case we want exactly the opposite. In this case, diversification works against you because if any of the issuers default, you get the worst one. It's not as if you have a portfolio and if one of them defaults the others are still performing. The investor gets the worst-performing bond. Assume that the underlying basket included only the Bank of China and the Korean Development Bank. Let's remove the U.S. companies from the basket. If the Bank of China defaults, probably the Korean Development Bank is not doing too well either. Should the investor care whether the basket included only the Bank of China or whether it was a basket of highly correlated assets? It's probably the same to the investor. On the other hand, the more uncorrelated the underlying securities are, the worse this structure is for an investor. How many investors actually realize that because the basket is highly diversified, it is a very dangerous structure to own? Most investors assume that diversification works in their favor.

Let's assume there is zero correlation between the probabilities of default of the issuers. We have to compute the probability of a default event, meaning that at least one of them will default. Based on the ratings agencies such as Moody's, we can estimate the probability of any of the issuers defaulting. Assume that the underlying basket is made up of five securities labeled A through E, from historical data we obtain that the probabilities of default (in one year) are as follows:

Probabilities of default
Bond A   = 2%
Bond B   = 1.5%
Bond C   = 3%
Bond D   = 2%
Bond E   = 3%

What is the probability that the basket CLN will be triggered in one year?

First we figure out the probability of survival for one year for each of the issuers.

Probabilities of survival
Bond A   = 98%
Bond B   = 98.5%
Bond C   = 97%
Bond D   = 98%
Bond E   = 97%

The probability of survival for each individual issuer is the complement of the probability of default. For example, bond A has a 2% probability of default and therefore a 98% probability of survival.

Assuming zero correlation, the probability of joint survival of all the issuers is the product of the individual survival probabilities: $98\% \cdot 98.5\% \cdot 97\% \cdot 98\% \cdot 97\% \approx 89\%$, or about 89%. We therefore can impute that the probability of a default event in one year is 11%. Of course, this has to be combined with the probability that the issuer (rated single A) will default.

One may look at these numbers and say that the average probability of default is 3%. Now assume that the default correlation is very high, close to 1. If the correlation is very high, then we can assume that if one of them defaults, they will all default. So the probability of default is around 3%. The most important thing here is the correlation. The probability went from 3% to 11% because of the low correlation.

There are mathematical formulas to calculate the default probabilities. If one can estimate the default correlation then one can calculate the probability of joint default using some theoretical formula (see Chapter 16). But, one of the most difficult things is getting a handle on the default correlation numbers, because defaults themselves are so rare. What is the default correlation of American Airlines and the Bank of China? Or the Korean Development and the Bank of China?

Recall the example of Ford and General Motors from Chapter 2. We don't know whether their default correlation is positive or negative.

TOTAL RETURN SWAPS

A total return swap is a vehicle for investors to establish a leveraged position in a reference debt instrument. This product is useful for leveraging relatively illiquid bonds. They might be distressed securities or bank debt. Many investors use total return swaps to enhance the return of a reference bond that might otherwise not meet their required return hurdle.

In Exhibit 6-10 we illustrate an MGM total return swap. The underlying is the MGM Grand Hotel finance 12% bond that has a current price of $109.50. The notional principal amount is $10 million, the face value of the underlying bond. Settlement is in one week. The total return payer is the bank. The bank pays all coupon and principal repayments for the investor two days after they are received. The investor is a fixed rate payer and the fixed rate is 8.50%. This looks very nice except that the bank is concerned about what would happen if the total return is negative. In this case, the bank would expect a payment of the fixed rate, 8.50%, plus the

Exhibit 6-10
TOTAL RETURN SWAP

MGM Grand—Total Return Swap
(as of 10/20/1994)

Underlying index:	MGM Grand Hotels Finance 12% due 5/1/02 (B1/BB-)
Current price:	$109.50 (Treasury 5/97 + 2.70%)
Notional principal amount:	$10.95 million ($10 million face value of the underlying index)
Settlement date:	One week
Maturity date:	May 5, 1997 (two days after call/put date)
Total return payor:	Bank
Total return payments:	The bank pays all coupon and principal repayments to the investor two days after they are received.
Fixed rate payer:	Investor
Fixed rate payment dates:	Quarterly
Fixed rate:	8.50% (or 3-month Libor + 1.25%), Act/360 paid on notional principal amount.
Collateral required:	$2,190,000 which is 20% of market value of the debt, in cash or U.S. Government securities. This transaction will be marked to market and the collateral adjusted on a weekly basis.
Settlement:	On the maturity date the investor will have the option to (a) take delivery of the underlying debt plus any cash or securities repaid, in exchange for $10.95 million plus the fixed rate payment, or (b) cash settle the transaction at the then-prevailing market rates.

negative total return on the bond. As we've seen previously, the bank is doubly exposed to the investor. They are exposed to the coupon payment and to any decline in prices.

The bank wants to avoid this exposure to the investor so it puts in a collateral requirement, $2.2 million or 20% of the market value of the debt. The transaction will be marked to market and the collateral adjusted on a weekly basis. It's not unlike a retail futures account. On maturity date you either take delivery of the underlying debt plus any cash or securities paid in exchange for the $10.95 million, or cash settle the transaction at the prevailing market rate.

In this transaction, the investor receives a leveraged return on the MGM Grand Hotel's 12% first mortgage bonds due 5/1/2002 (callable 5/1/97) and pays a fixed rate.

If no default occurs, and interest rates stay the same, then:

- The investor pays 8.50% * $10.95 million = $930,750 every year.
- The investor receives 12.00% * $10 million = $1,200,000 every year.

Note that the term sheet is a little misleading. It looks like a swap of 8.50% vs. 12.00%. But actually, the 8.50% is on a notional of $10.95 million and the 12% is on a notional of $10 million. It looks nicer than it actually is. Still, if there is no default, there is a positive result for the investor.

As already mentioned, a total return swap is very similar to an equity swap except that the two sides are exchanging payments based on a bond or a basket of bonds or debt rather than on an equity index.

Note: The investor in the total return swap illustrated in Exhibit 6-10 could lose its total initial collateral and then some. When the return on the underlying bond is negative, the investor must pay the bank not only the fixed rate, but also the decline in the value of the asset. Thus, the investor could end up owing the bank substantial amounts of capital.

MORE STRUCTURES USING CREDIT DERIVATIVES

We examine four more structures using credit derivatives. Our examples are based on actual trades.

Credit Default Swap Trade

In this trade, the Bank buys a credit default swap from a counterparty. The reference entity is the Czech Republic. The duration of the swap is one year. The Bank pays 37 bps per annum. If a credit event occurs, the counterparty agrees to accept a portfolio of reference obligations issued by the Czech Republic and pay $20 million USD.

Note the clause about dispute resolution.

(6)(b)(iv)(D)

The Bank AG London
SWAPS GROUP

Credit Default Swap Transaction

16 January 1998

xxxxxxxxx

Our Ref: xxx ######/xx

Dear Sir / Madam,

The purpose of this letter agreement is to confirm the terms and conditions of the Credit Default Swap Transaction entered into between us on the Trade Date specified below (the "Transaction"). This letter agreement constitutes a Confirmation, as referred to in the ISDA master agreement specified below. The Bank AG is referred to herein as Party A and xxxxxxxxx is referred to herein as Party B.

The definitions and provisions contained in the 1991 ISDA Definitions (as published by the International Swaps and Derivatives Association, Inc.) are incorporated into this Confirmation (and for the purposes thereof, this Transaction shall be a Swap Transaction). In the event of any inconsistency between those definitions and this Confirmation, this Confirmation will prevail.

This Confirmation supplements, forms a part of and is subject to, the ISDA Master Agreement dated as of 2 January 1997 as amended and supplemented from time to time (the "Agreement"), between you and us. All provisions contained in the Agreement govern this Confirmation except as expressly modified hereby.

The terms of the Transaction to which this Confirmation relates are as follows:

1. General Terms:

Trade Date:	14 January 1998
Effective Date:	20 January 1998
Termination Date:	The Scheduled Termination Date

If a Credit Event Notice and Notice of Publicly Available Information have been delivered on or before the date that is twenty-eight calendar days after the Scheduled Termination Date and the Conditions to Payment have been satisfied, the Termination Date shall be the day on which the Conditions to Payment were first satisfied.

Scheduled Termination Date: The earlier of
(1) 20 January 1999, and
(2) The Credit Event Date, if any

Floating Rate Payer: Party B (the "Seller")

Fixed Rate Payer: Party A (the "Buyer")

Calculation Agent: Party A

Calculation Agent City: London

Business Day Convention: Following (which shall apply to any date referred to in this Confirmation that falls on a day that is not a Business Day).

Reference Entity: Czech Republic and any Successors

Reference Price: 100%

Reference Obligation(s):   Czech National Bank 6.60% (JPY Samurai) due 9 August 2000
or
any senior obligation ranking pari passau that is issued or guaranteed by the Czech Republic.

2. Fixed Payments:

Fixed Rate Payer

Calculation Amount: USD 20,000,000

Fixed Payment Dates: Each 20 January, 20 April, 20 July and 20 October in each year and the Termination Date, commencing on 20 April 1998 and ending on the Termination Date.

Fixed Rate: 0.37 per cent

Fixed Rate Day Count
Fraction: Actual/360

Business Days: London and New York

3. Floating Payments:

Floating Rate Payer

Calculation Amount: USD 20,000,000

Conditions to Payment: The Conditions to Payment shall be satisfied when:

(a) Buyer has delivered a Credit Event Notice; and

(b) Such party has delivered a Notice of Publicly Available Information.

Upon satisfaction of the Conditions to Payment with respect to a Credit Event, (i) the Calculation Agent shall notify the parties of such satisfaction and (ii) the parties shall comply with the Settlement Terms.

Credit Event: The following Credit Events shall apply to this Transaction:

Failure to Pay
Bankruptcy
Restructuring
Repudiation
Cross Default

Obligation(s):   With respect to the Reference Entity, any obligation in respect of any present or future indebtedness for borrowed money issued by the Reference Entity, payable in a currency other than the currency of the Reference Entity which are at the time of determination quoted, listed or traded on any securities exchange or in any other securities market, other than any such indebtedness that was originally intended for sale in the domestic market of the Reference Entity. For the purpose of the foregoing the term "securities market" shall include but not be limited to an over-the-counter or dealer market in which price quotations for securities are customarily available and shall include securities avail-

<table>
<tr><td></td><td>able for resale in the United States pursuant to Rule 144A under the U.S Securities Act of 1933.</td></tr>
</table>

Payment Requirement:	USD 20,000,000 or its equivalent in JPY, DEM, ECU, CZK or the Euro (SWIFT Code EUR).
Specified Number:	One
Business Days:	London

4. Settlement Terms:

Settlement Method:	Physical
Physical Settlement Terms:	
Physical Settlement:	If the Conditions to Payment have been satisfied, Buyer has the right to Deliver to Seller the Portfolio and Seller shall pay to Buyer the Physical Settlement Amount on the Physical Settlement Date. For the purposes of the foregoing, any Delivery under this provision shall be made on a delivery versus payment basis.
Physical Settlement Date:	Three Business Days following the Termination Date.
Physical Settlement Amount:	The greater of (a) Floating Rate Payer Calculation Amount × Reference Price and (b) zero, payable in USD.
Portfolio:	Deliverable Obligations with an outstanding principal balance equal to the Floating Rate Payer Calculation Amount.
Deliverable Obligations:	The Reference Obligation(s).

5. Notice and Account Details:

Telephone, Telex and/or Facsimile Numbers and Contact Details for Notices:	Buyer:
	Seller:
Account	**Details**

ACCOUNT DETAILS OF BUYER:

USD
XXXXXXXXXX
Swift: XXXXX
A/c: xxxxxxxxxx

CHIPS ID xxxxxxxxx

Account Details of Seller: XXXXXXX

Account Number xxxxxxxxx

6. Other Terms:

(a) *Changes with respect to any Reference Obligation.* In the event that, in the opinion of the Calculation Agent, (i) the aggregate outstanding principal amount of any Reference Obligation has been materially reduced by redemption or otherwise (other than due to any regularly scheduled amortization or prepayments), (ii) if any Reference Obligation is an obligation guaranteed by a Reference Entity and, other than due to the existence of occurrence of a Credit Event, the guarantee of that Reference Entity is no longer a valid and binding obligation of the guarantor enforceable in accordance with its terms or (iii) for any other reason, other than due to the existence or occurrence of a Credit Event, any Reference Obligation is no longer an obligation of the Reference Entity, then the Calculation Agent, after consultation with the parties, shall identify one or more substitute obligations which rank equal in priority of payment with such Reference Obligation and which preserve the economic equivalent of the payment obligations of the parties to this Transaction and are issued or guaranteed (as to both principal and interest) by the Reference Entity to replace the Reference Obligation. Upon notice to the parties of a substitute obligation having been identified by the Calculation Agent, such substitute obligation shall without further action replace the Reference Obligation.

(b) *Additional Representations and Agreements.*

(i) Additional Representations and Agreements:

(A) Each party represents that, in connection with this Transaction, neither the other party nor any of the other party's affiliates has made any representation whatsoever with respect to the Reference Entity, any Reference

Obligation, or any guarantor of any Reference Obligation (a "Guarantor") on which it is relying or is entitled to rely.

(B) Each party acknowledges that this Transaction does not create either a direct or indirect obligation of the Reference Entity or any Guarantor or a direct or indirect participation in any obligation of the Reference Entity or any Guarantor owing to such party.

(C) Each party and its affiliates and the Calculation Agent may deal in each Reference Obligation and may accept deposits from, make loans or otherwise extend credit to, and generally engage in any kind of commercial or investment banking or other business with the Reference Entity, any affiliate of the Reference Entity, any other person or entity having obligations relating to the Reference Entity or any Guarantor and may act with respect to such business in the same manner as if this Transaction did not exist regardless of whether any such action might have an adverse effect (including, without limitation, any action which might constitute or give rise to a Credit Event) on the Reference Entity, any Guarantor or the position of the other party to this Transaction or otherwise.

(D) Each party and its affiliates and the Calculation Agent may, whether by virtue of the types of relationships described herein or otherwise, at the date hereof or at any time hereafter, be in possession of information in relation to the Reference Entity or any Guarantor that is or may be material in the context of this Transaction and that may or may not be publicly available or known to the other party. This Transaction does not create any obligation on the part of such party and its affiliates to disclose to the other party any such relationship or information (whether or not confidential).

(E) Each of the parties hereby represents that it is entering into the Transaction for either investment, financial intermediation, hedging or other commercial purposes. Each of the parties hereby further acknowledges and agrees that, subject to the Conditions to Payment, the parties will be obliged to comply with the Settlement Terms of this Transaction, irrespective of the existence or amount of the parties' credit exposure to the Reference Entity.

(F) Each party agrees that unless the parties are otherwise bound or subject to a confidentiality agreement, any information obtained from the other party with respect to this Transaction is not subject to any obligation of confidentiality.

(ii) Concerning the Calculation Agent: The Calculation Agent is not acting as a fiduciary for or as an advisor to either party in respect of its duties as Calculation Agent in respect of this Transaction.

(iii) Additional Representations and Agreements for Physical Settlement.

(A) Unless the Seller has specified alternative terms of Delivery, Buyer represents and warrants (which representation and warranty shall survive the Physical Settlement Date) that it has conveyed (or, if applicable, caused to be conveyed) to Seller (or, if applicable, its designee) all right, title and interest in the Portfolio free and clear of all claims, charges, liens and encumbrances (including without limitation any counterclaim, defense or right of setoff by or of the Reference Entity).

(B) Buyer agrees (which agreement shall survive the Physical Settlement Date) to execute, deliver, file and record any specific assignment or other document and take any other action that may be necessary or desirable and reasonably requested by Seller in connection with Buyer's Delivery of the Portfolio.

(C) If, due to an event beyond the control of the Buyer (including without limitation, failure of the relevant clearance system or due to any law, regulation or court order, but not including market conditions), it is impossible or illegal for the Buyer to Deliver any portion of the Portfolio on the Physical Settlement Date, then on such date the Buyer shall (1) Deliver that portion of the Portfolio that is Deliverable versus payment by the Seller of that portion of the Physical Settlement Amount that corresponds to such portion of the Portfolio and (2) provide a description in reasonable detail of the facts giving rise to such impossibility or illegality and as soon as practicable thereafter the Buyer shall Deliver (or designate the Delivery of) the portion of the Portfolio which has not been Delivered versus payment by the Seller of that portion of the Physical Settlement Amount that corresponds to such portion of the Portfolio. If upon the occurrence of any such impossibility or illegality the entire Portfolio is not Delivered to the Seller (or any of its designees) within 28 calendar days of the Physical Settlement Date (the "Final Delivery Date"), a

Termination Event with the Buyer as the sole Affected Party will be deemed to have occurred, with this Transaction as the sole Affected Transaction. For purposes of that Termination Event, it shall be deemed that Market Quotation cannot be determined and Loss shall apply and the Early Termination Date shall be the first Business Day following the Final Delivery Date.

(D) If, due to an event beyond the control of the Seller (including without limitation due to any law, regulation or court order), it is impossible or illegal for the Seller to take Delivery of any portion of the Portfolio on the Physical Settlement Date, then on such date the Seller shall (1) take Delivery of that portion of the Portfolio for which it is possible and legal to take Delivery versus payment of that portion of the Physical Settlement Amount that corresponds to such portion of the Portfolio and (2) provide a description in reasonable detail of the facts giving rise to such impossibility or illegality and as soon practicable thereafter the Seller shall take Delivery (or designate taking the Delivery) of the portion of the Portfolio which has not been Delivered versus payment of that portion of the Physical Settlement Amount that corresponds to such portion of the Portfolio. If, upon the occurrence of any such impossibility or illegality, the entire Portfolio is not Delivered to the Seller (or any of its designees) within 30 calendar days of the Physical Settlement Date (the "Final Delivery Date"), a Termination Event with the Seller as the sole Affected Party will be deemed to have occurred, with this Transaction as the sole Affected Transaction. For purposes of that Termination Event, it shall be deemed that Market Quotation cannot be determined and Loss shall apply and the Early Termination Date shall be the first Business Day following the Final Delivery Date.

(E) If an event which would otherwise constitute or give rise to an impossibility or illegality under either (C) or (D) immediately above also constitutes an Illegality, it will be governed by (C) or (D) immediately above, as applicable, and will not constitute an Illegality.

(F) Either party (the "designator") may designate any of its affiliates (the "designee") to Deliver or take Delivery, as the case may be and otherwise to perform such party's obligations to Deliver or take Delivery, as the case may be, in respect of this Transaction and the designee may assume such obligations. Such designation shall not relieve the designator of any of its obligations hereunder. If the designee shall have performed the obligations of the designator hereunder, then the designator shall be discharged of its obligations to the other party to the extent of such performance. If, as a result of such designation, (1) it would be illegal due to any applicable law or regulation affecting the transfer of Deliverable Obligations for the designee to so Deliver or take Delivery, (2) such Delivery gives rise to any Tax or (3) such Delivery gives rise to any loss or cost to the non-designating party, then such designation may not be made.

(G) Notwithstanding any other provision of this Agreement, if any Stamp Tax is payable in connection with the Delivery of (1) the Reference Obligation (or other Deliverable Obligations of the same type as the Reference Obligation), payment of such Stamp Tax shall be made by the party that would in the ordinary course bear such cost under a contract for purchase of the Reference Obligation or (2) other Deliverable Obligations, payment of such Stamp Tax shall be made by Buyer.

(iv) Each party represents to the other party as of the date that it enters into this Transaction that (absent a written agreement between the parties that expressly imposes affirmative obligations to the contrary for this Transaction):

(A) *Non-Reliance.* It is acting for its own account, and it has made its own independent decisions to enter into this Transaction and as to whether the Transaction is appropriate or proper for it based upon its own judgment and upon advice from such advisers as it has deemed necessary. It is not relying on any communication (written or oral) of the other party as investment advice or as a recommendation to enter into this Transaction, it being understood that information and explanations related to the terms and conditions of this Transaction shall not be considered to be investment advice or a recommendation to enter into the Transaction. No communication (written or oral) received from the other party shall be deemed to be an assurance or guarantee as to the expected results of this Transaction.

(B) *Assessment and Understanding.* It is capable of assessing the merits of and understanding (on its own behalf or through independent professional advice), and understands and accepts the terms and conditions and risks of this Transaction. It is also capable of assuming, and assumes, the risks of the Transaction.

(C) *Status of Parties.* The other party is not acting as a fiduciary for or adviser to it in respect of this Transaction.

(c) *Interpretation.* Each reference to the singular shall include the plural and vice versa.

(d) *Dispute Resolution.* In the event that a party (the "Disputing Party") does not agree with any determination made (or the failure to make any determination) by the Calculation Agent or the other party (the "Determining Party"), the Disputing Party shall have the right to require that the Determining Party have such determination made by a disinterested third party that is a dealer of derivative obligations and that is, or whose affiliates are, dealers in obligations of the type of the Reference Obligation but is not an affiliate of either party. Such dealer shall be selected by the Calculation Agent in its reasonable discretion after consultation with the parties. Any exercise by the Disputing Party of its rights hereunder must be in writing and shall be delivered to the Determining Party as soon as possible but no later than the Business Day following the Business Day on which the Determining Party notifies the Disputing Party of any determination made (or of the failure to make any determination). Any determination by a disinterested third party shall be binding in the absence of manifest error and shall be made as soon as possible but no later than within five Business Days of the Disputing Party's exercise of its rights hereunder. The costs of such disinterested third party shall be borne by (i) the Disputing Party if the disinterested third party substantially agrees with the Determining Party's determination or (ii) the non-Disputing Party if the disinterested third party does not substantially agree with the Determining Party. Determinations as to any amounts due shall (if possible) be calculated retrospectively with reference to the actual amount that was due on any Cash Settlement Date or Physical Settlement Date, and shall not account for subsequent changes with respect to any Reference Obligation. Interest on any amounts due that are subject to dispute shall be paid from (and including) the date of nonpayment to (but excluding) the date such amount is paid, at the Termination Rate. Such interest will be calculated on the basis of daily compounding and the actual number of days elapsed.

7. Definitions:

(a) Credit Event Definitions:

Failure to Pay means the failure by the Reference Entity to make, when due, any payment under any Obligation, if such failure is not remedied before the expiration of any applicable grace period to be limited to a period 10 business days.

Bankruptcy: the Reference Entity issuer (i) is dissolved (other than pursuant to a consolidation, amalgamation or merger); (ii) becomes insolvent or is unable to pay its debts or admits in writing its inability generally to pay its debts as they become due; (iii) makes a general assignment, arrangement or composition with or for the benefit of its creditors; (iv) institutes or has instituted against it a proceeding seeking a judgment of insolvency or bankruptcy or any other relief under any bankruptcy or insolvency law or other similar law affecting creditors rights, or a petition is presented for its winding-up or liquidation , and, in the case of any such proceeding or petition instituted or presented against it, such proceeding or petition (A) results in a judgment of insolvency or bankruptcy or the entry of an order for relief or the making of an order for its winding-up or liquidation or (B) is not dismissed, discharged, stayed or restrained in each case within 30 calendar days of the institution or presentation thereof; (v) has a resolution passed for its winding-up, official management or liquidation (other than pursuant to a consolidation, amalgamation or merger); (vi) seeks or becomes subject to the appointment of an administrator, provisional liquidation, conservator, receiver, trustee, custodian or other similar official for it or for substantially all of its assets; (vii) has a secured party take possession of all or substantially all its assets or has a distress, execution, attachment, sequestration or other legal process levied, enforced or sued on or against all or substantially all its assets and such secured party maintains possession, or any such process is not dismissed, discharged, stayed or restrained, in each case within 30 calendar days thereafter; (viii) causes or is subject to any event with respect to it, which under the applicable laws of any jurisdiction, has an analogous effect to any of the events specified in clauses (I) to (vii) inclusive; or (ix) takes any action in furtherance of, or indicating its consent to, approval of, or acquiescence in, any of the foregoing acts.

Restructuring: a waiver, deferral, restructuring, rescheduling, standstill, Obligation Exchange or other adjustment occurs with respect to any Obligation of the Reference Entity and the effect of such is the terms of such Obligation are, overall, materially less favorable from a credit or risk perspective to any holder of such Obligation.

Repudiation: the Reference entity disaffirms, disclaims, repudiates or rejects, in whole or in part, or challenges the validity of, any Obligation in any material respect.

Cross Default: means the occurrence of a default, event of default or other similar condition or event, other than a failure to make any required payment, in respect of the Reference Entity under one or more Obligations in an aggregate amount not less than the Default Requirement which has resulted in such Obligations becoming capable of being declared due and payable before they would otherwise have been due and payable.

(b) General Definitions:

Calculation Agent means the party to the Transaction (or a third party) designated as such for the Transaction. The Calculation Agent's calculations and determinations shall be made in good faith, in a commercially reasonable manner and be binding in the absence of manifest error.

Credit Event Notice means an irrevocable notice (which may be oral, including by telephone) to the parties and the Calculation Agent that describes a Credit Event that occurred on or prior to the Scheduled Termination Date. Any notice given orally, including by telephone will be effective when actually received by the intended receipt. A Credit Event Notice may be delivered between 9:00 a.m. and 4:00 p.m. in the Calculation Agent City on a Business Day. The notice given must contain a description in reasonable detail of the facts asserted. If the Credit Event Notice is delivered after 4:00 p.m. in the Calculation Agent City on a Business Day, then that notice will be deemed delivered on the next following Business Day. If the Credit Event Notice is delivered orally, a written confirmation will be executed and delivered confirming the substance of that notice within one Business Day of that notice. Failure to provide that written confirmation will not affect the validity of that oral notice. If that written confirmation is not received within such time, the party obligated to deliver it will be deemed to have satisfied its obligation to deliver it at the time that a written confirmation of the oral notice is received or otherwise deemed effective.

(c) Publicly Available Information Definitions:

Notice of Publicly Available Information means an irrevocable notice (which may be oral, including by telephone) to the parties and the Calculation Agent that confirms the occurrence of a Credit Event described in a Credit Event Notice with Publicly Available Information. Any notice given orally including by telephone will not be effective when actually received by the intended recipient. A Notice of Publicly Available Information may be delivered between 9:00 a.m. and 4:00 p.m. in Calculation Agent City on a Business Day. The notice given must contain a description in reasonable detail of the facts asserted. If the Notice of Publicly Available Information is delivered after 4:00 p.m. in Calculation Agent City on a Business Day, then that notice will be deemed delivered on the next following Business Day. If the Notice of Publicly Available Information is delivered orally, a written confirmation will be executed and delivered confirming the substance of that notice within one Business Day of that notice. Failure to provide that written confirmation will not affect the validity of that oral notice. If that written confirmation is not received within such time, the party obligated to deliver the confirmation will be deemed to have satisfied its obligation to deliver it at the time that a written confirmation of the oral notice is received or otherwise deemed effective. If a Credit Event Notice confirms the existence or occurrence of a Credit Event with Publicly Available Information, such notice will also be deemed to be a Notice of Publicly Available Information.

Publicly Available Information means information that reasonably confirms any of the assertions made in a Credit Event Notice and that has been published in or on not less than the Specified Number of internationally recognized published or electronically displayed news sources including each Public Source (if any), regardless of whether the reader or user thereof pays a fee to obtain such information. If, however, either of the parties hereto or any of their respective affiliates is cited as the sole source for such information, then such information shall not be deemed to be Publicly Available Information. Publicly Available Information need not state that such occurrence has met the subjective criteria specified in certain Credit Events including, without limitation, that such occurrence (i) is material (as required by Restructuring and Credit Event Upon Merger), (ii) qualifies under subclause (ix) of Bankruptcy, (iii) meets the Payment Requirement or Default Requirement (if any) and (iv) is the result of exceeding any applicable grace period.

(d) Physical Settlement Definitions:

Deliver means to deliver, novate, transfer, assign or sell, as appropriate, in the manner customary for the settlement of the applicable Deliverable Obligations (which shall include executing all necessary documentation and taking any other necessary actions), in order to convey all right, title and interest in the Portfolio to Seller free and clear of any and all liens, charges, claims or encumbrances (including without limitation any counterclaim, defense or right of setoff by or of the Reference Entity). "Delivery" and "Delivered" will be construed accordingly.

Please confirm that the foregoing correctly sets forth the terms of our agreement by executing the copy of this Confirmation enclosed for that purpose and returning it to us or by sending to us a letter or telex substantially similar to this letter, which letter or telex sets forth the material terms of the Transaction to which this Confirmation relates and indicates your agreement to those terms.

Yours faithfully,

for and on behalf of

XXXXXXXXXX

By: _____   By: _____

Name: Name:

Title: Title:

Confirmed as of the date first above written:

XXXXXXXXX

By: _____

Name:

Title:

The Bank AG London
SWAPS GROUP

Facsimile Transmission

RE: OUR REF.: XXX XXXXXX/XX

DATE: 01/14/99	Pages: (including cover sheet)
TO: xxxxxxxxxx	FROM: XXXXXXXXX —Swap Group
ATTN: xxxxxxxxx	ADDRESS: XXXXXXXX XXXXXXXXXX
TEL: xxxxxxxxxx FAX: xxxxxxxxxx	TEL: (+xx) xx xxx xxx FAX: (+xx) xx xxx xxxx

PLEASE RETURN TO THE BANK LONDON

Credit Default Swap Transaction

EFFECTIVE DATE: 20 January 1998

TERMINATION DATE: 20 January 1999

NOTIONAL AMOUNT: USD 20,000,000

Please find attached a confirmation for the above referenced Transaction

Please forward your acceptance for the attention of XXXXXXXXXX.

XXXXXXXX

XXXXXXXXX

XXXXXXXXX

Regards

XXXXXX XXXXXXXX

Credit Exposure Default Swap

In this transaction, the Bank takes on the credit exposure of the State of Israel. Note that this transaction is cash settled. The price being paid to the Bank is 52 bps per annum.

Indicative Maturity	Reference Entity	Indicative Spread
3 February 2003	State of Israel	52 bps pa

Key Points

- **The Bank** enters into a default swap with Investor whereby in exchange for regular payments **the Bank** agrees to take on credit exposure to State of Israel. If a credit event occurs **the Bank** pays cash settlement amount.

Terms and Conditions of Default Swap

Effective date: 30 June 1998

Scheduled termination: 3 February 2003

Date:

Seller: Bank

Buyer: Investor

Calculation agent: Bank

Reference entity: State of Israel

Reference obligation: State of Israel, State of Israel 6.375% issued on the 12 December 1995 and maturing on the 15 December 2005 (Cusip 465138LU7)

(provided that if the reference obligation is no longer an obligation of the reference entity for reasons other than the occurrence or existence of a credit event substitution shall apply)

Notional amount: USD 20,000,000

Buyer Payments

Payment dates: Semiannually, 3 February and August, starting on the 3 August 1998 and ending on the earlier of the scheduled termination date and the day on which the Conditions to Payment were first satisfied

Fixed rate and day: Count Fraction:	52 bps pa, (ACT/360) of the notional amount

Credit Event Provisions

Conditions of payment:	Delivery by buyer or seller to the other party on or before the day which is twenty-eight calendar days following the scheduled termination date of: a) Credit event notice; and b) Notice of publicly available information Upon satisfaction of the Conditions to Payment with respect to a credit event, (i) the calculation agent shall notify the parties of such satisfaction and (ii) the parties shall comply with the settlement terms.
Credit event notice:	Notice that describes a credit event that occurred on or after the effective date and on or prior to the scheduled termination date (or where the credit event is failure to pay where the payment was originally due on or before the scheduled termination date).
Notice of publicly available information:	Notice that confirms that information has been published on an internationally recognized published or electronically displayed news source that the credit event described in the credit event notice has occurred.
Credit event:	The following credit events shall apply to this transaction: a) Failure to pay b) Cross-acceleration c) Restructuring d) Repudiation
Obligations:	With respect to the reference credit, any obligation (whether present or future, contingent or otherwise, as principal or surety or otherwise) in respect of borrowed money, that ranks equal in priority of payment with the reference obligation.

| Payment requirement: | 10,000,000 |
| Default requirement: | 10,000,000 |

Settlement Terms

Settlement	If the Conditions to Payment have been satisfied the seller shall pay to the buyer the cash settlement amount on the cash settlement date.
Cash settlement: amount:	The greater of (a) notional amount * (100% –market value) and (b) zero.
Market value:	The highest of the bid prices for the reference obligation with an outstanding principal balance equal to the notional amount obtained by the calculation agent on the valuation date from five recognized dealers in the market for the reference obligation provided that if less than three dealers provide quotations then the market value shall be determined by the calculation agent on the next day on which at least three dealers provide quotations. If the calculation agent is unable to calculate the market value prior to the twenty-eighth calendar day following the applicable valuation date, then the calculation agent shall determine the market value for such valuation date in its reasonable discretion.
Valuation date:	One business day following the day on which the Conditions to Payment were first satisfied.
Cash settlement date:	Three business days following the valuation date.
Documentation:	ISDA.

One-Year Default Swap

The next transaction is a one-year default swap on the Monsato Company.

Indicative Maturity	Reference Entities	Indicative Spread
30 December 1999	Monsanto Company	48 bps pa

Terms and Conditions of Default Swap

Effective date: 4 January 1999

Scheduled termination: 5 January 2000

Date

Termination date: The scheduled termination date.

If a Credit Event Notice and Notice of Publicly Available Information have been delivered on or before the date that is fourteen calendar days after the Scheduled Termination Date and the Conditions to Payment have been satisfied, the Termination Date shall be the Physical Settlement Date.

Seller: The Bank

Buyer: Investor

Calculation agent: Bank

Reference entity: Monsanto Company.

Reference obligation: Monsanto Company 6% bond, issued on the 4th of August 1993 and maturing on the 1st of July 2000

Notional amount: USD 50,000,000

Buyer Payments

Payment dates: Semiannually, on the 30th of June and the 30th of December, starting from the 30th of June 1999 and ending on the termination date, subject to adjustment in accordance with modified following day-count convention.

Fixed rate and day: 48 bps pa, ACT/360 of the notional

Count fraction: Amount

Business days: London and NY

Credit Event Provisions

Conditions of payment:	Delivery by buyer or seller to the other party on or before the day which is fourteen calendar days following the scheduled termination date of: a) Credit event notice; and b) Notice of publicly available information Upon satisfaction of the Conditions to Payment with respect to a credit event, (i) the calculation agent shall notify the parties of such satisfaction and (ii) the parties shall comply with the settlement terms.
Credit event notice:	Notice that describes a credit event that occurred on or after the effective date and on or prior to the scheduled termination date.
Notice of publicly available information:	Notice that confirms that information has been published on two internationally recognized published or electronically displayed news sources that the credit event described in the credit event notice has occurred.
Credit event:	The following credit events shall apply to this transaction: (a) Failure to pay (b) Bankruptcy (c) Cross-default (d) Restructuring (e) Repudiation
Obligations:	With respect to the reference entity, any obligation (whether present or future, contingent or otherwise, as principal or surety or otherwise) in respect of borrowed money.
Default requirement:	USD 10,000,000
Payment requirement:	USD 10,000,000

Settlement Terms

Settlement: Physical

Physical settlement: If the Conditions to Payment have been satis-
                               fied the buyer shall deliver to seller the port-
                               folio and the seller shall pay to the buyer the
                               notional amount on the physical settlement
                               date. For the purposes of the foregoing, any
                               delivery under this provision shall be made
                               on a delivery versus payment basis.

Physical settlement   Ten business days following the day on
date: which the conditions to payment were first
                              satisfied.

Deliverable   The reference obligation(s).
obligations: Any obligations of the reference entity, either
                              directly or in its capacity as unconditional
                              guarantor, that rank equal in priority of pay-
                              ment with the reference obligation and (a)
                              that are denominated and payable in USD,
                              DEM, FRF, JPY, ITL, GBP, CAD, EURO, (b) are
                              repayable in an amount equal to their respec-
                              tive stated principal amounts, (c) that are not
                              repayable in an amount determined by refer-
                              ence to any formula or index, (d) the repay-
                              ment of which is not subject to any contin-
                              gency, (e) which bear simple interest at either
                              a fixed rate or a floating rate that is paid on a
                              periodic basis and computed on a bench mark
                              interest rate plus or minus a spread, if any, (f)
                              that do not have a remaining maturity greater
                              than 10 years. Deliverable obligations shall
                              not include any obligation (a) if the obligation
                              of the reference entity thereunder is subject to
                              any counterclaim, defense or right of setoff by
                              the reference entity, (b) if transfer thereof to
                              seller would require or cause seller to assume
                              or would subject seller to any obligation or
                              liability (other than immaterial, nonpayment
                              obligations), unless seller receives an appro-
                              priate indemnity from buyer with respect to
                              such obligation or liability satisfactory to sell-
                              er, (c) if there is any significant restriction in

the financial markets in the trading of the
obligation, other than as a direct or indirect
consequence of the creditworthiness of the
reference entity.

Portfolio: Deliverable obligations with an outstanding
                                    principal balance equal to the notional
                                    amount.

Documentation   ISDA.

Asset Swap Put

The last transaction is an asset swap put on the Republic of South
Africa. The Bank has the right to sell the asset swap at 100 to the
counterparty. The premium for the option is 1.00%, payable
upfront.

Put Option on Par Asset Swap on Republic of South Africa

Indicative Terms and Conditions as of April 1, 1998

Transaction type: An American style put option on a par
                                    asset swap transaction under which, if
                                    exercised, the option seller will purchase
                                    the nominal amount of the reference oblig-
                                    ations at par and enter into the below
                                    described swap

Option buyer: Bank

Option seller: Counterparty

Trade date: TBD

Effective date: Trade Date + 7 Days

Option type: Put

Option style: American

Premium: 1.00% on the notional amount payable
                                    upfront on effective date

Expiration date: One year following the effective date

Exercise: Telephonic notice from option buyer to option seller (between 9AM and 4PM NYC time) on a NY business day on or prior to the expiration date that it is exercising the option to enter into the underlying asset swap transaction

Terms of the Underlying Asset Swap Transaction

Asset seller: Option buyer

Asset purchaser: Option seller

Reference obligation: Republic of South Africa JPY 3.35% Due 1 of June, 2004.

Nominal amount: JPY 1,350,000,000

Price: Par

Settlement date: Three business days following the exercise date

Effective date: Same as settlement date

Termination date: 17th June, 2004

Notional amount: USD 10,000,000

Asset Seller Payments

Payment dates: The 17th of each March, June, September and December

Floating amount: Three-month LIBOR (Telerate 3750) + 1.20%, calculated on an actual/360 basis and payable in arrears at the end of each three-month period following the effective date on the notional amount

Asset Purchaser Payments

Payment dates: The 17th of each June and December

Initial fixed amount: An amount equal to the full coupon on the reference asset required to be paid on the interest payment date thereunder first following the effective date

Fixed rate: 3.35% on the nominal amount

Daycount fraction: 30/360

Initial and final exchange: There is initial and final exchange of prin-
                                   cipals.

Calculation agent: Bank

Asset purchaser payments: ISDA

SUMMARY

A casual observation of several term sheets reveals the richness
and diversity of the credit derivative markets. There are many different structures that are custom-made to fit the requirements of
the specific counterparties to each trade. However, all trades are
based on several simple concepts and a small number of basic
instruments.

CHAPTER 7

Credit Derivatives and the Repo Markets

In this chapter we examine the close connection between the total return swap and the classic repo trade. As it turns out, a total return swap plus a sale is very similar to a repo trade. This fact has not escaped many fund managers and we will see how they use it to their benefit.

CLASSIC REPO

A classic repo trade commits one party to sell and the other to buy securities and subsequently to reverse the trade at some preagreed future date. The counterparty supplying the collateral pays a fixed return to the party paying the cash. These trades are mainly used in the U.S. under a master agreement and provide more rights than sale-buybacks. Figure 7-1 shows what happens at the initiation of a repo trade. Party A gives bond C to party B. At the same time, party B gives cash to party A. In a sense, party B is lending money to party A and keeps bond C as collateral on the loan.

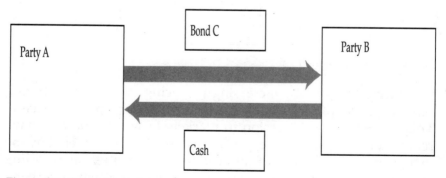

Party A

Bond C

Party B

Cash

Figure 7-1. Start of a repo.

Throughout the life of the repo trade, party A pays an interest rate on the amount borrowed while party B passes the coupons of the bond back to A. This is illustrated in Figure 7-2.

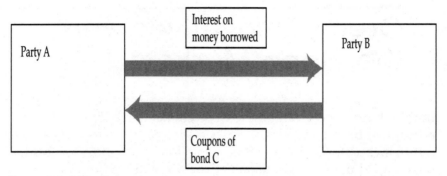

Figure 7-2. Life of a repo.

Finally, at the conclusion of the repo trade, party A returns the initial money borrowed back to B. At the same time, party B returns the bond back to A. This is illustrated in Figure 7-3. We can assume that the interest rate paid on the borrowed funds is Libor+x basis points.

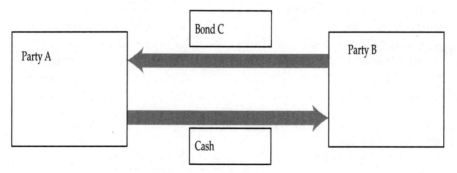

Figure 7-3. Conclusion of a repo.

Hedge funds are increasingly placing cash into emerging repo markets in Latin America, Asia, Eastern Europe, and Russia. This is a natural progression in markets in which volumes have rocketed in the past few years. This growth has been fueled by the increasing importance of international securities as funding sources. At the same time, repos are gradually replacing interbank depositing, blurring the distinction between banking and securities dealing.

The Bank of International Settlements (BIS) noted the massive impact repo transactions have had on international banking over the recent past. In its 1996–97 report, it said: "The slowdown in gross international banking flows would have been more severe had it not been for banks' on-balance-sheet transactions in securities, especially through repos. By improving funding and lending opportunities, the growing use of repos has enabled traditional players to maintain market presence and has allowed participation by new actors."

Repo markets are also helping to support the derivatives markets, according to the BIS: "The rapid growth of cash-based hedging strategies via the repo market has contributed to the continuing buoyancy of plain vanilla and exotic OTC products and the popularity of retail-oriented derivatives."

The biggest difference between emerging and developed repo markets is credit risk. In the latter markets, both collateral and counterparties are usually investment grade and the repo is an interest rate risk play. In emerging markets, the repo desk stands as principal in the middle and takes the credit risk of the emerging market counterparty while offering its own credit to the cash investor on the other side. The credit quality of the collateral is usually very weak and the credit quality of the counterparty is not very strong either. The repo trade is much more of a credit play.

REPO VS. A TOTAL RETURN (TR) SWAP

Let us consider a total return swap. Party A pays a floating interest rate to party B, say Libor + x basis points. At the same time, party B passes to A the total return on bond C. This is illustrated in Figure 7-4.

The TR swap is like a financed purchase of a bond, similar to a repo trade. Now consider a TR swap combined with the sale of the bond. Assume that party A already owns bond C and wants to finance it. Party A sells the bond to party B and simultaneously enters into a TR swap with party B. This is illustrated in Figure 7-5.

If party A were to repo the bond to party B, and if the repo rate were Libor + x basis points, then from a cash flow perspective the TR swap plus a sale would mimic the repo transaction. To see this, let us assume that at the initiation of the trade, the bond costs

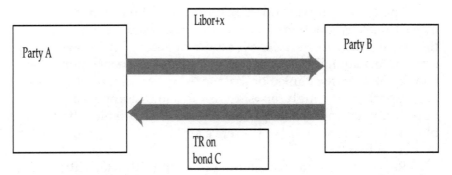

Figure 7-4. Total return swap.

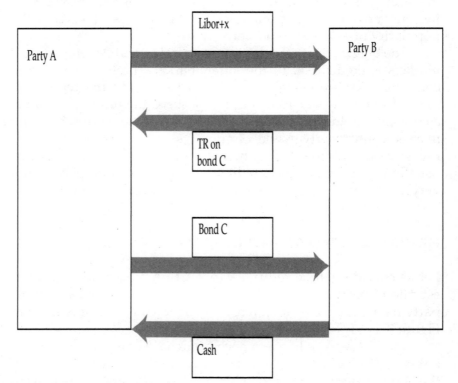

Figure 7-5. A total return swap + sale.

$100. The total return on bond C would only be due to capital gains and losses on that bond. The initial price of bond C is $100.

At the initiation of the repo trade, party A gives the bond to party B. Party B gives $100 to party A. This is illustrated in Exhibit 7-1. The exact same thing occurs in the situation illustrated in

Figure 7-5: Party A sells the bond to party B and party B pays $100 for it.

At the conclusion of the trade, the bond C may be worth more than $100, less than $100, or exactly $100. Assume that bond C increased in price to $110.

Bond C price	Repo (Figures 7-2 to 7-3)	TR+sale (Figure 7-5)
$110	A returns $100 to B.	B pays $10 to A.
	B passes the bond to A.	A pays Libor+x to B.
	A pays Libor+x to B.	

Exhibit 7-1.

In both types of trades, party A is now $10 richer. In the TR plus sale, party A receives $10 in cash. At the conclusion of the repo trade, A pays $100 to B but receives a bond that is now worth $110 in the marketplace. From a cash flow perspective, both trades are identical. If bond C were to decline in price to $90, both trades would still mirror each other, as party A would lose $10 in each case.

If bond C paid coupons, A would receive the coupons. Thus from a pure cash flow perspective we surmise that a total return swap combined with a sale of the bond is equal to a repo trade.

SIMILARITIES

There are clear similarities between a TR swap and a repo, a fact that has not escaped repo traders. Many repo traders use TR swaps because they may offer a more economical financing rate and also allow them to remove the bond from their balance sheets for the duration of the swap. The credit derivative market and the repo market are linked by the shared use of the structure. It is billed as a credit derivative but has other uses, including the financing function typically achieved by a repo or a sale-buyback. A dealer who wants to finance an asset for a short time (say, overnight) can do so in the repo market, especially if the asset is a U.S. Treasury security. Even a dealer who wants to finance for a longer time, say for a year, can do so in the repo market. However, longer-term deals and esoteric assets may require funding through the TR swap.

Therefore, the mechanics of the structure are similar. What is often different is the length of the deal. Repo trades are typically transacted over short time intervals, typically a few days and normally not more than a year. Total return swaps may be transacted for longer time horizons.

BALANCE SHEET CONSIDERATIONS

The TR swap plus sale mechanism has the capacity to remove the bond position from the balance sheet. One repo trader commented on the practices of a rival firm: "They balloon up the balance sheet inter-month and inter-quarter. Then they use total return swaps to get everything pared down for month-end and quarter-end reporting and for window-dressing. They'll do a one-week TR swap right over the reporting date. "

The reason the bonds go off the balance sheet in a sale plus a TR swap is that they are sold outright. A repo involves a commitment to buy the bonds back, so they are not removed from the balance sheet. A sale plus a TR swap includes no such obligation. The counterparty is not required to sell the bonds back to the original owner or even own the bonds at all. Presumably a firm will use classic repos intra-month and total return swaps combined with a sale when possible over the reporting periods.

SELLING CREDIT RISK

Repo teams, just like any other lenders of money, accumulate credit exposures. They may use some credit derivatives to lay off some of that exposure. Henry Lee, senior vice president at Lehman Brothers, said: "Typically the pressure to do a credit derivative or default swap comes from the internal risk management department, which may have a sour view on country exposure. For instance, Asia's recent stock market decline influences our total country exposures, so select country credit risks need to be reduced."

WHAT IS A CREDIT DERIVATIVE?

There is considerable uncertainty in the market about when an instrument is a credit derivative and when it is not. One definition of a CD is any contract whose economic performance is primarily linked to the credit performance of the underlying asset. This definition would technically rule out TR swaps, because their performance is only partially linked to the credit quality of the underlying and is mostly linked to the market risk of the underlying.

Walter Gontarek, director of the CD group at Toronto Dominion Bank in London, says: "Credit derivatives are over-the-counter products whose value is derived from the price of a credit instrument. Credit derivatives permit credit risk—and, occasionally, other forms of risk—to be transferred from a hedger to an investor. Total return swaps are clearly in the family of credit derivative products."

Gontarek notes that the use of TR swaps in pure financing transactions provides the same transfer of economic performance between counterparties that is achieved by other means in a classic repo. It is important not to get carried away by the jargon and to remember the concepts we are dealing with.

SUMMARY

A total return swap plus a sale mimics repo trade exactly from a cash flow perspective. The trades are different from a balance sheet perspective because in the repo trade the bond remains on the firm's books. A TR swap combined with a sale actually removes the asset from the books because the bond is physically sold. Another difference is the time horizon. Total return swaps are normally transacted over long time frames while repo trades are transacted for short horizon trades.

CHAPTER 8

Collateralized Bond Obligations

INTRODUCTION

In this chapter we introduce collateralized bond obligations (CBOs) and collateralized loan obligations (CLOs).

In the past few years a number of "weird" assets have been developed by Wall Street to appeal to traditional bond investors, for example, a bond whose payout was tied to the future earnings from David Bowie's songs. There was also a bond whose revenues were linked to the future sales of tequila and another whose revenues were linked to sales of secondhand Russian cars. Almost any asset can be sliced and diced now. In addition, the asset-backed securities market is exploding—credit card backed securities, car loan backed securities, and so on.

The reason for all this phenomenal growth is the search for yield. How can traditional bond investors earn respectable yields on their investments? Consider that returns on fixed income bonds have come down:

- Interest rates are low.
- Credit spreads borrowers of reasonable credit worthiness are low.

It is difficult to get adequate return in the traditional fixed income market.

CBO AND MBS

The idea behind a CBO is very simple. It is similar to the idea behind a mortgage-backed security (MBS). Consider a mortgage. What is really nerve-racking for the lender is that people prepay their mortgages. The lender receives a high interest rate on the loan, but just when interest rates in general are going down and the lender is happy to receive the high coupon, the borrowers pre-pay. This results in a negative convexity effect. To alleviate this problem, Wall Street came out with the idea of collateralizing the mortgages into MBSs. An MBS consists of many mortgage loans that are packaged into several tranches. The first principal payments are directed toward a specific tranche. Only after the entire principal has been paid on the first tranche do investors in the second tranche start receiving principal. CBOs are created using a similar principle.

A CBO is secured by a package of bonds. These are packaged into several tranches. The first defaults are absorbed by the first tranche. Only after the first tranche has been completely eliminated do investors in the second tranche begin to absorb defaults. Default-shy investors may now purchase CBOs that are based on less than secure credits.

Consider Figure 8-1. So long as all three bonds (A, B, and C) are performing, all three tranches receive payment. Now assume that a specific bond, say bond B, defaults. Whichever bond defaults, the investors in tranche 1 will stop receiving the coupon and may lose their principal. Investors in the other tranches (2 and 3) will continue to receive their coupons as if nothing had happened.

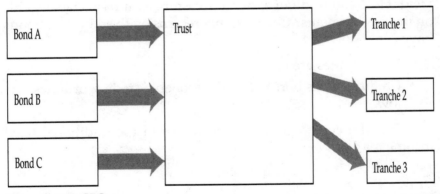

Figure 8-1. A CBO.

In a CBO, we are not concerned about prepayment. Rather, we are concerned about default. This is the same idea employed in

MBSs except that rather than being concerned with prepayment, we are concerned with default.

The principle behind a CBO structure is very simple. A special purpose, bankruptcy-remote vehicle purchases a basket of bonds or a basket of loans. In the case of loans, the structure is called a CLO (Collateralized Loan Obligation) rather than a CBO.

The trust is essentially a special purpose vehicle. It is rated AAA. The trust owns an underlying pool of assets. In our case, the underlying securities are bonds. For the sake of illustration, assume that these bonds are all rated A. The trust then carves them out into several pieces called tranches and sells the individual tranches. The tranches are subordinated or ranked in terms of seniority. If any one of the underlying bonds defaults, investors in the first tranche are going to lose. The second tranche is protected even if one of the underlying securities defaults. An investor in the second tranche will not lose. The third tranche is protected most of all. Obviously, the third tranche, which is protected from default by the first two tranches, is rated higher than A. The first tranche, which shoulders the risk that any one of the underlying securities will default, is rated lower than A. In a CBO structure, some tranches are highly rated. The first tranche is very risky, the second is less risky, and the third is even less risky. It is up to the credit rating agencies to rate the top tranches. For example, the third tranche that is most protected may attract a AAA-rating. An investor in this tranche will lose only if all three securities in the basket will default. If the basket is diversified enough, this may be quite unlikely.

Just as with the MBSs, CBOs typically have more than three tranches. Some MBSs have had up to thirty tranches and got quite complicated. In a similar fashion, the CBO is composed of a basket of many securities that are prioritized into several tranches.

JUNK DEBT

High-risk, high-yielding junk bonds have never been hotter.

- More than $46 billion were issued in the first half of 1997.
- In 1996, the total was $65 billion.

- In 1995, the record was set at $67.7 billion.

There is a huge explosion in the issuance of junk debt, else-where known as emerging market debt or high-yield corporate debt. This is a very hot market because investors need the yield, so they are willing to give their money to lower-rated debtors. The challenge facing Wall Street was to transform these lower-quality assets and repackage them into something that traditional fixed income investors could purchase.

CBOs enable a dealer to take a basket of high-yield junk debt securities and create an AAA-rated security or a AA-rated securi-ty. How is that done? By securitizing and prioritizing the CBOs, one class of securities is going to bear the brunt of the defaults. Other classes of securities are going to be isolated. If a default occurs, the first tranche is going to lose all the money while pro-tecting the other tranches.

Note that all defaults are shared by the holders of the junior tranche in a prorated fashion. You get paid based on your tranche, but you do not get differential treatment. Differential treatment of holders of the same security is not allowed under SFA or SEC laws.

SOME HISTORY

Drexel Burnham Lambert created CBOs as early as 1980. The CBOs were, in turn, sold to Drexel-managed mutual funds. Shortly there-after, Drexel closed its doors after being implicated in the Ivan Boesky insider trading scandal. Then, as the U.S. economy plunged into recession, there were a lot more defaults than expect-ed and even the investors who thought they were protected, were not protected quite enough. Defaults occurred in a tidal wave that swept many issuers and investors.

Supporters claim that CBOs were instrumental in the creation of the asset-backed market as we know it today. They say the early structures were truly groundbreaking. Critics say CBOs enable dealers to offload junk bonds that would not have been sold any-where else.

DIFFICULTIES

It is a fact that many of the CBOs packaged today are leveraged a lot more than the most leveraged structured note was. Some CBOs can be leveraged a thousand times or more. That is to say, there are a lot of issuers and if any of them default, the first tranche, which bears the brunt, gets hit. Investors in the first tranche face a much higher probability of default. While the first tranche loses, other tranches still keep on getting paid.

There is a lot more structural risk in CBOs than there was in structured notes because replication is very tough to do. It is nearly impossible to replicate the cash flows of a CBO without incurring a basis risk. One was able to replicate structured notes with positions in Libor futures and options. But CBOs are not just exposed to interest rates. Rather, they have to do with a specific issuer's defaulting. There are no fungible building blocks to a CBO. In order to replicate the cash flows, one really needs the specific bonds of those specific issuers. In addition, there is no liquid secondary market, so prices are not very transparent.

CBOS AS COMPLEMENTARY VEHICLES TO CREDIT DERIVATIVES

Collateralized bond obligations are complementary vehicles to credit derivatives. Assume a bank has a basket of loans on its books. The bank can either purchase a credit derivative to protect itself or it can securitize the portfolio and sell the loans off to investors. This is also a type of hedge. Also, CBOs are useful in removing high-risk credits from a portfolio. A bank can achieve that objective either with a CBO or with a credit guarantee. Both choices are available.

The bank chooses between the alternatives based on cost. Credit derivatives are typically issued on one specific underlying reference bond. To create a CBO you have to collateralize the whole package of underlying securities and sell out the different tranches.

FINANCIAL ENGINEERING

This is the challenge for the financial engineering team:

- On one hand, the market is hungry for yield. The sales team mentions that it has ample buyers for high-yielding securities.
- On the other hand, the reference assets that are available have low yields.

How can we take low-yielding assets and convert them into high-yielding assets? This was the challenge facing financial engineering teams. Even relatively risky bonds do not provide enough yield.

Financial engineering is used to create high-yielding CBOs that:

- Ensure that the yield is enough to compensate for the extra risks, and
- Ensure that investors can adequately assess the risks.

MARKET SIZE

In 1996, $8 billion CBOs were issued and the same amount was issued in the first half of 1997. This is a rapidly growing market. It's growing hand-in-hand with the asset-backed securities market. The whole idea of collateralization has taken off.

Banks are originating and passing on the credit risk via CBOs. Alternatively, they are originating and passing on the credit risk via credit derivatives. Standard and Poor's rated more than $4.5 billion worth of CBOs toward the end of 1996. Note that you cannot expect to sell any structure to an institutional investor unless it's rated. In the beginning of 1997 there were $22 billion of securities in the pipelines that were waiting to be rated by Moody's or S&P. We do not know the exact market size. Just like credit derivatives, CBOs are privately placed. As of March 1997, traders believe that there are approximately 50 structures worth more than $12 billion.

In January 1997, Capital Markets Assurance Corporation of New York provided the first financial guarantee to a CBO consisting only of Asian corporate bonds. In March 1997, Nomura launched a structure aimed exclusively at Japanese retail investors backed by U.S. investment grade bonds.

FEES

The reason that creating CBOs is such a fast-growing field is, of course, that there are a lot of structuring and placement fees embedded in these structures. Fee-hungry banks are rapidly moving in on this business. For example, one CBO issued generated $18.5 million in management and placement fees on a $200 million face value deal. The fees are almost 10% of the face value of the entire deal. There are structuring and placement fees as well as investment management fees:

- $3.1 million in placement fees,
- $2 million in structuring fees, and
- $1.4 million a year in investment management fees.

To date, much of the underlying paper has come out of the U.S. junk bond market and a little bit less from the emerging markets of Latin America.

THE JUNIOR TRANCHE

By subordinating or ranking tranches in terms of seniority, the issuer protects the senior tranches from bankruptcy risk. The junior tranches bear that risk. Obviously, it is difficult to get a credit rating for the bottom tranche. Typically, no one even wants to worry about a rating for the bottom tranche. It behaves very much like an equity. An increase in interest rates by 25 basis points or reduction by 25 basis points will affect the top tranches, which behave like pure fixed income bonds. Slight changes in interest rates will not have much of an effect on the junior tranche. What affects the junior tranche is the fortunes of the underlying securities. If the firms that issued the securities are doing well, so will the junior tranche. If there is a reason to worry about any of the issuers of the underlying securities, the junior tranche will deteriorate. For example, one of the underlying bonds is Kmart or EuroTunnel, or another name is hovering on the brink of bankruptcy. The investor is really nervous about the underlying securities. Is a reduction of rates by 25 basis points really going to save them at this stage? The investor thinks like an equity trader rather than like a fixed income investor.

While the bottom tranche rarely attracts a rating, it is pivotal to the entire deal. If you don't have a bottom tranche, you cannot create any of the other tranches. The rule of thumb used by the credit rating agencies is that to get the AAA rating, the senior unsubordinated securities must be collateralized approximately 1.5 times. That is, if you have $500 million worth of assets, you would not be allowed to issue more than $330 million of AAA securities. You would have to source $170 million of junior subordinated securities to get the deal done. The precise numbers depend, of course, on the quality of the underlying securities.

To receive a AA rating on the senior securities, you need a lower ratio. The rule of thumb is 1.25. You could issue $400 million of senior tranche and $100 million of junior tranche debt. Obviously, it is much harder to sell the risky junior tranche to investors.

According to the head of one of the U.S.' largest CBO dealers: "You know exactly where you can place AAA-rated Libor-plus paper. The problem is finding buyers with the risk appetite to take on the rump. Quite simply, until you preplace the bottom rung, you don't have a deal—the only way to get investment grade ratings on the senior tranches is to source and sell the junior tranche and thus guarantee at least some credit enhancement."

So somebody has to buy the bottom tranche. The dealer will rarely go long the entire deal with the hope of selling the junior tranche later on. The dealer does not want to be stuck with the junior tranche. This can be contrasted with regular bonds. In a normal bond issue, security houses usually buy the entire bond issue and then sell it later on. For a period of time between purchasing and selling they warehouse the bond. Dealers are quite nervous about warehousing the junior tranche in a CBO deal because if they do this and sell the senior tranches, then they may be stuck with the junior tranche. If the dealer is stuck with the junior tranche it is also stuck with an enormous credit risk. The reason for the creation of the CBO in the first place was to pass on the credit risk. Therefore, the junior tranche must be placed.

Placement is not impossible. While the senior securities come at 15 to 20 basis points over Libor, the junior tranches might generate annual yields in excess of 25 to 30%, so long as nobody defaults. In 1996, Moody's Investor Service's speculative grade total return index outperformed U.S. Treasuries by 13%, and some emerging market CBOs have posted annual gains of up to 50% on the back of the strong rally in the emerging markets.

The party that buys the junior tranche thinks like a pure equity investor. It is taking a bet that the rally will continue. It is not so concerned with the 25-basis-point increase in interest rates. Clients include special opportunity fund managers, insurance funds, and banks. Rather than putting a pool of assets on the balance sheet that would result in a regulatory capital hit of the entire pool, an investor can get exposure and the high return that goes with it by buying the junior tranche. A small amount of the junior tranche is leveraged up many times.

The junior tranche of the CBO guarantees a level of protection to the senior tranche and thus affords its higher credit rating. The size of that tranche is determined by the losses that the asset pool is likely to sustain from defaults.

Size of the Junior Tranche

The junior tranche must be:

- Large enough to absorb any expected losses to protect the senior tranche, and
- Small enough for the issuer to place.

The junior tranche is very hard to sell. Consider the sales team of the dealer. Everybody wants to sell the senior security; that's easy. The sales department just makes a few phone calls and it's done. The junior tranche is much harder. The size of the junior tranche has to do with the probability of default of the underlying securities, the recovery rate of the underlying securities, and the default correlation between them.

Probability of Default

One method of estimating the probability of default is to use historical data. It is very tricky to figure out which historical data to use. In 1997, the annual default rate in the junk bond market was 1.6%. This is well below the 3.6% default rate that has been the historical average. In 1991, one in every ten speculative securities defaulted. Is the probability of default 1.6% or is it 10%? Using these two numbers, one would get totally different answers.

Correlation

Once we start considering a specific portfolio, we are talking about defaults of very specific securities. We need to compute the correlation of default events. Many investors use an index as a proxy. An emerging market CBO might be pegged to the J.P. Morgan Brady Bond index. A U.S. domestic CBO might be pegged to the Merrill Lynch High Yield Bond index. In general, many participants use a basket as a proxy. Of course that is not entirely accurate. There are substantial basis risks. The basket is not identical to the specific pool of underlying securities of the CBO.

The quoted default rates on benchmark indexes are about 1.5 to 2%. Moody's put the probability of default in the next 3 years on some investment grade corporate names at 8%, rising to 40% over the next 10 years.

Why are the default rates of the benchmark index so low while Moody's estimates are so high? The Moody's estimate is 40%, but if you take the benchmark index default rate, it only comes to 18.29%. It's less than half. Why is that? It turns out that the index is composed of very young bonds. Junk bond issuance rose from almost nothing in 1991 to 500 deals in 1996, so almost all the bonds in the index are of young, well-capitalized companies. These companies have enough funding to survive for at least a few years. Later on they may collapse. When the funding runs out and the companies have to survive on their own, they may find it difficult. If you use the index, which is a brand new index in which all the bonds are brand new, you get a low probability of default. That default rate is then exponentialized to 10 years.

Call Risk

There is also call risk with CBOs. If the credit rating of the issuer improves, it will tend to call its debt and repay it early. If the underlying bonds get called, the CBO investors get paid sooner than they expected. Even though the CBO has a high coupon, if the underlying bond get called, you don't lose principal, but you also don't realize the yield you expected. You were planning to get a nice yield on the coupon for a long time, but then it got called and disappeared. Of course, getting called is not as bad as bankruptcy, which results in your getting nothing. In a call situation you get par back. Regarding the bonds in the underlying pool, the winners get called and the losers default.

The Sweetener

The dealer has to offer the investor a sweetener to take on the junior tranche. One way is to offer the investor who buys the junior tranche the opportunity to do the investment management chores—and collect the fees. The dealer offers the client investment management responsibility for the entire basket.

This is very similar to the scheme a foreign currency option desk might have with a hedge fund. The option desk invests $2 million in the hedge fund. In return, the hedge fund has to do all of its option business through that options desk. Under this arrangement, the option desk earns the fees from the hedge fund and also gets the return on the $2 million.

The same arrangement applies to the CBO. The client who purchases the junior tranche will get a nice coupon if none of them defaults. In addition, it will also collect the investment management fees. The entire investment management process is given over to the party that buys the junior tranche. That fee can be as high as 70 to 100 basis points per year. Remember that the fee applies to the whole deal, while the client buys only the junior tranche.

Investment management fees on the entire portfolio are quite substantial. Consider 70 to 100 basis points on a $200 million deal for approximately 8.5 years. The client only has to buy the junior tranche, which is about $50 million or so. Hence collecting the fees is a sweetener.

A SAMPLE CBO DEAL

- Approximately $200 million collateral
- 65% high-yield, 35% emerging market collateral
- Interest rate cap to hedge if Libor rises to above 8%
- Structuring fee: 100 bps

- Collateral management fees: 75 to 100 bps per year
- Securities issued:

Size ($ million)	Rating	Maturity	Coupon	Placement Fee (in bps)
50	AAA	7 years	Libor+35	62.5
110	Aa2	12 years	Libor+80	87.5
10	Baa2	12 years	U.S. T+275	275
30	Unrated	12 years	n/a	500

Collateral pool:
$200 million of high-yield and emerging market debt, largely B-rated

$142 million—U.S. domestic high-yield

$ 22 million—fixed income emerging markets

$ 31 million—floating rates emerging markets

$ 5 million—cash

Consider the sample CBO deal. There is approximately $200 million of collateral. The structuring fee is 100 basis points. The investment management fee on the collateral is 75 to 100 basis points. The securities that were issued in this case were in four tranches. The bottom one is unrated and has a small size. The lowest tranche has the largest placement fee, 500 basis points. The dealer that can sell this tranche will receive a big bonus. The top tranche is rated AAA and has the smallest placement fee.

The top tranche is rated AAA based on the credit rating agency's assumptions. If there are more defaults than expected, even the top tranches might get hurt. So the AAA rating is based on today's assumption, but it will not necessarily remain at that level.

Assume that there is a 1.6% probability of each of the issuers in the collateral defaulting. What happens if this probability changes to 1.7%? A small change in the individual default probabilities of the reference security will have a tremendous impact on the probability of default of the junior tranche.

CREDIT RATING AGENCIES

The credit rating given to the senior tranches by the credit rating agencies is pivotal to the deal. Some CBOs include hundreds of bonds or loans as collateral. The credit rating agencies typically do not check all of the loans in the collateral. They do not have the resources to do so. Instead, they "spot check" a small group of the collateral loans, perhaps 5% to 10% of the entire collateral. The credit rating agency also has to verify the methods by which the issuer has assigned ratings to the individual loans in the basket and also their methodolgy in creating the tranches.

SUMMARY

CBOs are complementary vehicles to credit derivatives in that they enable banks to offload the risks involved in loan or bond portfolios. CBO structures also enable slicing the credit risk and apportioning it between different buy-side parties who may have differing risk profiles.

CHAPTER 9

Locating the CD Function within a Bank

INTRODUCTION

Many organizations are starting to dabble in credit derivatives. From an organizational point of view, where should the credit derivative function be placed? Organizationally, there are five main alternatives for incorporation of credit derivatives:

1. The loan portfolio management function.
2. The derivatives group.
3. The syndication and loan trading group.
4. An independent, freestanding CD desk.
5. A decentralized approach whereby each unit transacts its own CDs.

In this chapter, we examine the pros and cons of each alternative. In reality, most banks start with the last alternative. Several groups within the bank might use credit derivatives independently of each other. Then, as time passes and the credit derivative becomes mainstream, the bank establishes a credit derivative function.

REQUIREMENTS

As with any other derivative function, to establish a credit derivative function of good quality, the bank must address six necessary functional tasks:

1. Back-office and operational support.
2. Regulatory and documentation management.

3. Pricing.
4. Trading.
5. Marketing and distribution.
6. Credit analysis.

CDs As Part of the Loan Portfolio Department

- The end users of CDs are the credit portfolio managers.
- There are informational advantages to holding the CDs within that group.
- Portfolio managers may be advantageous buyers or sellers of specific credits due to their effects on the portfolio—the marginal risk that a specific credit will add to a portfolio.
- Portfolio pricing is a double-edged sword. It allows you to buy credits at prices that are attractive to the portfolio but less than attractive to the market.
- Trading in CDs can lead to disregard of market prices and sentiments.
- The portfolio management function should not be at an information disadvantage in terms of pricing within the bond and loan markets.
- Limited involvement in the markets also leads to limited distribution capabilities.
- The portfolio management function should not be diverted from its primary responsibility by secondary market trades.
- In any case, the portfolio is the best client of the CD product. The portfolio managers should be kept well aware of the available CD products.

CDs in the Derivatives Unit

- Credit derivatives belong here because they are a "D" group.
- The derivatives team is knowledgeable about documentation issues, off-balance-sheet instruments, creation of complex structures from simple ones, etc.
- The main disadvantage is that the derivatives unit does not usually have the credit analysis expertise required.
- Derivatives departments are typically unaware of loan sales; they do not know of the latest events or trade flows and are

less capable of explaining a structure or a situation to a potential client.

Loan Syndication and Trading Unit

- The loan syndication and trading unit is related to CDs in much the same way as the spot desk is related to the derivatives group.

- The clients for CDs are the same as for the loan syndication unit, so there are synergies in marketing, distribution, and information flow.

- Synergies are also available in back-office operations.

- The disadvantage is that there is no portfolio on which to add the CDs as an overlay.

Independent Group

- An independent CD unit is difficult to create from scratch.

- The CD unit needs information from the other groups, so it is better placed within an existing group.

Decentralized Units

- Each department can do its own thing.

- With several departments, each specializing in its own type of product, more and more contact points are generated, and these generate more information. The information needs to be shared.

- On the other hand, CDs are specialized instruments. They must be placed within expert hands. Allowing decentralized CD units is like allowing a decentralized exotic option operation.

SUMMARY

There is no one single unit where a CD department naturally fits:

- Loan portfolio already possesses a portfolio of credit risks that allows it to trade CDs, but it lacks the necessary client focus.

- Derivatives have the back-office systems but lack the credit analysis capabilities that are crucial to CDs.
- An independent unit can be created but it will lack back-office systems as well as daily contact with the cash markets.
- A decentralized approach can be adopted, but this is quite dangerous because CDs should be traded by experts.
- A syndication and loan trading group generally lacks the large inventory to deal effectively in CDs, but has good distribution channels and excellent market knowledge.

Each bank assesses the strengths and weaknesses of its desks and places the credit derivatives function accordingly. In reality, placement of the CD desk is often a political process. The manager with the most connections will get the desk placed within their department.

CHAPTER 10

Credit Risk Management in Asia

INTRODUCTION

One of the biggest problems in the credit derivative market is the lack of data from which to draw valid statistical measurements. This is especially true in Asia. On the other hand, credit risk management is even more important in Asia than in the established markets. In Asia, the volume of derivative trading has grown by phenomenal amounts in the 1990s.

Dealers have to set aside enough capital to deal with:

- market movements, and
- defaults of counterparties.

Any over-the-counter derivative product carries with it a credit risk exposure. If the counterparty goes bust or refuses to pay, the dealer must replace or unwind the position at prevailing market rates. The dealer may not be able to unwind a commitment from a bankrupt counterparty.

The dealer has to compute:

- How much it will lose in the event of default.
- The probability of default.

Dearth of Data

In Asia there is a lack of both credit information and a liquid corporate bond market, making it difficult to compute the spreads.

There is little data available on company defaults. Most borrowing has been done by private loans rather than by publicly traded bonds. Even the rating agencies have been active only since the beginning of 1996. Therefore, not much historical data is available. The lack of data means that the dealers have to rely on guesswork rather than on models. Miles Draycott, regional head of Deutsche Morgan Grenfell in Singapore, says: "You can throw science out of the window. There just isn't the universe of rated credits to use as a benchmark in estimating the probability of default."

Lower Credit Quality

A much higher proportion of the borrowers in Asia are of lower credit quality. Miles Draycott, regional head of Deutsche Morgan Grenfell in Singapore, said: "The whole universe of borrowers is below investment grade, so by definition, you have to be prepared to face more credit risks."

Loose Disclosure Requirements

Disclosure requirements for Asian companies are extremely loose. Experienced dealers have commented that:

- The transparency is the main problem for assessing credit risk, both for derivatives and for standard corporate lending.
- The biggest hurdle to doing business is disclosure.
- Some of the publicly available information is at best opaque.

A dealer in U.S. companies gets timely financial data via the 10-Qs, 10-Ks, and other reports that companies are required to file. The dealer can access the Edgar database on the Internet and see the latest financial information or observe every announcement via FirstCall or other data vendors. Dealers in Asian companies do not have the luxury of having that kind of information available.

A dealer in Asia might have all the publicly available information, which is quite scant. Before approving a deal it may also augment that information with several due diligence meetings. The result is still much less information than is required by an agency for credit assessment. Dealers in Asia need to be committed to finding sufficient information and need to have the risk appetite to handle the credit risk. They cannot expect that any information will simply be handed to them.

Recovery Rates

When defaults occur, the recovery rates in Asia are much lower than in the U.S.

- In the U.S., average losses in the event of default are 30 to 35%.
- In Singapore, the rate rises to 40 to 50%.
- In the Asia-Pacific region as a whole, loss rates can be above 50%.

COURTS

Another problem with trading in Asia is the lack of highly developed financial laws and case histories dealing with defaults. There isn't a history of rulings based on default events. Dealers cannot be sure of their chances in court, and they see the court as a last resort.

The legal system in Asia is slow. Even if the dealer wins a case, it will take quite some time to receive access to the counterparty's assets. A dealer may get a judgment in the U.S. or U.K., but the only way to get payment from a company may be to get the local courts to compel them to pay. The local court may not recognize the overseas decision. Even if it does, the process may be very slow. This is sometimes known as cross border legal risk. One bit of advice is to make sure the Asian counterparty has assets overseas that can be grabbed by the U.S. or U.K. courts. If you win the case you may be able to seize those assets.

In mid-February 1998, it became known that J.P. Morgan stood to lose as much as $350 million due to a Korean court's decision that a domestic brokerage firm does not have to pay up on a credit support. SK Securities argued that it was not adequately informed of the risks. There were many issues on which the Korean courts ruled in favor of the local firm.

DEFAULT MODELS

Traders in Asia use default models that are similar to the ones used in the U.S. or U.K. The data going into the models, however, is quite different. There is tremendous flexibility and guesswork in the calibration of the models used for trades in Asia.

For example, a U.S.-based model might require the input of corporate spreads. We have already seen that the spread, the recovery value, and the probability of default are all related by a formula. In the U.S., one can estimate the spread and the recovery value. In Asia, these are only rough guesses. As one head trader commented:

"The subjective element of credit analysis remains vitally important—especially in the developing world."

ILLIQUIDITY

Because the derivative markets are less liquid, you need to allow for a longer holding period before you can unwind a trade. The closeout period becomes longer. The longer it is, the more market risk you are taking because the market may move in that elapsed time. Consider a dealer who does a back-to-back transaction in an interest rate swap. The dealer has one swap with counterparty A and has the opposite swap with counterparty B. Now assume that one of these swaps is in the money. Just as the dealer expects to receive funds, counterparty A goes into default. On the other hand, the dealer still has the mirror position with counterparty B, and the dealer still has to pay B. The dealer would like to close out the losing position with counterparty A by paying some other institution to take the swap. This process is called "unwinding the position." How long will it take to unwind the position? If the dealer can't unwind that swap within a reasonably short time frame, the market may move again before the position is unwound. This will cause even further losses.

- In developed countries, one typically assumes a one-week closeout period.
- In developing countries, a two- or three-week period is the norm.

The longer closeout period contributes to a higher market risk that must be added on to the credit risk being considered.

Liquidity in Asia is difficult to judge. Even at the height of the crisis in the last quarter of 1998, some CD dealers were talking of liquid markets. "Rubbish," says one CD dealer based in Hong

Kong. "This is symptomatic of the hype that so often surrounds credit derivatives."

Geoffroy Wallier, the Hong Kong–based head of Credit Derivatives for North Asia at J.P. Morgan, says: "You could—and can—almost always do trades of up to $20 million on a few top names in each country." He cites, for example, the Korean Development Bank (KDB) or the Malaysian state-owned oil major Petronas. Other dealers are quick to remark, however, that $20 million is not a "liquid" market.

BANKERS TRUST

Bankers Trust incorporates liquidity risk into its models by requiring a higher return on risk-adjusted capital. This is done rather than using a different method of calculating exposure. The higher return is required to address the concerns about uncertainty in the input parameters.

GOVERNMENT INTERVENTION

There is some good news. In Asia, many financial institutions pose less of a credit risk than expected. The local government may step in and save the institution rather than let it go bankrupt, so there is weight given to the prospect of government or regulatory support or intervention. The intrinsic creditworthiness of an Asian bank is probably higher than it would be if the same bank were located in the U.S.

COLLATERALIZATION

A counterparty will generally post a margin in cash or highly rated securities with the dealer to cover costs in the event of a default. The practice is common in the U.S. and Europe. It is not as popular in Asia. While the dealers would like to require collateralization, the process is unpopular with companies that would rather use the cash elsewhere. Derivative dealer's salespeople and marketers have to convince Asian companies that collateralization is a required part of the deal. It is common practice for companies to threaten the dealer. If you require us to post collateral, we will take the deal somewhere else. In reality, however, it turns out that if one dealer requires a collateral, so will most other ones.

In Asia, client education in credit enhancement is necessary. Collateralization takes up extra time and work in calculating margins, calling them, making sure they are posted, and so on.

SPECULATION

In Asia, some companies or individuals use derivatives to speculate. Many times, a company wants to enter a derivative transaction without any business reason. The entrepreneur who owns the company may wish to speculate on the company's assets, for example, a local beer manufacturer playing on some unrelated exchange rate. The best advice for the dealer is to try to avoid deals in which shareholder voting is controlled by one rich individual and deals that involve punting with the company's money. There is a long list of speculation-driven disasters. It serves as a reminder that high-margin exotic deals have turned into catastrophes.

Rather than flatly refusing a deal, an alternative is for the dealer to convince the owner to do the deal through a personal account, using collateral to back it up. This way, there is no possibility of the shareholders voting to renege on the commitments.

STAFF

It is very difficult to find personnel who are qualified and understand the statistical methods of dealing with credit risk in Asia. There is no shortage of traditional credit officers who make decisions based on a company's cash flow criteria. However, people familiar with the highly quantitative approaches required for calculating the credit risk of a derivative counterparty are rare. Hong Kong headhunters say that derivative credit risk managers are able to earn much higher salaries in the Asia-Pacific region than in the U.S.

The demand for credit risk managers has exploded. In March 1997, *Euromoney* reported that in Hong Kong, senior staff are making $1,000,000 a year while in London the range is between $160,000 and $480,000 for juniors, going up to $800,000 for those with more experience. Headhunters in Asia are looking for credit risk managers.

In Europe, the prospect of a single currency is driving the demand. Issuers, arrangers, and investors all know that the element of risk in international bonds will disappear, so what counts is credit. In Asia, bond issuance is growing at a rapid pace but there is little credit research and the level of disclosure is poor. Anyone who can decipher opaque balance sheets and explain the inner workings of a company is in demand. In the U.S., there are special research teams for each type of industry. In Hong Kong, the entire field started up only in the late 1990s.

HOW TO DEAL WITH THESE ISSUES

The simplest way to deal with these issues is to avoid one-way transactions with counterparties that have poor or unacceptable credit risk profiles. Citibank identifies the counterparties it wants to deal with and the products it wants to transact with them. The Citibank system includes a detailed, forward-looking microanalysis of the business environment through which sectors and individual companies that are likely to be successful are identified. Credit Suisse First Boston rates every counterparty internally and individually. A deal has to fit within its book or it isn't transacted. For smaller banks with fewer resources, such heavy analysis is impossible to manage.

CREDIT DERIVATIVES

Many times you want to make a deal but are afraid of the counterparty risk. "Your appetite to deal is larger than your appetite for risk." For example, a dealer wants to transact a deal with an attractive risk-adjusted return on capital, but the credit lines are all used up. Credit derivatives allow the dealer to separate the deal from the credit risk. It means finding a third party who is willing to take on the credit risk without taking on the market risk, which is the raison d'etre of the derivative structure.

Because of the special difficulties of conducting business in Asia, credit derivatives are gaining popularity in the region. Local banks can leverage their knowledge of individual companies and local creditors and receive a premium for taking on the credit risk.

CREDIT MEDIATION

In Asia, one popular type of deal is credit mediation. A U.S. bank may want to deal with a Filipino company but does not have the required credit lines to do so. It may find a local Filipino bank with a high credit rating.

- The U.S. bank makes the deal with the Filipino bank.
- The Filipino bank transacts a mirror trade with the local Filipino company.

The U.S. bank takes on only the credit risk of the Filipino bank. The Filipino bank is exposed to the local company. The local bank has taken on the risk of the end user defaulting. The U.S. bank has only taken on the risk of the Filipino bank defaulting. The Filipino bank incorporates a premium into the deal and so earns a spread between the deals to compensate it for the risk taken. It is very much a familiarity issue. The U.S. bank cannot be expected to be familiar with 100 counterparty names. Instead it transacts with the three or four local banks that have the local expertise.

An alternative way of structuring the deal is for the U.S. bank to deal directly with the counterparty and then transact a credit swap or a credit option with the local bank to remove the credit risk from the deal. This means that the local bank agrees to guarantee the obligations of the local end user in case of default or downgrade.

ASIA AFTER THE CATASTROPHE

There are two ways of looking at the Asian markets:

1. As a vicious circle of low liquidity and worsening credit quality, or
2. As one of the best opportunities to make money since the region was opened to trading in the 1980s.

There are two corresponding courses of action:

1. Close down the credit lines.
2. Set up a proprietary Asian credit trading desk.

The name of the game is relative value. "Relative value is a term that gets bandied about. Some people refer to today's yields on Asia's distressed assets as holding relative value at Libor+ 500 bps, compared with Libor + 50 bps eighteen months ago," said Drake Pike, Executive VP at Tokai Asia in Hong Kong.

After you decide to go into Asia you discover that one half of your competitors have left, and the other half are in default mode strategy—they are not trading.

The players in the market are those with cash to invest, notes Mark Davies, director of asset trading and credit derivatives for CSFP in Hong Kong. He moved from London to Hong Kong in February 1998 to set up a proprietary trading desk.

"It comes down to capital. There are people who did not get burnt by the financial crisis and who are looking for cheap assets and cheap markets to invest in. Players could be banks or funds that didn't get in on the first wave and are now looking for a chance, or they could be banks that have good credit departments and have managed to escape the turmoil without getting hurt."

"If I go long 10 to 20 million dollars on a local bond and my trade blows up, I lose 10 or 20 million. But if I win I could make 80, 90, or 100 million," said Luigi Bernas. Bernas recently left Bankers Trust and joined Bear Stearns to head up credit trading business in the region. He notes that vulture funds are typical investors. "Many vulture funds did well in the first quarter of 1998 when Asia temporarily bounced back, but their gains were short-lived as more bad news came out of Asia." Bernas adds, "Credit analysis and research ability are far more important than trading ability if you want to make a profit. We look at companies that have a decent chance of overcoming the turmoil." This is a very labor-consuming process because a big credit team is required.

Instead of buy-and-hold strategies on risky debt investments, some desks are opting for short-term "carry trades." A trader will be paid a high yield for holding a risky position in local debt. For example, if you hold the view that the currency turmoil is likely to continue, you can hedge out into U.S. dollars. The yields are so good that you will carry a positive spread in U.S. dollar terms even though the forward on the currency is very high. Alternatively the bank could hold a local currency sovereign debt without hedging, on the assumption that sovereign default risk is quite minimal or that the long-running currency crisis is over.

CREDIT NEUTRAL STRATEGIES

Added volatility means more opportunities and pricing anomalies, arbitrage opportunities between different credits. For example, the Korean Development Bank (KDB) issues debt at significant discount to Korean government sovereign debt.

KDB issues carry very similar credit risk to Korean government debt. The KDB was formed with a special Korean government act. The rating agencies, however, distinguish between the two. There is always a possibility that the Korean government will revise the rules regarding the KDB.

A trader can pick up a profit by trading the arbitrage between yields on the government issue and the quasi-government issue with minimal credit risk. The assumption is that even if the government revamps the KDB act, it will give ample warning. Of course, credit derivatives feature heavily in these types of strategies.

The view is that volatility will remain high in the market as governments flip-flop on macroeconomic policies. Japan is seen as a major source of volatility as it tries to decide on the value of the yen, tax cuts, and the next prime minister.

Bernas of Bear Stearns adds:

> We think the secret is not to get caught long sovereign credits and to buy volatility. We look for cheap credit default puts on sovereign entities and major corporate issuers and wait for volatility to hit before taking returns. Credit risk premiums are high in Asia. But ultimately, as long as the probability of default increases significantly, the premium will be a small price to pay.

High premiums mean there are more risk takers willing to sell credit protection and make markets. Selling credit protection has a similar risk profile to investing in the underlying asset, and the premiums are often attractive.

Credit derivatives are also used in establishing credit-neutral strategies: "Our proprietary trading desk has a risk mandate three times the size of our securities market-making business and we are making good money on our book. But we prefer to opt for credit-neutral positions in tumultuous times and look for arbitrage opportunities rather than taking a view in a market that has yet to bottom out," said John Ellis, head of Asian debt capital markets at Bank of America in Hong Kong.

One popular strategy is to go long the physical asset and buy a credit protection against it. In this way you establish a credit-neutral position.

Chris Iley, managing director at CIBC in Singapore, says: "Liquidity in Asia-related credit derivatives is not as good as many make it out to be. There are products on sovereigns and some of the top corporate names that trade, but usually it's very difficult to match out many of the exposures banks are holding on their books."

CREDIT DERIVATIVES HELP THE ASIAN MARKETS—IN THEORY

Some banks have bought credit protection on corporate debt issues they own. When a borrower is facing liquidity problems and tries to renegotiate the maturity terms of its debt with the banks, it may get a nasty surprise. While it may be easy for the bank to roll over the bond, it may not be possible to roll over the credit protection. Invariably, the bank would then prefer to see the company default, rather than lose the premium it paid for the protection and wait for the corporation to repay the loan. Credit derivatives are changing the game for borrowers.

An analogy is someone whose house is burning down. If the homeowners have substantial fire insurance, they are not as motivated to make a big effort to put the fire out. They will be less inclined to run and get pail after pail of water.

SUMMARY

In Asia, credit analysis is complicated because there is very little publicly available information. There also isn't a lot of activity by the credit rating agencies. The traditional means of performing credit analysis are missing. This fact has contributed to the growth of credit derivatives in the region.

CreditMetrics

INTRODUCTION

Just as important as mitigating credit risk is the problem of measuring and assessing the risks within an organization. In recent years, risk management in general has been a rapidly developing field. More specifically, the credit risk management process can be broken down into several parts:

1. Data collection—Collecting the raw exposure numbers for each counterparty is a huge information technology challenge. Within a financial institution, each department accumulates credit risk. Consider a bank. The individual branches accumulate credit risk when they make personal or business loans. The main office accumulates risk. Each department might keep its data on different systems, on different computers, in different formats, and so on. The act of collecting and merging the data becomes very difficult.

2. Analysis—Once the data is collected it has to be analyzed. We compare two popular systems: CreditMetrics by J.P. Morgan and CreditRisk+ by Credit Suisse Financial Products.

In Chapters 11 and 12, we compare and contrast the two systems.

CREDITMETRICS

J.P. Morgan introduced RiskMetrics in 1994 and it put financial risk management on the map. In 1997 it released CreditMetrics for credit risk management. CreditMetrics is based on three elements:

- A technical document.

- A historical database with a wealth of information on default probabilities, recovery rates, correlation, and credit migration probabilities.
- A software package.

The database and technical documents are free. The software costs a $10,000 one-time fee plus $25,000 a year. It is obvious that J.P. Morgan spent a lot of money and effort to develop these tools. Why is it giving them away or almost for free?

J.P. Morgan is not giving out these tools because it is a charitable institution. It is giving the tools out because it wants its clients and potential clients to use them and then come back to J.P. Morgan to buy derivatives to protect themselves against losses. Another reason it gives these tools out is that the only thing a bank can do to add value to a bank–client relationship is to give the client a way to utilize information. The raw information is already widely available. Knowing how to use the information is what is important.

J.P. Morgan's goal was to establish an accessible benchmark to:

- Measure and manage credit risk across an institutional balance sheet.
- Create integrated value-at-risk statements for creditors that seek to capture the cost of concentration risks and the benefit of diversification.
- Incorporate a multistate view of the credit risk that recognizes the lesser effects of upgrades and downgrades on the trauma of default.

The important issue is that of diversification. Traditionally, the credit analyst looks at the company individually and either approves it for another $10 million loan or does not approve it. Credit analysts base their decisions upon that company in a vacuum. They do not consider the fit of this borrower into the existing portfolio.

One of the main goals of the CreditMetrics tool is to answer a question like, "What are the extra risks that adding this borrower into our loan portfolio will add?" If the loan helps to diversify the existing portfolio, it may be very desirable. On the other hand, if the borrower is very correlated with the rest of the loan portfolio, it may be less advantageous to make that loan. Traditional credit analysis looks at a potential borrower only in isolation, so it would not even notice these effects. That's one of the big differences between credit analysis and credit risk management.

Another goal of CreditMetrics was to look at a multistate view of the credit risk that recognizes the lesser effects of upgrades and downgrades versus the big crash of default. Upgrade, downgrade, and default: Rather than saying "Yes, we approve another $10 million" or "No, we don't approve it" arbitrarily, based upon a decision that has nothing to do with the loan book, CreditMetrics enables an institution to talk about risk and reward framework, similar to an option.

CREDIT RISK VS. MARKET RISK

RiskMetrics was the initial system J.P. Morgan developed. Market risk management is quite different from credit risk management. RiskMetrics evolved from the need to measure market risk exposure in a trading environment. Later it was realized that the model could be used in portfolio management theory. CreditMetrics is a more sophisticated tool. Risk management and technology have improved a lot during the 1990s, and credit risk is a much more complicated problem than market risk.

The market goes up or down in a more or less symmetrical fashion. With credit there is a small probability of a huge loss, in case of default, and a large probability of a small gain, the spread on the interest rate of the loan. So the distribution is much more skewed. The very nature of credit makes the downward bias or the asymmetry quite difficult to hedge away. Because of this bias, it is difficult to measure the credit risk within the context of a portfolio, but it is also vital to do so.

One finds less correlation in a credit portfolio than in an equity portfolio. Almost all stocks move up and down with the market. When the S&P goes down by a lot, the number of advancers is small and number of decliners is large. On a big day when the market moves down, almost all equities move down, so there is a high correlation in an equity portfolio. Credit risks are not independent either, because there are market forces that operate on all companies together. One of the toughest problems is to find enough accurate, unbiased data to draw credit quality correlation. The J.P. Morgan approach was to establish an open-ended methodology that users could modify to their needs.

Because of these issues, the mathematics involved in CreditMetrics are much more complicated than those of RiskMetrics.

SKEWED DISTRIBUTION

With credit, we have a very skewed distribution. This is illustrated in Figure 11-1.

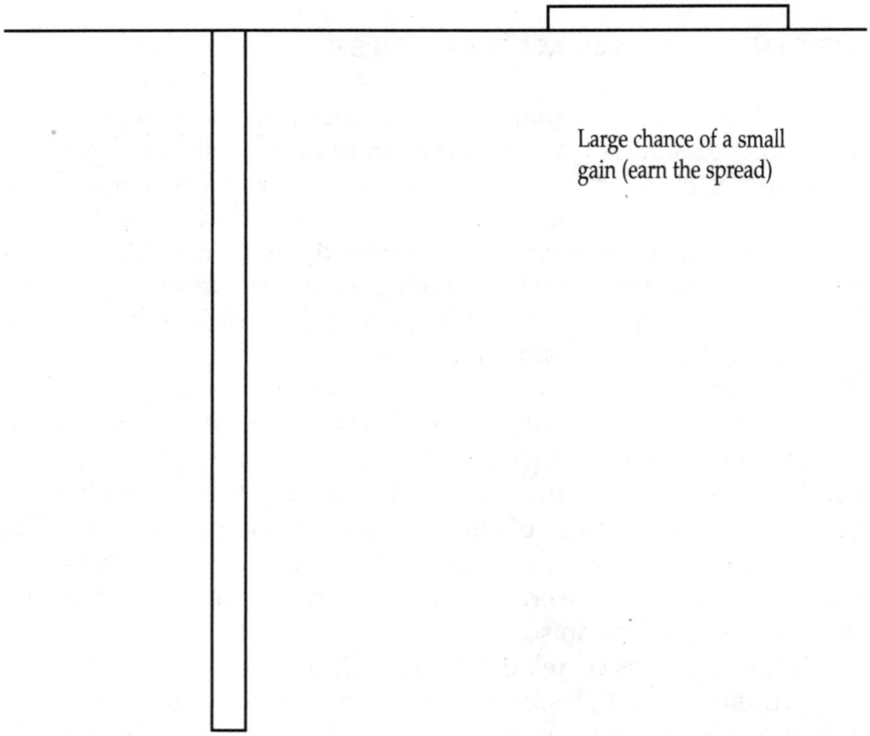

Large chance of a small gain (earn the spread)

Figure 11-1. Small chance of a big loss.

ACCEPTANCE

To ensure the acceptance of CreditMetrics, J.P. Morgan invited dealers to put their names on the initiative. Many dealers and market participants agreed to do so. They include:

- BZW
- Swiss Bank Corporation and Union Bank of Switzerland
- Bank of America
- Deutsche Morgan Grenfell
- Industrial Bank of Japan
- KMV Corporation

THE METHODOLOGY

The methodology arrives at a credit value at risk using three steps:

1. Calculate exposure to each individual creditor. As well as conventional instruments such as floating rate bonds and drawn loans, the model can handle loan commitments, commercial credit agreements, and soon. It can also handle market-sensitive instruments such as swaps, forwards, and options. In these instruments, the credit exposure bears little resemblance to the notional exposure.

CreditMetrics distinguishes between principal risk and market value at risk. A $10 million swap does not have the same credit risk exposure as a $10 million loan. In the swap, the notional never changes hands; the payments are merely netted out. The credit risk is much smaller. The credit risk is the cost of replacing the swap as it goes into the money, or the replacement value.

2. CreditMetrics estimates the probability of each creditor being subject to a credit event such as an upgrade, downgrade, or default. It then calculates a distribution of values for each of the credit migrations.

3. Individual value distributions are merged throughout the portfolio using the appropriate correlation numbers.

The crux of the system is that as a basis of correlation number, CreditMetrics relies on historical equity prices. The assumption is that if two companies' equities move more or less in tandem and the companies have high correlation, then they are going to default together. This, in turn, implies high default correlation.

High equity correlation implies high default correlation. This is a concept that one may believe or may not believe. Perhaps there are high equity correlation numbers because the stock market is just moving up all the time.

CREDIT RISK OF A SWAP

Figure 11.2 is an illustration of the credit risk embedded in a five-year interest rate swap which is settled semiannually.

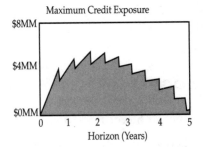

Figure 11-2. The credit risk of an interest rate swap.

Assume that you have entered into an interest rate swap agreement and that your swap counterparty defaults tomorrow. In this case, you do not have any credit exposure. You have not made any payments to your counterparty and neither have they made any payments to you. The replacement cost of the swap is zero because the present value of the fixed rate payments is set equal to the present value of the expected floating rate payments.

As time passes, the swap might become in the money. Suppose you are paying fixed and the counterparty is paying floating. Then, as interest rates rise, you will collect payments from the counterparty. Just as the counterparty is supposed to make payments to you, it goes into default. The more time passes, the more the swap can be in the money. After six months and just before the fixing date, a counterparty default could have disastrous consequences. Not only have you failed to receive your payment on the fixing date, but the entire value of the swap has been lost. As soon as the fixing date arrives, you receive a net payment from the counterparty and your exposure to it drops.

The more time passes, the more interest rates can move and the higher the potential replacement value of the swap. On the other hand, as more time passes fewer fixing dates remain. Thus the potential amount that could be lost dwindles down and so does the potential credit exposure. At the end of the five years, the swap also has zero replacement value. After all payments have been exchanged, you are no longer at risk if the counterparty defaults.

For a swap, we can consider several exposure measures: the potential exposure, the peak exposure, and the expected exposure. The precise definitions of those are set by the user. For example, the peak exposure may be set at the 2% limit while the expected exposure is set at the 10% limit. The expected exposure is a measure of the exposure that the swap is expected to stay within 90% of the time. The peak exposure might be defined as the 98th percentile, and so on.

PROBABILITY OF DEFAULT, DOWNGRADE, OR UPGRADE

Much of the difficult work is found in stages 2 and 3. What is the probability of default? Consider a single bond rated BBB. Table 11-1 is a copy of Table No. 8 from the S&P *Credit Week* of April 15, 1996.

| | | Next Year's Rating | | | | | | | |
		AAA	AA	A	BBB	BB	B	CCC	Default
Today's	AAA	90.81%	8.33%	0.68%	0.06%	0.12%	0.00%	0.00%	0.00%
Rating	AA	0.70%	90.65%	7.79%	0.64%	0.06%	0.14%	0.02%	0.00%
	A	0.09%	2.27%	91.04%	5.52%	0.74%	0.26%	0.01%	0.06%
	BBB	0.02%	0.33%	5.95%	86.92%	5.30%	1.17%	0.12%	0.19%
	BB	0.03%	0.14%	0.67%	7.72%	80.45%	8.83%	1.00%	1.16%
	B	0.00%	0.11%	0.24%	0.43%	6.43%	82.83%	4.04%	5.91%
	CCC	0.21%	0.00%	0.21%	1.25%	2.28%	10.79%	62.24%	23.03%
	Default	0	0	0	0	0	0	0	100%

Probability transition table
Source: *S&P Credit Week*, April 15, 1996, Table #8

Table 11-1. Probability transition table.

A more up to date version of this table is presented in Table 11-2.

The table assesses the probability of a rated creditor being upgraded, being downgraded, or defaulting. Suppose an issuer is rated AAA today. Its chances of staying at AAA next year are 90.81%. Its chances of going to AA are 8.33%. Its chances of going to A are 0.68%. Another issuer is rated CCC. Its chances of staying at CCC are 62.24%. Its chances of going into default within one year are 23.03%. Its chances of being upgraded to B are 10.79%.

There are slightly weird numbers in Table 11-1. For example, BB has a 1% of going to CCC, but a 1.16% chance of going directly

One-Year Transition Matrix from Standard & Poor's
Based on 1981–1997 period
Weighted average across all industry sectors and across all 17 annual static pools
(weighted by number of obligors).

	AAA	AA	A	BBB	BB	B	CCC	D	N.R.
AAA	88.77	7.80	0.68	0.05	0.10	0.00	0.00	0.00	2.60
AA	0.69	88.25	7.32	0.56	0.05	0.14	0.02	0.00	2.98
A	0.07	2.25	87.86	4.88	0.61	0.25	0.01	0.05	4.03
BBB	0.03	0.28	5.37	82.96	4.44	1.00	0.11	0.18	5.62
BB	0.02	0.06	0.53	7.12	74.44	7.29	0.79	0.90	8.85
B	0.00	0.08	0.25	0.41	6.15	72.96	3.32	4.72	12.11
CCC	0.16	0.00	0.32	0.81	2.27	9.87	53.07	19.09	14.40

Table 11-2. An up-to-date credit transition matrix.

to default. Why is it that the probability of default is higher than the probability of a downgrade? Intuitively, it does not make sense. Note the 1.00% versus 1.16%. The extra 0.16% might be one or two companies, because these are such rare events. All the non-diagonal entries in the table are compiled from rare events. They are not statistically meaningful. It's not as if you have tested millions of companies and these are accurate data. Not at all. How many single-A companies go into default? The table says 0.06%. This may have been a single company that happened to go into default and therefore the number is not simply zero.

THE VALUE OF A BOND

Consider a single bond rated BBB. That bond can go to any one of the other ratings—AAA, AA, etc.—or it can default. There are eight possibilities and eight corresponding probabilities of each of those events happening. We can also compute the value of the bond under each of those conditions, using the yields and spreads that are available today. For example, we know how much the bond is worth in case of default: In case of default, the bond will be worth its recovery value.

In case the bond stays at BBB, we can calculate the forward yields and the forward spreads and the forward price. If it moves to AA, assuming interest rates stay the same, there is a different spread and, therefore, a different price.

We illustrate this computation in Figure 11-3. The BBB annu-al-pay three-year bond has just been issued. The three-year spread on BBB-rated bonds is 68 basis points. Thus the bond was issued with a coupon of 6.68% to be priced at par. In one year, this bond will become a two-year bond. Assume the credit rating has improved to AA. The two-year spread for AA rated issuers is 20 basis points. We assume that the risk-free rate stays at a flat 6% level. In one year, we have a two-year bond paying a coupon of 6.68%, which must be discounted at 6.20%. The 6.20% comes from the 6% riskless government debt rate plus the 20 basis points of the spread. Now discount that $6.68 to be received in one year at 6.20% to then discount the $106.68 to be received in two years at 6.20% and come up with a new value. This is the sum of the present value of the cash flows. In our case, the bond will be priced at $100.878 one year from today.

A three-year BBB bond changes to an AA-rated bond in one year.
Assume government yields are fixed at 6%.
Suppose it changes to AA.

Year	Cash Flow			Total	Discount		PVCF
	Principal	Riskless	Spread	Cash Flow	Riskless	Spread	
1	0	6.00%	68	6.68	6.00%	20	6.29002
2	100	6.00%	68	106.68	6.00%	20	94.5875

100.878

Figure 11-3. A BBB bond moves to AA.

If the bond moves to AAA instead, we discount by 6.05%. Every credit rating will imply a somewhat different discount rate. This in turn will result in different prices.

In addition, from the probability transition table, we also have the probability of the credit rating migrations. From these we can compute the expected value. This is illustrated in Figure 11-4. If the bond rating changes to AA, its price will move to $100.878. The probability of such a move is 0.33%. If the bond were to move to AAA, the price would be $100.970 with a probability of 0.02%.

In Figure 11-4, we calculate the expected value of the bond in one year. It is computed as the probability times the price. Thus the expected value of the bond in one year is $99.859.

	Probability	Spread	Value	
AAA	0.02%	15	100.970	
AA	0.33%	20	100.878	
A	5.95%	30	100.694	
BBB	86.92%	62	100.109	
BB	5.30%	200	97.646	
B	1.17%	300	95.919	
CCC	0.12%	1100	83.641	
Default	0.19%		53.800	← recovery value of senior secured debt
Expected value of the bond			99.859	

Can also compute the standard deviation around that mean.

Figure 11-4. Expected value of the bond.

A PORTFOLIO

Assume we have a portfolio of just one bond. Using the probability times the price method, we can calculate what its value is going to be one year from today.

Now let's say we have two bonds in the portfolio, Bond ABC and Bond XYZ. ABC can migrate to 8 places and XYZ can migrate to 8 places. Theoretically we have an 8 by 8 tree for one year. For example, ABC's credit rating can get upgraded to AAA, and XYZ can also get upgraded to AAA. Or ABC can get upgraded to AAA and XYZ can move to AA, and so on. All in all we have 64 different cases and each one has a joint probability based on the probability of a move down or up and its correlation. Theoretically at least, we can price that. If we have three bonds, the tree is 8x8x8. If we have ten bonds, it is 8x8x8x8x8x8x8x8x8x8.

If we have ten bonds, there are more than a billion possibilities. Even if it takes only one millisecond to compute each event, the trader will want to trade before the computation is finished.

Instead of exploring all possibilities, CreditMetrics chooses a reduced set of outcomes chosen randomly and concentrates on those. CreditMetrics randomly chooses a million scenarios out of all existing ones. The ones that have higher probabilities have a higher chance of being chosen and the ones that have lower probabilities have a lower chance of being chosen. There is a Monte Carlo simulation technique behind the theory. (Any technique that has to do with random numbers is called a Monte Carlo algorithm, so named after the casino.)

Based on all these scenarios, we can compute:

- The average return that we expect to earn on this portfolio.
- The standard deviation of the portfolio's return.
- The specific confidence levels, and the likelihood of the return falling below a specific confidence level.

The confidence levels are very much like the value at risk calculation. They measure the likelihood that the portfolio manager will lose more than $10 million, more than $50 million, and so on. Standard deviations are much simpler to compute but are not as applicable in the case of skewed distributions. Remember that we are not dealing with lognormal distributions here. Confidence levels are much more appropriate to our task from a statistical point of view, a tool with which we can identify the credit risk and measure it.

MARKOV CHAINS

Consider Figure 11-2 again. The probability of a BBB issuer moving to A is 5.95% and the probability of its being downgraded to BB is 5.30%.

Suppose our company is rated BBB and that it has just been downgraded from A. What are the chances of it being downgraded again? The chances that it will be downgraded again are higher, because this is a company on the way down. Once a company is downgraded, there is a high probability it will be downgraded again. The fact that it has been downgraded before increases the probability that it will be downgraded again.

Consider the opposite scenario. The fact that a company was just upgraded from BB to BBB means it is very unlikely that it will be upgraded again in the near future. It has just been upgraded and that's a big achievement. It still has to do a lot more work to be upgraded again. A recent upgrade reduces the probability that a company will be upgraded again.

Compare this to foreign exchange rates. Looking at U.S. dollar–Deutsche mark exchange rates, we know that the rates form a Markov chain. That is, the rates have no memory. Where the price is going to be tomorrow does not depend on where the price was yesterday or the day before yesterday; it only depends on where the price is today. So to calculate a forward price or an option value on the U.S. dollar–Deutsche mark rate, we only need a price today to calculate the lognormal distribution. It doesn't matter whether rates have just increased or decreased in the case of the U.S. dollar–Deutsche mark rate or any other commodity or currency or equity. We assume that they have no memory and thus form a Markov chain.

On the other hand, with credit ratings, we do not think that there is a Markov chain. There is a memory, in fact. The probability transition table in Table 11-1 has nothing to do with memory. It just lists where the credit rating is today and where it is probably going to be next year. It's very hard to compile the data just for this table. Look at the numbers: 1.16%, 0.19%, etc. If we started differentiating between creditors on what they are today and what they were last year, we would need a 64 by 8 table. A specific creditor was BBB last year but was AA the year before. What are its chances of defaulting next year? You are going to have many empty cells.

Because it is so difficult to obtain the data, CreditMetrics ignores the effects of memory.

CREDIT RISK OR MARKET RISK?

Assume that our bond is rated BBB. The BBB spreads are 68 basis points today. In one year, spreads for BBB have moved to 115 basis points. In this case, the holder of the bond would lose money. CreditMetrics is not designed to capture changes in the value of a portfolio due to swings in the spreads. It is only designed to capture changes in ratings.

Are changes in ratings to be considered market risk or are they credit risk? According to CreditMetrics, changes in spreads not due to rating movements are market risks.

PROBABILITY OF DEFAULT

Is the probability of default related to the exposure of the counterparty?

Assume a bank enters into an interest rate swap with a small company. The swap itself could represent a major exposure of the company. If the swap is in the money (for the bank) and the company has to make large payments to the bank, the company may be forced into default. On the other hand, assume the bank enters into the very same swap with a highly diversified derivative dealer. The swap represents just a small portion of the dealer's activities. It is highly unlikely that the single interest rate swap will cause the dealer to default.

In the case of the small company, it is likely that the exposure is correlated with the probability of default.

Is the probability of default also negatively correlated with the recovery value? Consider a real estate company whose holdings are in a rapidly deteriorating area of the city. The real estate company finds it difficult to rent its properties, which leads to a decline in its cash inflows which, in turn, leads to an increased probability of default. At the same time, the undesirable properties drop in value, which leads to a deterioration of the recovery value.

Needless to say, most models, including CreditMetrics, do not consider these correlations.

WHAT-IF QUESTIONS

We now have a tool to identify the credit risk in a portfolio, and the tool knows how to take the correlation into account. If there are two BB bonds and they are highly correlated, this will be reflected. Suppose that we have two bonds and they are highly correlated. The probabilities in our 8x8 tree will be different than they would have been if there had been a low correlation.

The tool allows one to consider the effects of buying another bond and adding it into a portfolio. What will that do to the portfolio? The tool allows one to consider making another loan or entering into another swap. Just plug the new instrument into the portfolio and calculate the new risk and return numbers. The tool allows one to compute the incremental effect of the added risk on the overall portfolio. Rather than just studying the risk by itself, we have the potential to see much more, stress-testing credit exposures along any dimension. Let's just take out all of the U.S. bonds and see what happens. Or let's double our exposure to French bonds and see what happens to our portfolio. Let's quantify our exposure to the finance industry, or to the tobacco industry. What is the exposure on each one?

RISK LIMITS

Risk limits are not set in stone anymore. Traditionally, credit risk managers would allocate a $10 million loan to a company. It was a binary decision: yes or no. Now we can consider a softer version of credit limits based on a risk–return profile. We can consider taking on extra exposure to underconcentrated names, even if they are riskier. Even a risky credit that has low correlation with the portfolio may reduce the overall risk of the entire portfolio. *Moody's Investors Services* issued "Modern Credit Risk Management and the Use of Credit Derivatives," a report by Samuel Theodore and Michel Madelain (March 1987) that said:

> ...The growing emphasis on modern credit risk management techniques and the development of the budding credit derivatives market will in time have positive effects for banks' creditworthiness if they are pursued consistently and effectively. This will probably not happen any time soon. Some of the benefits: more accurate loan loss provisions, risk adjusted loan pricing and more earnings stability.

Federal Reserve Chairman Alan Greenspan is also a strong supporter of quantitative measurement techniques.

HISTORICAL DATA

The use of historical data is tricky. Should one use default data when interest rates were at 14%? How long a historical data set do you collect? That's a big question nowadays because there is very little inflation now and even a little deflation.

Every time you try to stress-test a model like CreditMetrics, you end up with differing results. But it's not a problem with the model; it's a problem with the credit markets themselves, and with limited data on default and recovery rates. There is very little data on non-U.S. names. Even that 0.16% estimate in Table 11-1 is already a luxury; in many other places we don't even have that much data.

TRADITIONAL CREDIT ALLOCATION

The traditional way of looking at credit was in notional terms, on a name-by-name basis, for example:

Name	Notional Limit
Texas Instruments	$150 million
Exxon	$200 million
Marriott Hotels	$ 80 million

This is similar to the way institutions looked at market risk:

Instrument	Notional Limit
Currencies	$150 million
Government Bonds	$200 million
Equities	$ 80 million

When we consider concentration risks without the portfolio approach, the limits are our input. With the portfolio approach, the limits are the output.

ADVANTAGES OF THE PORTFOLIO APPROACH

Rather than lending $150 million to a particular creditor, we are going to examine the effects of adding $150 million exposure to our already existing portfolio. What is the addition going to do? This will allow us to make a more rational decision based on diversification or concentration.

The portfolio approach has the following advantages:

- It creates a framework in which to consider all concentrations: by name, industry, sector, country, or product.
- It calculates the "costs" of overconcentration: What is the total effect on the risk of the entire portfolio?
- It integrates diversification as a risk reduction factor.
- It should improve pricing decisions.
- It provides a methodology for more rational limit setting.
- It results in a better allocation of capital.

ARCHITECTURE OF THE SYSTEM

Figure 11-5 illustrates the architecture of the CreditMetrics system. The machine accepts the position data, computes the volatility of each possible instrument, and then calculates the correlation coefficients between them. All this information is fed into a portfolio risk calculator, which produces the final results.

Table 11-3 is an illustration of the raw data fed into CreditMetrics. First, it needs the positions: exposure type, notion-

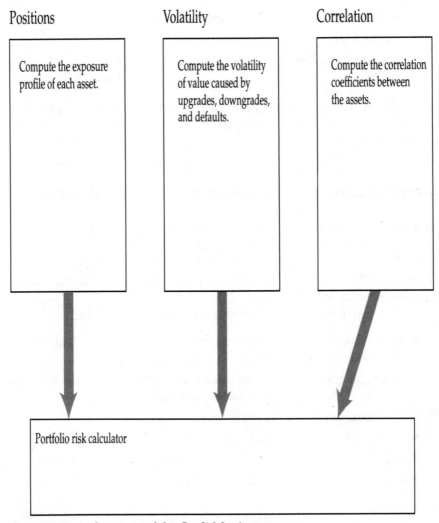

Positions

Volatility

Correlation

Compute the exposure profile of each asset.

Compute the volatility of value caused by upgrades, downgrades, and defaults.

Compute the correlation coefficients between the assets.

Portfolio risk calculator

Figure 11-5. Architecture of the CreditMetrics system.

	Positions	Volatility of value due to credit events			Correlation
Raw Data	Exposure type, notional amount, maturity, rating, seniority	Raw credit rating data from Moody's, S&P	Recovery rates upon default	Market spreads by maturity and credit ranking	Equity and bond historical default data
Models	Conversions of different product positions into common terms	Transition matrices: Moody's, S&P		Present value bond calculation	Factor analysis to determine economic sector that relates one firm to another
Parameters	Mean and standard deviation of exposure profile	Standard deviation value for each credit rating and maturity σ_i			Name-specific firm value correlation ρ_{ij}

Table 11-3. A schematic of the CreditMetrics system.

al amount, maturity, ratings, seniority, etc. It accepts the raw credit rating data from Moody's and S&P. The system also accepts the recovery rates of bonds in case of default. We also have to input the market spreads with maturity and credit rating as well as equity and bond historical default data.

Then we have the models. First, CreditMetrics converts the different product lines and positions into common terms. Here is where we equate the swap with the loan with the bond. Then we take the probability transition matrices. CreditMetrics also has a present value of a bond calculation, as already illustrated.

As for parameters, we have the mean and standard deviation of the exposure profile, a standard deviation value for each credit rating and maturity, and the name-specific firm value correlation.

CreditMetrics has a separate model to handle swaps and what it calls "market-driven exposures." These are then equated to common terms; see Table 11-4.

RECOVERY VALUES

What are the effects of default? In Table 11-5 we list some loss ratios in case of default. These are taken from Moody's. Recovery

	Loans & Bonds	Swaps	Commitments	Letters of Credit
Raw Data	Notional exposures	These "market-driven exposures" are processed by a separate model	Notional exposures	Notional exposures
Models	Adjustment for time horizon		Adjustment usage by credit rating	Adjustment for usage by credit rating and type
Parameters	Exposure amount profile: mean and standard deviation for each instrument			

Table 11-4. Adjustment of data by CreditMetrics.

Type of Debt	Percentage Lost
Senior secured	46.20%
Senior unsecured	48.87%
Senior subordinated	61.26%
Subordinated	67.50%
Junior subordinated	82.50%

Table 11-5. Loss ratios on default. *Source:* Moody's.

values depend on the type of debt and also depend on the type of company we are dealing with.

If the debt is a junior subordinated bond, you will probably lose much more than if it's a senior and secured debt. Also, you have to consider the type of company to determine the recovery value. A hotel owner has many properties that could be sold in the event of default. A consulting company might have a lot less in the form of tangible assets.

Note that the Moody's data are valid only for the U.S. In other countries, spread and recovery data are much harder to obtain. For example, in Canada it is difficult to estimate the credit spread for a Canadian CCC corporate entity. There is some data for foreign markets but not a lot. In less-developed countries, even less data is available.

CORRELATION

There are several methods of imputing the correlation between companies.

1. **Use equity data.** The equity market is the most liquid and efficient market. Assume that debt will mirror equities: As the equity goes down, so will the debt.

2. **Use bond spreads.** This method directly addresses the "proper" correlation for bond portfolios. There may not be enough available data; for example, South Africa has only one corporate bond outstanding. Remember that bond spreads also depend on other factors, such as liquidity, recovery rates, and supply and demand.

3. **Use historical ratings and default data.** This method provides an objective representation of actual defaults. It also ties the model to public credit ratings.

4. **Use one constant factor.** If it includes one constant factor, the model can highlight overconcentrations.

5. **Use factor analysis.** The method focuses on the essentials: Firms are correlated if they are sensitive to the same underlying economic factors. You will need to focus on a handful of factors rather than on thousands of companies. Choose the factors you wish to consider from among thousands of counterparties, 50 to 100 industry types, and 5 to 10 risk factors.

SUMMARY

Correlation coefficients are extremely difficult to estimate accurately, but they are crucial to producing more tailored pricing. Correlation allows for more interesting stress testing, and better portfolio management.

Now the risk manager can ask, "What if I allow the trader to buy more CCC names? How will that affect the portfolio returns and how will that affect the risk?" The bank manager can make a more informed judgment, asking, "What if the risk manager increases the trader's limits on France? What will that do to the portfolio?"

Not all CCC creditors are the same, because one is highly correlated with the portfolio and one is less correlated. CreditMetrics is a tool that enhances the formulation and analysis of credit risk management questions.

CHAPTER 12

CreditRisk+

CreditRisk+ was released on October 14, 1997 by Credit Suisse Financial Products. The CreditRisk+ model attempts to answer some of the same questions as CreditMetrics but from a totally different angle. It is quite interesting to compare the two.

WHAT ARE THE RISKS IN DESIGNING A MODEL?

There are three risks inherent in designing a credit risk model:

1. **Process risk.** This risk arises because the actual observed results are subject to random fluctuations even though the model and parameters used to compute them are appropriate.
2. **Parameter uncertainty.** There are difficulties in estimating the parameters used by the model. We may be able to get historical parameters, but there is no guarantee that today's parameters will be the same.
3. **Model error.** This is the risk that the model does not represent reality. It is the hardest risk to track down.

Suppose a scientist conducts an experiment that fails to show the expected result. Is it a mistake in the experiment or is it a mistake in the model? Because defaults are rare events, we are not sure whether the default rate is 0.16%. Is it 0.16% or is it 0.19%? We are very uncertain. If four more companies default, the rate is a whole new number because defaults are so rare.

As for parameter uncertainty, how do you estimate the parameters used by the models? Consider the problems encountered in the estimation of volatility. Correlation is even harder to assess.

Model error is a huge problem. What if our model does not represent reality? For many thousands of years people believed that the sun rotates around the earth and not the other way around.

CREDIT RISK IN LOANS

There are two types of credit risk in loans:

1. The credit spread risk applies to portfolios that are marked to market. Changes in credit spread will impact the price of a portfolio.
2. The credit default risk, that the obligor will not return the debt due to bankruptcy, applies to all loans.

The CreditMetrics approach tries to answer both of these risks because it is concerned with credit rating changes and also with defaults.

CreditRisk+ only addresses the default risk. It's concerned more with default than with rate changes because loans are not rated. CreditRisk+ is more geared toward loans. With a loan, you really only care whether or not you receive your principal back. You are not as concerned about marking the loan to market.

DEFAULT RATE

Default rate can be modeled as either a continuous or a discrete variable.

- Continuous variable: The data required for analyzing credit default risk is similar to the data required for stock options: a forward stock price and stock price volatility.
- Discrete variable: This is the technique used when assigning credit ratings to obligors. Each obligor is assigned a specific credit rating.

A continuous variable can have any value, such as 5% or 5.5% or 5.6%. A discrete variable goes into bins like a credit rating: AAA, AA, A, and so on. The discrete variable is assigned into windows. It operates via a credit rating and credit migration table. That is the

Treatment of Default Rate	Data Required
Continuous variable	Default rates Volatility of default rates
Discrete variable	Credit ratings Credit migration table

Table 12-1. Default rate models.

approach used by RiskMetrics. CreditRisk+ uses a continuous variable approach.

TIME HORIZON

We can think of two possible time horizons for analyzing risk:

1. A constant time horizon such as one year; corrective action can be taken over that year.
2. Hold to maturity.

CreditRisk+ suggests using a one-year horizon. It is likely that corrective action could be taken within a year.

OUTPUT OF THE MODEL

CreditRisk+ identifies two types of output reports:

1. Distribution of loss—How much can I lose for a given confidence level, e.g., 2% of the cases?
2. Identification of extreme outcomes—What can I lose in a catastrophe?

CURRENT MANAGEMENT PRACTICES

Banks and financial institutions have been managing credit risks for many years. It is useful to examine their current modus operandi and determine the reasons behind their successes. There are four main types of limits being used:

1. Limit the exposure to a particular obligor.
2. Limit the tenor of each obligor.
3. Limit the extent to which you are exposed to a particular rating or "credit bucket."
4. Limit the concentration of exposure by country or industry.

Each of those limits directly affects a corresponding type of credit risk.

1. The size of the exposure.
2. The maturity.
3. The probability of default.
4. The systemic or concentration risk of the obligor.

The systemic or concentration risk of the obligor is almost like the correlation. It's another way of saying that well-diversified portfolios are less risky than more diversified ones.

Current management practices involve limiting each of the risk factors individually. Applying these limits creates well-diversified portfolios. Current practice is to limit the size of the exposure, limit the tenor, limit the maturity, and impose credit rating limits and country and industry limits. The banks already have these limits in place. That is how they manage traditional loan books. Hence, applying these limits is a reasonable way to proceed, to build upon this knowledge. But there is no single measure of the benefits of diversification. There is no way to measure the extra risk of concentration. CreditRisk+ uses techniques from the insurance industry to model the sudden event of default of an obligor.

CreditMetrics used Monte Carlo simulation to model one million out of the billions of possibilities. CreditRisk+ does not use simulation at all, so it's computationally tractable and quite fast.

MODEL INPUTS

CreditRisk+ has four types of model inputs:

1. Credit exposures.
2. Obligor default rates.
3. Default rate volatility numbers.
4. Recovery rates.

Exposures are determined by the instrument. A letter of credit should be taken at full face value because it will probably be drawn down. An interest rate swap will have a much smaller exposure than its notional principal amount.

Default rates can be taken from Moody's. Note that one-year default rates show significant variation from year to year. In a recession, there are many more defaults.

Default rate volatility numbers are used by CreditRisk+ in addition to default rates. The standard deviation of the default rates may be quite significant compared to the default rates themselves. If one were to take only the historical default rates, the result may be an underestimation of the true default rate. Because the default rate is not a stable number, it's necessary to look also at the volatility of the default rate.

Recovery rates depend on seniority and the type of security. Recovery rates from bonds can be obtained from statistical studies available from the rating agencies. For loans, we can use statistical studies available from the Loan Pricing Corporation's database and figure out what the default rate is for the type of loan in question.

CreditMetrics took the default rate as represented by a single fixed number. CreditRisk+ doesn't consider the default rate a static number; it has to have some volatility around it.

DEFAULT RATES AND CORRELATION

Default rates appear to be auto-correlated. A high default rate in one month means the economy is not doing very well and there are likely to be more defaults next month. In addition, default rates are also correlated across different companies and even different sectors. A high default rate in the manufacturing sector will be correlated with a high default rate in the banking sector.

There is a background process (e.g., the economy) that affects defaults. One possibility is to develop an econometric model that ties the economy to default rates. This is a daunting task because:

- It is very difficult to establish causal relationships.
- There is little available default data by country or industry.
- The relationship found will probably not remain stable over several years.

It is very difficult to develop a model tying the default risk to the economy. What is the causal relationship between the economy and default rates? One may be able to come up with a theory, but none has been established precisely. Practitioners know that there is some correlation, but they don't know exactly what the precise model is. One would have to model the economy versus the default rates, the industrial production index versus default rates, and many different types of models. One of the problems is that there is very little available default data by country or industry, so it's very hard to develop this model. Even if one were to develop such a model, does it mean that the relationship that is found is going to be stable over the next year? We are moving from a production-based economy to an information-based economy. Consider the yardsticks that we now use to measure the economy, numbers such as the industrial production index and the nonfarm payroll. Are those numbers useful for the new economy in which more people are working at home? Maybe what counts is PC sales or number of hours logged on the Internet or some other measure.

CreditRisk+ allows the default rate itself to exhibit volatility, and the system can use default correlation numbers. These will give you a fat-tailed distribution. Rather than using a normal distribution that gives low probabilities for out-of-the-money events, we would like to use a fat-tailed distribution that would account for the higher default rate in periods of recession. Statisticians call this a leptokurtic distribution, one with fat tails. In Figure 12-1, we show a table of the default rate and volatility of that rate for obligors with various credit ratings.

Default correlation numbers are difficult to obtain and are unstable over time. In a retail loan portfolio there are no share prices, so we can't even get equity correlation numbers. CreditMetrics can rely on share prices as they are available for publicly traded companies. For rated companies that have bonds, we can observe their credit rating and can see their correlation.

If there is no default rate volatility, the distribution of the number of default events will be similar to what statisticians call a

	Probability of Default in One Year	Std. Dev. of That Rate
Aaa	0.00%	0.0%
Aa	0.03%	0.1%
A	0.01%	0.0%
Baa	0.12%	0.3%
Baa	1.36%	1.3%
B	7.27%	5.1%

Carry & Lieberman, Moody's Investor Services Global Credit Research, 1997

Figure 12-1. Probability of default and the volatility of that probability.

Poisson distribution. Poisson distributions measure the occurrences of events.

Think of yourself sitting in a bus station and consider how long it takes for the bus to arrive. The arrival time follows a Poisson distribution. You don't know precisely when the bus will arrive, but you do know that the longer you wait, the higher the probability it will arrive. If you don't include a default rate volatility, the default rate is modeled with a Poisson distribution. Default arrives in a similar fashion to the bus. Intuitively, the Poisson distribution says: "The bus is expected to come in about five minutes but we cannot be sure that it will come exactly then."

Figure 12-2, taken from the CreditRisk+ manual, illustrates the difference between a distribution with and without volatility. In Figure 12-2 the Poisson distribution is depicted by a white line. It is very centered around the mean. Default rate volatility has the effect of widening out the tails. This is depicted by the dark line in the graph. There is now much more uncertainty as to the exact arrival time. In a recession there are more defaults because the

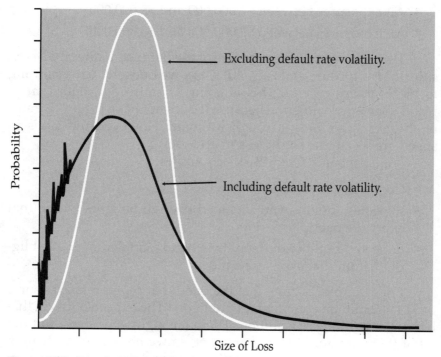

Figure 12-2. Distributions with and without volatility.

economy is not doing well. This is depicted clearly by the dark line. Note that the left side of the distribution is jagged. There is a big difference between two defaults and three. The right side of the distribution is smooth as there is very little difference between 500 defaults and 501.

DEFAULT EVENTS AND DEFAULT LOSSES

Given the number of defaults, we now consider the total loss to the portfolio. Even if the defaults themselves follow a Poisson distribution, the losses do not. The actual losses depend on the exposure to different obligors. This is no longer a Poisson distribution.

CreditRisk+ considers each exposure (net of recovery values). The exposure is the one that was input less the recovery value. Exposures are then bucketed according to the size of the exposure. For example, separate buckets could be created for:

- All exposures under $1,000,000.
- All exposures between $1,000,000 and $2,000,000.
- All exposures between $2,000,000 and $3,000,000.

This is done to reduce the size of the data set. Rather than consider each exposure at its absolute size, we bucket them according to more grainy criteria. This is going to cause our algorithm to result in an approximation because it does not have the precise size of the exposure, only a rough estimate. However, the gains in speed are worth the slight loss in accuracy.

For each band, CreditRisk+ computes:

- Common exposure level in band j.
- Expected loss in band j, totaled over all obligors within that exposure band.
- Expected number of defaults in band j, totaled over all obligors within that exposure band.

For example, assume that the band that represents exposures of $1 to $2 million contains eight obligors. The expected loss in that band is not 8 times $1 million. There are eight exposures, but not all of them are going to go bankrupt, so we have to total them in each band. How many are actually going to default? A certain percentage of the loans in each bank will default.

SECTOR ANALYSIS

In CreditRisk+, sector analysis is used to further capture the effects of diversification and concentration. In finance we differentiate between:

- Systematic factors—Factors that affect the fortunes of all obligors within the same group (for example, all obligors in the same country).
- Specific factors—Factors that impact a specific obligor.

Diversification of the portfolio usually mitigates the exposure to specific factors. In CreditRisk+ the factors are called sectors, as in sectors of an industry. Sector analysis is used rather than directly estimating the correlation.

USE OF THE MODEL

CreditRisk+ offers three methods of using the model:

1. Allocate all obligors to a single sector without considering diversification.
2. Allocate obligors to one of several sectors so that each obligor is mapped to a specific sector (e.g., the country).
3. Apportion obligors among sectors so that each obligor is distributed to a specific risk sector.

The first and simplest method is to assume that there is only one risk factor—the state of the overall economy—and everybody goes up and down with that same economy. There is no diversification. There is no correlation. Since there is no diversification all companies are in the same boat.

The second method is to allocate each obligor to one of several sectors. Each obligor is mapped to a specific sector. An obligor from Italy will receive a 100% allocation to Italy. An obligor from England will receive a 100% allocation to England.

The third method involves apportioning obligors among sectors. Each obligor is distributed among specific risk sectors. Suppose companies ABC and DEF operate in different industries in the same country. Both companies will be affected by the general market conditions of the country but they will not be perfectly correlated because they are in different industries. In CreditRisk+ we will assign a common country factor to both companies but different industry factors. In this fashion we capture the fact that both companies share exposure to some of the same risk factors. This is similar to an orthogonal basis for a vector space. In another example, Company GHI conducts half its business in Italy and half in the U.K. Such a company will be allocated 50/50 between Italy and the U.K.

CreditRisk+ recommends including a single global "specific risk sector" to take into account the specific risk.

Of course, more sectors reduce the expected loss in the 99th percentile. Each sector has a default rate and a volatility of that rate. A sector can be thought of as a collection of obligors. A large number of sectors or very low default rate probabilities have the same effect—the fat tails are eliminated. The reason we eliminate the fat tails is that the more sectors we have, the more diversification we have, the less concentration we have, and the less the probability of a fat tail. When the economy worsens they are all diversified so that the massive amount of defaults that leads to fat tails disappears. One company goes up while the other one goes down. The probability of a joint default goes down. This has a tendency to reduce the loss in the case of extreme moves.

ECONOMIC CAPITAL

Sufficient earnings should be generated by loans to cover any expected losses. This is the reason banks charge higher spreads on low-quality loans. Economic capital is used by the bank to cushion itself against unexpected default losses, because the level of defaults in any one period might be greater than was originally expected.

In Figure 12-3, the expected loss is illustrated at the 50% mark. That's how the bank priced the spread on the loan in the first place. The unexpected loss is depicted at the 99% level. That's where one should allocate the economic capital.

In 1997, most banks were stressed when the "Asian flu" hit because the Asian defaults were a five standard deviation move, not a two. A move of five standard deviations could result in larger losses than were originally budgeted for.

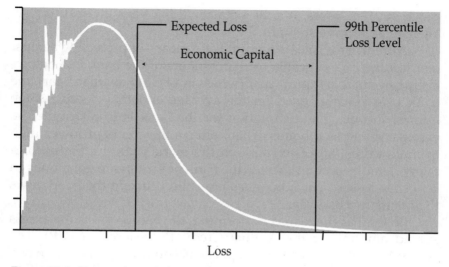

Figure 12-3. Economic capital.

- Up to the expected loss, banks rely on adequate pricing.
- From the expected loss to 99% you add the economic capital that we see the bank tacking on, to cover the extra risk for that obligor.
- Beyond 99%, the bank needs to do scenario analysis because the standard mathematical model cannot predict what will happen in a five standard deviation move. In those faraway regions, risk is controlled via limit settings.

CREDIT PROVISIONS

Current economic practices recognize credit income and credit loss at two different times. Loans are typically held in a "hold to maturity" account. The bank gets the benefit of credit income and the credit loss is deferred until later. Credit loss provisions are only made when a loan is not performing.

In a typical year, the bank will suffer credit losses that are much smaller than average. This is because the average includes defaults of really big exposures that only happen rarely. If you look at a historical time frame or average, in the average there may have been a recession that included a lot of big losses. So the average is not a fair representation because in a typical year the bank suffers much smaller losses. It's the occasional big year that caused the average to become so high.

A credit provision is required as a means of protecting against distributing excess profits to shareholders of the bank in a below-average year. In a typical year (which is a below-average year), the bank uses pricing based on the average and they receive some interest income. The temptation for the bank is to distribute the excess income as a bonus. Then, after a few years of lower than average losses, all of the sudden the market takes a big hit and many defaults occur. Where is the bank now going to get money to cover the losses? The bank needs to collect during the good years to anticipate a bad year.

So long as the loan is performing, the bank collects the excess spread amount, or the Annual Credit Provisioning (ACP). The bank places these profits in a special account to budget for when the loan defaults. The special Incremental Credit Reserve (ICR) account is set up to protect against unexpected losses. This is depicted in Figure 12-4.

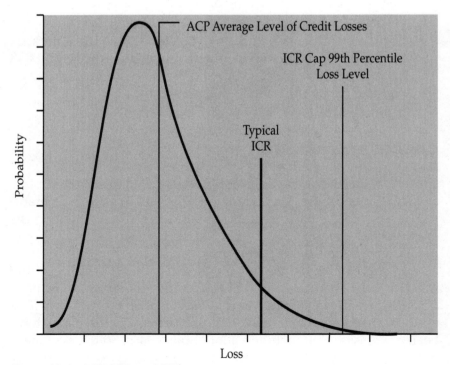

Figure 12-4. ACP, ICR, and ICR cap.

Every year the bank adds the proceeds from the ACP to the ICR. Only when the ICR is fully saturated and has reached the ICR cap should the bank consider that it has enough of a cushion to distribute the excess profits.

SUMMARY

CreditRisk+ attempts to answer very similar questions as CreditMetrics. While the uses of the systems are similar, their methodologies are quite different. This is not surprising given the origins of the systems. CreditRisk+ was developed mostly for non-rated loans held in a "hold to maturity" account. CreditMetrics was developed for a trading situation.

There are currently four products on the market designed to measure and manage the credit risk of a portfolio. They are:

- J.P. Morgan—CreditMetrics/CreditManager
- CSFP—CreditRisk+
- McKinsey and Company—CreditPortfolioView
- KMV—PortfolioManager

We can classify them into three general types:

- Merton-based—CreditMetrics and PortfolioManager
- Econometric—CreditPortfolioView
- Actuarial—CreditRisk+

The Merton-based models work on the assumption that a default is associated with a drop in the stock price of the issuer. The econometric models look at the general state of the economy and use that to predict default rates. The actuarial models use techniques from the insurance industry (e.g., a Poisson distribution) to model default distribution.

The art and science of credit risk management are continually evolving and the methods keep improving. Additional models and techniques are constantly being developed and tested.

CHAPTER 13

Credit Derivatives and Bank Loans

INTRODUCTION

There are currently big changes being made in the environment of bank loan portfolios. Trade barriers are being eliminated. This is especially true in Europe. The fact that U.S. investors can trade in eastern European debt is quite new. There is a growing secondary market for bank loans. It is still tiny and the clients are still resisting it, but at least there is a secondary market. Non-investment-grade loan portfolios are actively trading in the secondary market. Subsequent sales are increasingly used by banks. The secondary market is also used for portfolio growth. Banks are buying existing loans whether by bank mergers or by bank acquisitions. Alternatively, they just buy a bank's loan book.

Pooled investment vehicles for institutional investors are rapidly becoming more available: asset-backed securities (ABS), mortgage-backed securities (MBS), collateralized bond obligations (CBO), collateralized loan obligations (CLO), etc.

We are now beginning to see some benchmarks for performance emerge, as well as a growing commitment to portfolio management by banks. Credit derivatives have become a necessary addition to the secondary market for loans.

THE ROLE OF CREDIT DERIVATIVES IN THE LOAN BOOK

Credit derivatives are not a just a product group. Rather they are a derivative approach of looking at risk, quantifying exposure, including correlation, and managing exposure in a portfolio context. A trading book requires marking to market, netting, taking collateral, allocation of risk capital, and so on. This is an entirely different approach to loans than managing them on a hold-to-maturity basis. Within this context it is possible to minimize portfolio volatility, maximize risk-adjusted returns, and maximize shareholder value.

At issue is the difference between an actively managed trading book and an accrual book in which loans are held to maturity and the only thing that matters is the net interest margin (NIM). Rather than considering NIM, we are moving toward a risk-adjusted return on capital (RAROC) approach.

The idea is to treat default risk as fungible. It is an asset in its own right that can be traded. Further, derivative products can be created from that risk if we consider the loan as an "index" in which the actual physical asset does not have to be owned by any of the swap counterparties.

For example, consider a total return swap. The physical asset that is used as the reference asset is not part of the deal. It does not have to be owned by any of the swap counterparties. The same is true of a credit default swap. No one has to actually own the reference securities. One can use bank loans or bond reference to hedge untraditional risks, bearing in mind that there will still exist some basis risk.

IMPROVING RETURNS

Credit derivatives can improve returns for nonbank loan investors. The operating costs for derivatives are lower than the operating costs of managing a loan portfolio. The regulatory and economic capital allocated to the derivative may be lower than in the cash market.

Credit derivatives can also improve returns for banks. Credit derivatives:

- Permit reinvestment of funds in higher-yielding issuer exposures. Thus a bank can lend money to a high-yield, high-risk issuer and, at the same time, purchase a credit default swap to protect against issuer default.

- Provide an opportunity to move toward optimized portfolios, reducing the economic capital requirement. Regulatory guidelines are changing to permit properly structured credit derivatives to reduce regulatory capital requirements.

USING CREDIT DERIVATIVES
FOR RISK MANAGEMENT

When a credit risk manager is thinking about using a credit derivative, there are some questions that need to be asked:

- Which borrowers should be used?
- How much to use of each borrower?
- How much of the line to free?
- Who pays for the risk reduction? There is an option premium associated with the credit derivative. Who pays for the premium—the facility revenues or the hedge differentials?
- Who approves the transaction?

There are quite a few issues to consider.

The last recession convinced banks that they have to manage credit differently. The Asian collapse reinforced that lesson. In the United Kingdom, for example, the default rate is growing and so is volatility. Credit derivatives are attractive tools; but to succeed, the credit derivative must be integrated into the bank's credit culture. It's not enough to establish a credit derivative desk. Rather, the entire commercial banking division of the bank has to be integrated into this culture. Currently, this is rarely the case in most banks. Most banks are still coming to grips with the technological problems involved in measuring their credit exposure.

The proper use of credit derivatives involves changing the culture from a yes–no, buy and hold risk management approach, whereby one places loans into an accrual account and hopes that things will turn out all right. It involves changing the culture toward a mark-to-market mentality, whether that's done by explicitly putting the loans into a trading book or by actively and dynamically managing the portfolio's risk level. In the U.S., regulators actually encourage banks to place loans in a trading book because that reduces regulatory capital requirements. The same loans, placed in an accrual account, would require higher regulatory capital. Most regulators in Europe have not taken that step yet.

Many banks have come to the conclusion that they must manage risk better. They've developed systems to measure current credit risk exposure and have instituted dynamic management of credit risks. Models have been purchased or developed to figure out:

- default probabilities,
- obligor concentrations and risk contributions, and
- optimal hold levels for individual loans.

Mechanisms are also being developed to analyze volatility.

VOLATILITY OF DEFAULTS IN A LOAN BOOK

It is customary to separate the bank's loan portfolio into several types of borrowers or obligors.

- Large multinational or multiproduct corporations—These are the biggest clients, of which there are only few, but each one has a huge line of credit. Think of the major companies.
- Small and medium enterprises (SME)—A typical bank has many thousands of such clients.
- Personal loans—Individuals borrow on their credit cards or home equity lines of credit.
- Nonperforming loans.

We now consider each type of borrower and examine where the volatility of defaults occurs for each of type of loan.

Large Multinationals. The volatility of defaults in this group comes from what has been called the "bad" risk. This is the risk that can be diversified. There are only very few credit lines in this group and they are highly concentrated in several large borrowers. The bank may have a large exposure to a big multinational or some other specific company. If that one company were to default, it could have drastic consequences to the bank.

Small and Middle Enterprises. For small and middle borrowers, the bank typically has a concentration in the domestic country, because that's where the bank does most of its business. It could also be a home state, home province, etc.

Personal Sector. In the personal sector, there is a battle over who issues the most credit cards or who issues the most loans. In the rush to issue more and more credit cards, banks are accepting more and more borrowers with deteriorating credit quality.

Nonperforming Loans. The difficulty with nonperforming loans is in figuring out the value of the collateral. What's a piece of real estate really worth? Is it going to be worth the same under a collapse? The drop in the value of the collateral has been blamed for the demise of the U.S. Savings and Loans industry.

The ability to manage the volatility of defaults is worth a lot to any investor. What are the techniques employed by the banks?

Big Exposures to Single Names

Some techniques that help reduce the volatility of a loan portfolio are:

- The bank buys bonds issued by other borrowers. This has the effect of increasing diversification and reducing the correlation.
- The bank reduces hold levels after syndication. This reduces the exposure to the specific name.
- The bank sells the loans in the secondary market to reduce exposure.
- The bank uses a credit derivative solution.

As illustrated in Figure 13-1, managing exposure is an ongoing process. There is some ongoing loan origination, as the bank has some loans, bonds, derivatives. On the other hand, there is some ongoing repayment. These loans are a bank's biggest exposures, and the bank can create and use custom-made solutions to manage the risk involved.

Small and Medium Enterprises

A bank can't act on these loans on a case-by-case basis, because there are many thousands of them. The bank can use an index, but several questions arise: How is the index calculated? How is it produced? What is the basis risk between the index and the bank's actual loan portfolio? Another alternative is to reduce

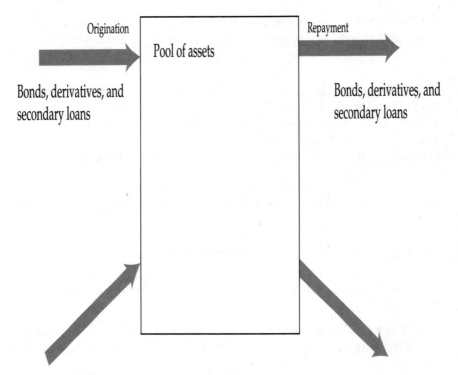

Figure 13-1. The ongoing process of origination and repayment.

hold levels by securitization. Banks create asset-backed securities (ABS), loan-based securities, collateralized loan obligations (CLO), and collateralized bond obligations (CBO) and sell them to the public. Securitization imposes a lot of data requirements. The bank has to persuade the rating agencies of the worth of its internal grading models. It has to convince the credit rating organization that the collateralized bond obligation or the asset-backed security is overcollateralized enough to merit a rating of AAA.

Note that these are not standard, approved models. Among other things, the bank has to compute the probability of default of each of the underlying companies. Can the bank convince the credit rating agency that it calculated the probabilities correctly? Typically, only very large issuers rely on securitization. For example, in the U.S., car makers relied on car-loan-based securities much more in the past than they do today. There is an increasing tendency on the part of the car makers to borrow capital based on their own balance sheets and credit ratings. Since U.S. car makers have improved credit ratings, their cost of funds is lower when they borrow on their own. Others who use securitization are the major credit card issuers.

Nonperforming Loans

Of course, nonperforming loans are typically referred to a specialist team. Most of the loans are secured by property. Specialist teams may use property derivatives or sales of the property to manage risk.

RISK CAPITAL

Return on risk capital is the driving force behind risk management in general and the spectacular growth of these markets in particular. The credit spread is compensation for holding the risky asset. It's compensation for the expected losses. The expected loss can be thought of as the loss on a BBB index composed of many BBB bonds.

The unexpected loss is the one specific BBB issuer that surprises us and actually defaults. Even though the issuer is supposed to default only 0.2% of the time, it actually defaults in practice.

Risk capital is the capital set aside to fund potential losses. The credit spread in the market only compensates for the expected loss. The unexpected loss is not compensated for by the market. Obviously, the greater the diversification in a portfolio, the lower the unexpected losses, the more the actual losses behave like the expected losses, and the lower the risk capital that must be assigned to the portfolio. All other things being equal, diversified portfolios have a greater return on risk capital than concentrated portfolios.

Thus, risk capital should be attributed to new assets according to an asset's incremental contribution to the portfolio's risk. The risk capital analysis should take into account the current portfolio and the asset being considered, and not just the asset by itself, which is what has been done traditionally.

The lower the correlation between the asset and the portfolio, the lower the attributed risk capital. Risk capital varies according to a portfolio's composition. Diversified portfolios have higher returns on risk capital because of the attribution of less capital to the new assets. Therefore, diversified portfolios can pay more for an asset.

Capital always flows to portfolios with greater returns. This means that credit risk and return should be owned by those who can diversify it best. We will return to this issue later in this chapter.

ORIGINATORS OF LOANS

To date, banks have had the comparative advantage in originating and holding loans.

- Banks comprise the only major investor class that employs risk capital, so they have leverage. Relationship banks have superior access to the loan market, and banks have little motivation to reduce concentration. They are asset-hungry. Every bank wants to be the biggest bank.

- One study says that there will only be six major banks by the year 2010. Union Bank of Switzerland and Swiss Bank Corporation merged in 1997 because they wanted to be one of the big six. There is a drive toward increasing asset size and loan book size. There are also relationship benefits to consider. The major clients of a bank will not be very pleased if the bank turns down their loan request.

- Banks lack centralized portfolio management. Consider a bank that has 300 branches and 60 divisions. A client company's different divisions may have different deals with the different branches and departments of the bank. For the bank to determine precisely its exposure to the company is a daunting task. It has to collect data from all the branches and departments, probably using systems that are not connected. Just collecting the data is an information technology problem.

- Currently, there is scant regulatory guidance to motivate banks to reduce concentration.

- For the most part, compensation in the banking industry is based on the net interest margin (NIM), not on risk-adjusted return on capital (RAROC). Consider a portfolio manager or a derivatives trader whose compensation is based on returns, not on volatility. The trader, for example, is presented with a chance to make a punt. The upside for the trader is that the move will succeed, the bank will make $300 million, and the trader will earn a $10 million bonus. The downside for the trader is that the bank might lose $300 million, and the trader will be fired.

- Compensation based on net interest margin encourages traders to take high risks on behalf of the bank. There is talk of changing the bonus scheme to base it on RAROC and several financial institutions have already done so. This is a very sensitive topic because traders do not like to have their compensation played around with.

HOLDER OF LOANS

Banks have a competitive advantage in being the source of loans. However, the banks are not the most efficient holders of loans. Figure 13-2 summarizes the differences between banks and nontraditional investors.

Commercial banks have a high cost structure. They employ a binary approval process for loans: It is a yes or no decision. There are only two alternatives: Either we approve the loan or we do not approve the loan. Banks have a relationship bias that causes portfolio concentration.

Nontraditional investors have low cost structures. They have a disciplined approach to pricing risk. Such investors employ a continuous pricing discipline, much like an option methodology.

Banks:
    High cost structure
    Binary pricing   >> Yes/no decision
    Relationship bias   >> Portfolio concentrations

Nontraditional investors:
    Low cost structures
    Continuous pricing   >> Disciplined approach to pricing risk
    Risk aversion   >> Portfolio diversity

Figure 13-2. Holding loans: banks vs. nontraditional investors.

These investors have a natural risk aversion, so they are biased toward portfolio diversity. An example of a nontraditional investor is a hedge fund.

THE ATTRACTION OF LOANS

On a risk-adjusted basis, loans have outperformed almost all other asset classes. Figure 13-3 illustrates the Sharpe ratio of different U.S.-based instruments for the period 1991 to 1996.

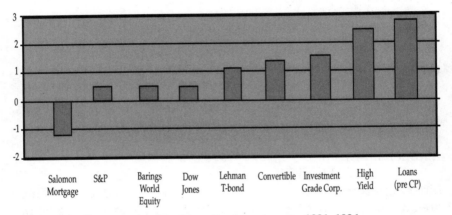

Figure 13-3. Sharpe ratios for alternative investments, 1991–1996.

The Sharpe ratio is the outperformance of an investment divided by its volatility. The excess performance is the return that was received for an investment minus the risk-free rate.

$$\text{Sharpe ratio} = \frac{\mu - \surd}{\sigma}$$

μ = return of the asset

$\surd$ = risk free rate

σ = volatility

That number is divided by the volatility. A high Sharpe ratio indicates a great asset, one with high excess return coupled with low risk.

As illustrated in Figure 13-3, loans were the top-performing U.S. asset from 1991 to 1996. Banks could charge a lot of interest, and there was little default and little variability, so loans were at the top. If we included data from 1980 to 1990, the picture might look somewhat different. But for right now, that's the picture that people are looking at and that's why people are really interested in loans as investments.

OPENING THE LOAN MARKET TO NONTRADITIONAL INVESTORS

Hedge funds would like to get access to loans as an asset class. Everybody wants access to loans. Credit derivatives enable non-traditional investors to access the loan market.

A variety of features help make credit derivatives popular:

- Leverage.
- Ease of access.
- Administrative simplicity—The commercial bank already has a huge book of loans. The hedge fund can get a piece of it without starting a whole commercial lending operation.
- Better net pricing than is available in a cash market.

Credit derivatives will enable assets to leave the banking system and flow to portfolios better suited to holding them. Banks are the best originators of loans, but not necessarily the best holders of loans. The following examples illustrate how credit derivatives can improve return on capital both for the bank and for the hedge fund.

ECONOMIC CAPITAL EXAMPLE 1

Note: In our examples we set Libor at 5.75%.

Consider an outright cash ownership of a high-yield loan by a high-quality bank. This is illustrated in Figure 13-4.

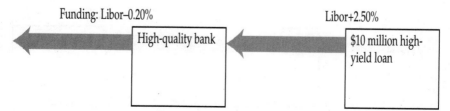

Figure 13-4. A high-quality bank makes a high-yield loan.

High quality bank:

Capital: 8%

Net revenue: $248,400 (spread on $9.2 million) + $44,400 (Libor–0.20% on 8%) = $292,800

Return on capital: 36.60%; this is $292,800/$800,000

Libor–0.20% is not an investment, it is a "saved funding."

Assume the high-quality bank can fund at Libor minus 20 basis points. Let's say that the bank makes $10 million high-yield loan and the interest rate is Libor plus 250 basis points. Because this is a bank making the loan, assume that the economic capital example is set at 8%. The bank's net revenue is $248,400. The spread of 250 basis points plus the funding spread of 20 bps is 270 basis points. The loan is $10 million, the capital is 8% or $800,000 so the spread is computed on $9.2 million. This gives $248,800. The bank also saves funding. It saves $44,400, which is Libor-0.20% on the 8%. The total is $298,800. The denominator of $800,000 is the capital that was set aside. Thus the return on capital is 36.60%.

Hedge fund:

Capital: 100%

Net revenue: $825,000 (Libor of 5.75% + 2.50%)

Return on capital: 8.25%

Figure 13-5 illustrates a hedge fund that makes an identical loan. We assume that the hedge fund has to fund itself by issuing equity. The hedge fund issues stock and sells it. People pay the hedge fund for the shares, and the hedge fund makes the loan. The interest received is Libor plus 250 basis points. The revenue is $825,000, which is Libor of 5.75% plus 250 basis points on the entire $10 million. The hedge fund's net return on capital is 8.25%.

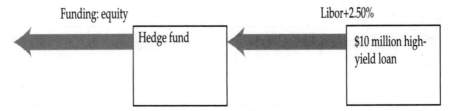

Figure 13-5. A hedge fund makes a high-yield loan.

ECONOMIC CAPITAL EXAMPLE 2

In Figure 13-6, the hedge fund engages in a total return swap with the high-quality bank. The high-quality bank has a $10 million high-yield loan. The bank collects Libor plus 250 basis points and passes it to the hedge fund. The hedge fund gives the bank Libor plus 75 basis points. Note that the high-quality bank still funds at Libor minus 20 bps. Consider how this picture has changed from an economic capital point of view. Look at Table 13-1.

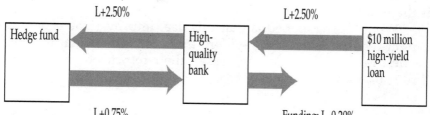

Figure 13-6. The bank and the hedge fund engage in a total return swap.

	Hedge Fund	**Bank**
Capital	10% (initial margin)	1.5%
Net revenue	$175,000 (spread) + $55,500 (Libor–0.20% on 10% capital) = $212,500	$93,575 (spread) + $8,325 (Libor–0.20% on 1.5% capital) = $101,900
Return on capital	21.25%	67.93%

Table 13-1.

Let's start with the hedge fund. The hedge fund opens a margin by posting collateral. Let's say that in this case the initial margin is 10%. What's the revenue? $175,000. The hedge fund earns $175,000 by receiving 250 basis points and paying the bank 75 basis points back. It is left with a net of $175,000.

The hedge fund also receives $55,500, which is Libor-0.20% on the 10% collateral that was posted in cash. The total received is $212,500. The capital employed was $1,000,000, so the net return on capital is 21.25%.

From the point of the view of the bank, the bank reduces the economic capital requirement to 1.5%. Why can the bank reduce the economic capital? It was 8% before, now it is reduced to 1.5%. The bank reduces the economic capital because there is a hedge with a total return swap. The bank is not exposed to the default risk of the borrower anymore. Furthermore, the hedge fund is collateralized by the margin. So the bank has very little remaining exposure. The economic capital is allocated by the bank itself. It is not regulatory capital. Other banks in similar situations might charge 1.00% or 2.00%; in any case, it is less than 8.00%. In our example, the charge is 1.5%.

Now, $93,575 is the spread of 95 basis points on $9.85 million as the bank funds at Libor-20 bps and receives Libor+75 bps. There is also Libor-0.20% on the 1.5% capital that the bank set aside, which is $8,325. The total return is $101,900. The return on capital is therefore 67.93%.

What has happened is that this deal improves the economic capital requirements and therefore the return on capital for both parties. Both parties have increased their return on capital. The deal is useful for both parties.

REGULATORY CAPITAL EXAMPLE 1

Consider an outright cash ownership of a BBB-rated loan by a high-quality bank. This is illustrated in Figure 13-7.

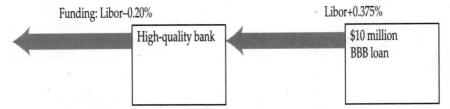

Funding: Libor–0.20%   Libor+0.375%

High-quality bank $10 million
                           BBB loan

Figure 13-7. A high-quality bank owns a BBB-rated bond.

High-quality bank:

Risk weighting: 100%

Net revenue: $52,900 (spread on $9.2 million) + $44,400 (Libor–0.20% on 8%) = $97,300

Return on capital: 12.16%; this is $97,300/$800,000.

The high-quality bank is the same one in the previous example. The bank funds at Libor minus 20 basis points. The bank owns a $10 million BBB loan that pays an interest rate of Libor plus 37.5 basis points. From a regulatory capital standpoint, the risk weighting is determined by the Bank of International Standards (BIS). The BIS requires a 100% risk weighting because the borrower is not an OECD government (in which case the risk weighting would be zero) or an OECD bank (in which case it would be 20%). The net revenue is $52,900. This is derived as follows: 37.5 basis points plus 20 basis points on the $9.2 million. In addition, the bank earns Libor–0.20% saved funding costs on the 8% capital or $800,000. The total revenue figure is $97,300. The return on regulatory capital is 12.16%. This is calculated as $97,300 divided by $800,000.

Lower-quality bank:

Risk weighting: 100%

Net revenue: $11,500 (spread) + $46,000 (Libor on $800,000) = $57,500

Return on capital: $57,500/$800,000 = 7.18%

In Figure 13-8 we consider a lower-quality bank. This bank funds at Libor plus 25 basis points. Its risk weighting is also 100%, as the loan is not made to an OECD government or a bank. The net revenue is $11,500, which is calculated as 37.50 basis points minus 25 basis points times the $9.2 million. The bank also earns Libor on the $800,000 capital, or $46,000. The total revenue is $57,500, which brings the return on regulatory capital to 7.18%.

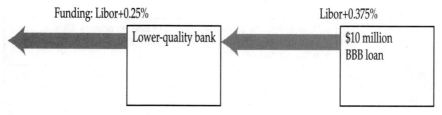

Figure 13-8. A lower-quality bank owns the same BBB-rated loan.

REGULATORY CAPITAL EXAMPLE 2

In Figure 13-9 we show both banks engaged in a default swap. We first consider the high-quality bank. The bank earns Libor+37.5 basis points on the $10 million BBB loan. The high-quality bank passes the 37.5 basis points premium to the lower-quality bank, and the lower-quality bank has an obligation in the form of a default contingent payment.

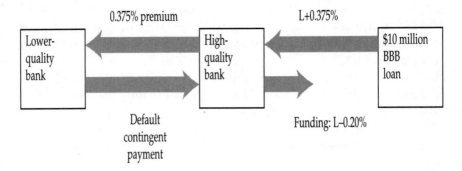

Figure 13-9. The banks engage in a default put.

In Table 13-2 we see that the lower-quality bank gets saddled with a risk weighting of 100% because it wrote an option. The option is written on a loan whose obligor is not an OECD bank or a government. The net revenue for the lower-quality bank is $37,500. This is the 37.5 basis points premium on the $10 million. The lower-quality bank also earns Libor on the 8% capital, or $46,000. The total revenue number is $83,500. Now, $83,500 divided by $800,000 is 10.438%, which is the return on regulatory capital figure for the lower-quality bank.

	Lower-Quality Bank	**High-Quality Bank**
Risk weighting	100%	20%
Net revenue	$37,500 (0.375% premium) + $46,000 (Libor on 8% capital) = $83,500	$19,680 (spread) + $8,325 (Libor–0.20% on (8%*20%) capital = $28,005
Return on capital	$83,500/$800,000 = 10.438%	$28,005/(800,000*20%) = 17.5%

Table 13-2.

As for the high-quality bank, it now has a 20% risk weighting. The high-quality bank is now dealing with a lower-quality bank that is, nonetheless, an OECD bank. The structure receives the risk weighting of the lower-quality bank. It is dealing with an OECD bank, so it gets a 20% risk capital weighting. Thus regulatory capital for a high-quality bank is 8% multiplied by the 20% risk weighting. The bank earns a $19,680 spread. Where is the spread coming from? The bank receives Libor+37.5 basis points from the loan and meanwhile funds at Libor minus 20 basis points. The bank keeps the Libor for itself. It passes the 37.5 basis points to the lower-quality bank, but it keeps the Libor and, meanwhile, funds at Libor minus 20 basis points. The 20 basis point spread is applied to the loan of $10 million minus the regulatory capital of (20%·8%=1.6%).

In addition, the regulatory capital requirement is now 20% of 8%, or only 1.6%. The bank earns Libor–0.20% on that capital. This amounts to $8,325. The total earnings are $28,005. We now have $28,005 divided by $800,000 times 20%, because of the 20% regulatory capital requirement, so the total is 17.5%. Again, you can see that with credit derivatives the return on regulatory capital increased for both participants in the deal. It's good for everybody.

AN INTERNAL CONFLICT

The previous two examples showed how credit derivatives could be used to reduce the economic and regulatory capital requirements to very low levels. By reducing the capital required to perform a deal, banks can inflate the return on capital. Banks have two conflicting goals:

1. Increasing the return on capital; this is done by reducing the required capital through the use of various derivative products.

2. Increasing the size of the balance sheet and the actual profits earned.

Increasing the return on capital will, in most cases, cost a price—the premium paid to buy the options. The bank has to decide whether to seek maximal profits or to maximize its return on capital. These two goals may be in conflict.

For example, in Figure 13-4 the bank earned $292,800 per annum using the cash transaction and only $212,500 when using the derivative overlay. The annual profits have been reduced by a substantial amount. On the other hand, the return on capital has increased from 36.60% to 57.93%.

In the past, banks used to focus solely on maximization of profits. The current trend is to focus more and more on return on capital.

JOINT DEFAULT

Credit derivative dealers trade correlation risk. The basic structure of a credit derivative trade is illustrated in Figure 13-10.

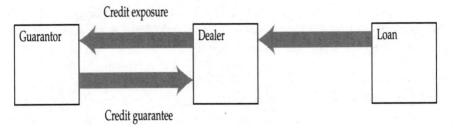

Credit exposure

Figure 13-10. A credit derivative trade.

From Figure 13-10 it becomes obvious that in order for the dealer to lose:

- The loan must default ... and ...
- The guarantor must default.

Small joint probability of default gives the dealer a high return on risk capital. Credit derivatives add value by finding the investors who are best suited to hold the risk.

This leads to a new paradigm in which lower-rated borrowers can invest in higher-rated assets, which is the reverse of the cash market. In the cash market, a low-rated borrower who can fund at Libor + 25 basis points would not be able to earn anything from investing in an asset that pays less than that. For example, the low-rated investor would not be able to invest in an asset paying Libor + 10 basis points. Such an investment would result in a negative cash flow of 15 basis points per year. Using credit derivatives, it can invest in such assets.

- In the traditional world the return on an investment would be computed as:

Borrower's credit spread – Investor's credit spread

This is similar to the net interest margin (NIM).

- In the new world, the return is:

Borrower's credit spread – Investor's credit spread
adjusted for conditional default probability

This is similar to the risk-adjusted return on capital (RAROC).

THE CREDIT PARADOX

A typical bank is often faced with the following dilemma, often called the credit paradox. The situation is summarized in Table 13-3.

Relationship Banker	Credit Line Manager
Familiar credit Ongoing business Profitable structured transaction	Increasing concentration Missing other credit opportunities Consuming capital
More exposure	Less exposure

Table 13-3. The credit paradox.

In Table 13-3, we have a situation in which one of the major clients comes to the bank and asks for another loan.

On one hand, we have the relationship manager arguing to grant the loan, which would result in more exposure. On the other hand, we have the credit risk manager arguing to decline the loan and reduce exposure to the borrower.

Glaxo borrowed 6.5 billion British pounds from only nine banks. The Reichman Brothers in Canada borrowed significant amounts from a handful of banks. Lending is a primary resource in maintaining client relationships. Selling loans is just as bad as refusing them outright. Banks can free up credit lines using the confidentiality inherent in credit derivatives.

Loan originators are not the best holders of these loans. As illustrated in Figure 13-11, the risk increases nonlinearly with the concentration. As the bank becomes exposed to more and more concentration, it needs more and more required returns, because now the bank is also faced with an unexpected loss. The more concentration the bank has, and the more the unexpected loss risk grows, the more the required return to make up for the added risk.

On the other hand, there is a limit to how much a specific borrower will pay the bank. The bank cannot charge too much inter-

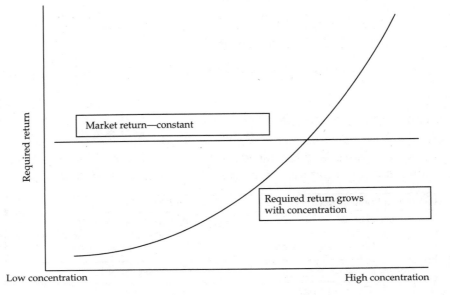

Figure 13-11. Required return vs. concentration.

est, or else the client will borrow somewhere else. While the required return grows with the concentration, the market will only pay a specific return.

ADDRESSING CREDIT LINE CONSTRAINTS

The problem we have just discussed occurs when a bank has too much exposure and its credit line is full. The client wants to borrow, but the credit manager says "No, the line is full." The cash market solution would be to sell the position. This may cause difficulties because the loan might be an illiquid asset. There are also relationship consequences because the client will be upset about the sale. There are also mark-to-market and tax consequences. The loan may be held in an accrual account and if it is going to be sold, there will be tax consequences. Credit derivatives, on the other hand, are confidential. The physical asset remains on the balance sheet. The client is not aware that the credit risk has been "sold." In addition, there are many situations in which sales of cash assets may be difficult to transact or harmful to a client relationship.

Finally, if the exposure is associated with other desired market risk levels (e.g., duration, convexity, or foreign currency), then replacing the original market risks will result in additional transaction costs. The default swap allows the bank to maintain confidentiality yet frees up the credit line constraint.

SWAP GUARANTEES

We have already seen that the exposure of an interest rate swap is a function of time and market prices (see Figure 11-2). It is difficult to hedge a credit book dynamically. In a swap position, both counterparties are exposed to counterparty credit exposure. This exposure is a combination of the current mark to market of the swap as well as future replacement costs.

The credit exposure of the swap counterparty can be highly correlated with the market. Just as you are in the money on a swap, you find that the credit quality of your counterparty has deteriorated significantly. This is especially true if the swap itself represents a major portion of the assets of the counterparty. The counterparty may owe you so much under the swap that it goes into default.

A possible credit derivative solution is a swap guarantee. This is a credit swap with a notional directly linked to the mark to market of the underlying reference swap. The contingent payment is triggered by a default on the swap.

The swap guarantee could be structured to provide:

1. A full guarantee for the replacement value of the swap.
2. A guarantee for any loss above $10 million (so there is a $10 million deductible).
3. A guarantee for any loss up to $10 million.
4. A guarantee for the first year of marking to market.
5. A guarantee between margin calls or collateral postings.

The buyer of a swap guarantee will lose only if both the original swap counterparty and the guarantee seller default together. The chance of a joint default is smaller than the chance of each one defaulting individually, so the protection buyer is well protected.

Every time a credit derivative desk transacts a swap guarantee, it's a totally different structure. The concept is to develop a kind of production line approach to these trades.

RELATIVE VALUE

Correlation means that the protection buyer wants to buy protection from a seller that is unaffected by the risk being hedged. For example, it will not want to buy protection on Belgium sovereign default risk from a Belgian bank. The Belgian bank already has enough exposure and may not be able or willing to receive a low premium.

It makes more sense to buy that credit risk protection from a counterparty who is uncorrelated. A non-Belgian bank has very little exposure to Belgian sovereign risk and will be willing to accept that risk in return for a lower premium.

What is the exposure of a non-Belgian bank to Belgian sovereign risk? This is very difficult to ascertain. The correlation between the bank and Belgium might be higher than expected. The bank may already have transacted a lot of off-balance sheet deals in Belgium that we don't know about.

In the marketplace, we often find that the only one who is willing to insure Korean sovereign risk is a Korean bank. The Korean bank knows that if Korea defaults, it will be in much worse problems than the default guarantee would cause.

So, even though we bought the Belgian derivative from a non-Belgian bank, it was subsequently sold and sold and sold and ended up back in a Belgian bank. To our dismay, we now own protection from a counterparty we were reluctant to purchase it from.

INCREASING OFF-BALANCE-SHEET CREDIT RISK

A client would like to increase credit risk off its balance sheet. In the cash market it can buy a cheap bond or initiate an asset swap. There are problems associated with the cash market solution. The securities may be scarce, illiquid, or expensive. The credit derivative solution would be to write a credit swap. No relationship is necessary. The credit derivative could be structured with any maturity and any seniority that the client prefers. The notional amount is tailored to suit the client, and there is no market risk. That is, there is no interest rate risk. The client does not actually hold the bond and therefore isn't exposed to interest rate risk.

CULTURAL CHANGES WITHIN A BANK

The successful integration of credit derivatives in the bank portfolio will require a few cultural changes within the bank.

Dynamic Credit Risk Management

Dynamic credit risk management is currently practiced by very few outfits. It entails:

- Analyzing and quantifying the risk and reward of the entire loan portfolio.

- Allowing the portfolio manager to have buy, hold, or sell authority abilities to take on nontraditional exposures if that will help the book.

- Attributing risk capital to each deal according to an incremental basis. In Figures 13-4 through 13-9 we saw quirks in the risk capital and the economic capital. The reason for these quirks is that in the examples we allocated risk capital according to the 0%, 20%, or 100% rule. Risk capital allocation was totally divorced from the portfolio. If one were to allocate risk capital according to the incremental risk to the portfolio, it should result in much smoother transitions. The question that should be asked is, "How much extra risk does a new deal add to the existing portfolio?" rather than, "How much is this deal worth by itself?"

Mark to Market of the Entire Portfolio

- Currently many loans are held in an accrual account that is not marked to market. In the U.S., ISDA recommended to Fed regulators to encourage the movement of loans into the trading book by assigning less regulatory capital to loans held in the trading book.

- Integration of credit risk management to the trading function itself might be considered. The trading function already has to handle market risk and hedge exposures dynamically. It may be best suited to deal with the credit risks also. The trading function can buy or sell options on market risk to hedge its cash desk; for example, if it has a U.S. dollar–Deutsche mark exposure, it can buy or sell foreign exchange derivatives to hedge its market risk. These could be options or futures or whatever other solution required. But what if the trading function accumulates credit risk? Currently, it is stuck with the risk. We need to enable the trading function to trade credit derivatives.

Compensation Based on RAROC

- This is the most politically charged debate.
- Are you going to compensate traders on RAROC and not on NIM? The traders on the desk are opposed to compensation based on RAROC. They claim that if you compensate them on RAROC, it will cause problems. Consider a trader with a portfolio that is growing steadily. The trader will get a nice bonus because even though the portfolio has a low return, it has a very low volatility; so the bonus will be quite nice. Then, all of a sudden the trader spots a very short-lived opportunity. Even if the trader were to make a lot of money for the bank, the sharp increase in value would result in high volatility for the portfolio. The trader makes more money, but the volatility of the portfolio goes higher. This scenario may result in a lower bonus. In this situation the trader may pass, and refuse to act on the opportunity. The opposite of this argument is that the reason this opportunity has such a high return is that it is risky. The proposed trade could also go down. The bank may want to discourage the trader from acting upon this opportunity because it might be loaded with risks. With compensation based on NIM, the trader who makes $300 million earns a $10 bonus. The trader who loses $300 million loses his or her job. Compensation based on NIM may encourage traders to take on high-risk trades. As one can imagine, this is a politically charged question. Most traders agree that limits should be set with a RAROC model because this tends to give traders somewhat higher limits; but most traders do not want to be compensated based on RAROC.

- The cost of a hedge or a purchase of a credit derivative should be charged to the relationship manager's P&L. This will force quantification of the relationship benefit. The relationship with the client benefits both the bank and the relationship manager. When the client brings a bond issue to the bank, the relationship manager gets a bonus. If the client floats equity through the bank, the manager gets a bonus. Every time the relationship manager brings a new deal, he or she gets a bonus, but the risk is not charged against the manager. The new idea is to charge the risk against the relationship manager. This is another very touchy, very sensitive idea.

Use Credit Derivatives as a Risk Management Tool

- Credit risk managers are traditionally used to making yes or no decisions. They either approve a loan or decline it. They are not used to approving a loan contingent on a default protection purchase.
- The loan portfolio is the best client of the credit derivative desk. Frequent communications (at least daily) are required between the two functions.

The hope is that, in the future, loans will be more efficiently priced. The assets will be held by those best suited to hold them. Bank portfolios will become more diverse. That's utopia; plan for the realistic future: Banks will become more fee-driven than relationship-driven.

In summary, loan portfolios can benefit immensely from the judicious use of credit derivatives.

CHAPTER 14

Creation and Analysis of Structured Credit Derivatives

In this chapter, we cover the processes involved in the creation of structured notes (financial engineering) and the analysis of them (reverse engineering). Much has been written about the pricing of structured CDs. It is important to understand that pricing is just one aspect of the process.

ANALYSIS OF A NOTE

When analyzing a structured note, many market participants have found that the following six issues are useful as a framework for a discussion.

The first four issues can be considered "buy side" issues. Assume the dealer on the sell side sends the portfolio manager on the buy side a fax listing the terms for a structure. Assume that the portfolio manager in the investment management department is contemplating the purchase of the structure. Then these are some of the questions that the portfolio manager should ask.

1. The first issue concerns motivation. Why is there a buyer for this security? Why is there a seller of such a note? This is a general question that should be asked about any structure, whether you are looking at an exotic option or a financially engineered structured note. What are the buyer and seller trying to accomplish? What views are they expressing?

2. The second issue we want to look at is the risk and reward of the note. Initially, one can think of the performance in the best-case and in the worst-case scenarios. What is the maxi-

mum I can earn with this note? For example, before we begin to analyze how is it priced exactly, it would be useful to know that the maximum I can earn is 10 basis points, but the worst that can happen is that I can lose my entire principal. That note would be a bit different than one that enables me to double my money in the best scenario and the worst that can happen is that I lose 10 basis points.

3. The pricing issue has to do, of course, with the expected case. What return can I expect from this note? The price of any instrument is basically the present value of the expected value of the cash flow. If I can figure out the expected value of the cash flows, I can arrive at a reasonable price for the structure. While it's easy to figure out the best and the worst in most situations, it's harder to figure out the expected value, because you also have to consider probabilities, such as the probability of receiving a certain payout. That becomes quite a bit harder.

4. The fourth issue to consider has to do with sensitivities. What type of risks is this note sensitive to? That is to say, is this note sensitive to interest rates, to default rates, to the state of the economy, to foreign exchange rates?

Another set of questions must be considered if you are on the sell side. If you are on the sell side, you also have to think of some other problems.

5. Consider the hedging issue. If you created this note and you sold it, you are now short the note. How would you hedge your position?

6. Another issue is the alternatives question. It may be formulated as follows: Suppose I am on the sell side and my competitor comes up with this particular note. Maybe I am not allowed to trade credit derivatives yet. Maybe I am not allowed to trade this particular structure. How do I find an alternative to this structure that will let the client express very similar views? For example, I may not be able to sell a digital option to a client, but I can sell a very aggressive bull spread that lets the client express almost the same views.

THE CREATION PROCESS OF A NOTE

How does the process of creating a structured note work?
There are three steps to the creation of a note:

1. Conceptual stage.
2. Identification stage.
3. Structuring/construction stage.

Conceptual Stage

In the conceptual stage, a request typically comes from a client or an investor with one or more of the following requirements:

- **View.** In Chapter 6 we looked at a very complicated structure that involved Argentine Bocon bonds versus Argentine pars. The participants had a particular view on the capital structure of Argentina. A client may have a view that Brazil will improve more than Argentina, or that Canada will stay intact and that Quebec spreads will come in. Another example is a hedge fund that wants to take a specific view. The client can take a view that the spreads between France and Germany will stay narrow, or that the Italian spread to the U.S. will stay narrow, or that either one will widen out significantly.

- **Risk management.** Commercial banks have a lot of outstanding loans and they want to manage the risks on the loans. They are afraid of default. They have concentration problems, but they cannot access the secondary market to sell the loans. How do we help them with risk management?

- **Cash flow.** Consider a client who is long on bonds, but the bonds will only pay in the future. Can we somehow allow the client to sell us a credit derivative and get some premium right now? Can we help the client realize cash flow now rather than in the future?

- **Arbitrage or timing.** Consider a capital structure arbitrage. In some situations one level of capital structure is cheaper than other levels.

- **Diversification.** This is an extremely important area of motivation for the existence of credit derivatives. A commercial bank may be overconcentrated in several borrowers and want to reduce its exposure to those borrowers.

- **Asset allocation.** A hedge fund, on the other hand, wants to diversify its assets. It would like invest in a loan portfolio that have high returns and low standard deviations, but hedge funds are not equipped to lend money themselves. We have already seen how total return swaps can reduce the exposure of a bank and, at the same time, allow nontraditional investors to invest in the loan market.

- **Regulatory arbitrage.** Many structures exist to take advantage of quirks and flaws in the regulations of a particular country. At one time, products involving equity swaps were popular in Germany because Germany taxed equity dividends differently depending upon whether the holder of the asset was based in Germany or outside the country. Other examples involve clients who would like to purchase certain asset classes but are forbidden to do so because of regulations. For example, an investment management corporation may not be allowed to purchase options, but is typically allowed to buy option-embedded bonds.

The request for a structured note may come from one of two sources:

1. **The client**—The sales team of the dealer talks to clients all day long. They become familiar with the needs and requests of their clients. It is up to the financial engineering desk to find solutions to those needs and requests.

2. **The dealer**—The financial engineering team becomes aware of a new tax or regulatory arbitrage. They create a structured note that would result in a better financing rate for the borrower and a higher yield for the investor. Then they find appropriate clients to pitch the idea to.

The sales team works closely with the financial engineers to conceptualize ideas for new products.

Identification Stage

The identification stage takes place once the idea has been conceptualized. The equivalent views that are necessary to the construction of the note can be distilled from these concepts. The general type of the structure can then be selected based on these views. The components required for the assembly of the structure are identified.

In this stage we are asking what views are necessary to the construction of the note. What view is the investor taking? Is the investor expressing a view that Argentine bond spreads will tighten, or that Italian bond spreads will widen? We select a general type of structure based on the investor's view. Do we need a binary credit-linked security, one that pays out nothing upon default, or do we need one that pays out the recovery value upon default? Do we need a security that pays a fixed coupon, or one that has a floating coupon? In this stage we determine the components that are required for the assembly of the structure and identify them as options, forwards, or credit options.

The identification stage usually covers six areas: nationality, rate profile, risk/return, strategic view, maturity, and credit quality.

1. **Nationality**—The investor is taking a view on the underlying in which country or countries? For example, the investor may be based in the U.S. but may want to take a view on Argentina. Alternatively, an Italian investor may want to take a view on the U.S. high-yield market.

2. **Rate profile**—What is the interest rate profile of the investor? Is the investor bullish on rates or bearish on rates? Should we construct a floating rate note or a fixed rate note? Is this a note that has to gain value when the yield curve steepens, when it shifts and twists? The two main questions to consider are: a) What is the investor's view on short-term rates? and b) What is the investor's view on the steepness of the yield curve? Based on the answers to these two questions, we can generally construct a structure that will respond favorably.

3. **Risk/return**—The higher the desired potential return, the more risk is embedded in the structure. The investor's

risk–return profile is crucial in determining the amount of risk to be embedded in the note. The risk tolerance for coupon and principal payments must be examined. Some investors are more risk averse than others. If you are going to sell the structure to a hedge fund that wants to take high-risk punts, you will structure it differently than if your target audience is investment managers who want to earn a few extra basis points but do not want to risk losing any of the principal. Table 14-1 shows the coupon enhancement that can be made available for various risk categories.

Risk/Return	Coupon Structure	Principal Structure
Low	Minimum coupon > 0 Incremental yield pickup	No principal risk
Medium	Minimal coupon = 0 Medium yield increment	No principal risk
High	Minimal coupon = 0 High to very high-yield increment	Principal risk

Table 14-1. Risk and reward tradeoff.

Suppose the risk and return are both low. Those types of structures are typically appropriate for an investment manager. Assume that such a client purchases a credit-linked note. That client will not want its principal to be at risk. It will want to be sure that at maturity, it will receive par. This client will also require a coupon. If there is no default, the investor will receive a few extra basis points; but if there is a default, the investor still wants its principal repaid and a minimal coupon. For example, consider a zero coupon structure in which, if the spread stays between 400 and 600 basis points, the investor will receive a 111% payout. If the spread goes outside these boundaries, the investor will receive 102%. In this case, the investor receives 102% and gets its principal back and even some minimal coupon. This investor would not want a structure in which it risked the entire principal. (See Exhibit 6-2.)

Another type of investor has a medium risk and return appetite. This investor is willing to accept that its coupon could go down to zero if it is wrong; and if it is correct, it wants a medium-yield increment. However, such an investor does not want to put any principal at risk.

The third type of investor is the most aggressive. This investor is willing to put principal at risk, to accept that at maturity of the bond, it will either get zero or par, depending on whether the reference security defaults. These are pretty dangerous structures. The investor is placing its principal at risk and also accepting that it might not receive any coupons. Consider a one-year note, a zero coupon note. Either the note pays par if there is no default or, in case of default, the note pays zero. This is a binary structure. The client either gets the entire principal back or gets zero, in case of default. Who would buy this security? Somebody who is willing to put the entire principal at risk.

4. **Strategic View**—Embedded within the risk–return profile is the investor's strategic view. The two basic strategies are buy and hold, or trading.

Buy and Hold
- A structure with low leverage, enhanced coupon at low risk, and no principal risk.
- Time horizon equals maturity.
- These investors often wish to obtain a steady level of return over the life of the note and thus prefer to avoid high leverage.
- The investor is willing to accept a low measure of risk to obtain an incremental yield enhancement. The enhancement can range from 5 to 200 basis points.
- Investors prefer a non-zero coupon to protect themselves if interest rates move in an adverse direction.
- Investors wish to obtain par at redemption to protect themselves if interest rates move in an adverse direction.
- Typical investors are pension funds, banks, and regionally based investors.

Trading
- A structure with high leverage, high risk, and high return, that may include principal risk.
- Time horizon equals intermediate date.
- A smaller class of investors may consider a trading strategy in structured notes.

- Investors require a structure that can gain value very quickly if rates move in the right direction.
- Trading horizon is usually short term.
- However, the maturity of the note can be longer to provide greater leverage.
- Investors would like high potential returns and will accept the high risks that go with them.
- Redemption-linked structures (they may like a 60 to 70% floor) may be appropriate. They have a lower floor than required for buy-and-hold strategies.

It is crucial to understand the difference between the two strategies. In a trading mentality, you are interested in structures that you go in and out of very quickly. In that case, you expect high leverage, high risk, and high return. In Hong Kong, for example, some equity warrants have been traded approximately 50 times in the two years since they were issued. The warrants would expire in two years, but people traded in and out of the warrants 50 times, passing them around. An investor is not going to buy such a structure and then sell it two days later if it increases by 2 basis points. The trading-mentality investor wants a big increase or wants to get out of the structure. Such traders need high risk and high return. They don't want to pay the bid and ask spreads and get hit by commissions for only 2 basis points. They just won't make any money this way.

The buy-and-hold strategy entails low leverage and enhanced cash flows. The enhancement is from 5 to 200 basis points over the relevant index. Minimum coupon protection required, even if the investor is wrong, is 2% coupon and no redemption rate risk. At least investors will get par, so there is no risk. Pension funds, banks, and regionally based investors are found in this group.

5. **Maturity**—When we talk about the maturity of a credit derivative note, we have to distinguish between several maturity dates. There's the maturity of the reference security and the maturity of the credit-linked structure itself. For example, a total return swap may last for two years, but the reference security could be a thirty-year bond. As we have seen, a client can finance for two years and get a return that is tied to the thirty-year index. Table 14-2 summarizes the maturity and form of many structured notes.

Maturity	Form	Issuer
Under 1 year	CP	A1/P1
1 to 3 years	CD, MTN, Bank notes	Banks, Corporations
More than 3 years	MTN, Bond	U.S. Agencies

Table 14-2. Maturity and form of many structured notes.

6. Credit quality—There are two aspects of credit quality that we need to consider: the credit quality of the issuer and the credit quality of the reference security. What would the investor be comfortable with?

It is crucial to understand that some of these products involve taking real risks. Even if the issuer is rated AAA, that doesn't mean that the investor will receive payment. The credit rating agency is rating the ability of the issuer to pay, but it's not rating the obligation to pay.

Structuring Stage

In this stage, the dealer prices all the elements required for creation of the note. A spread is added to the total and, finally, the complete note is priced and brought to the market.

CHAPTER 15

The Valuation of Credit Derivatives

INTRODUCTION

When considering a model to price any derivative instrument in general and credit derivatives in particular, we have to consider three questions:

1. How do I choose a model? What assumptions should it contain, and what mathematical formulations is it based upon?
2. What data does it require and what output values does it produce? The model must require data that are easily obtainable and must produce the required pricing and hedging parameters.
3. Which instruments does it handle? The model must be flexible enough to handle many types of instruments within the same framework.

As a general rule, we price derivatives by modeling the behavior of the underlying. For example, a U.S. dollar–deutsche mark option is priced by a Black-Scholes formula. The formula is predicated on a set of assumptions about the underlying process: the Brownian motion assumption, etc.

For credit derivatives we have three general types of models:

1. Equity value models.
2. Spread-based models.
3. Ratings-based models.

Equity Value Models

These models rely on modeling changes in the issuer's stock prices. The main advantage to these models is that the dynamics behind stock price movements are well understood. After all, there are numerous pricing models for equity options.

We assume that:

- We understand the process.
- We have the data.
- Default always occurs when we expect it to.

Many difficulties arise when the issuer does not issue equity, for example, in the case of credit derivatives on sovereign debt. Because countries do not issue shares, these models are not applicable in a straightforward fashion. However, some participants model the country's currency as a proxy for default. If the country defaults, its currency is likely to be massively devalued. Another possibility is to model the main stock index of that country.

The main assumptions behind equity models are that default is correlated with a drop in equity and that we understand the combined process.

Spread-Based Models

Spread models are based on modeling changes in the credit spreads. The model considers the spread between a risk-free bond and the corresponding corporate bond of the relevant issuer. One such model is attributed to Longstaff and Schwartz; see Chapter 16.

These models assume that:

- We understand the process.
- We have the data.
- Markets price credit fairly.
- We know the recovery value.

The creation of a model for credit spreads involves determining how they behave. Are credit spreads normally distributed? Are they lognormal? Are credit spreads mean reverting? Are they correlated to interest rates?

Then, a reasonable database of credit spreads must be collected. This may be difficult to do except for very large issuers with many outstanding bonds. For example, consider a small corporation. If the corporation only has a single ten-year bond outstanding, how can we determine its two-year spread?

Credit spread models rely on the assumption that the spread in the markets is entirely due to credit considerations. In fact, this is not so. Corporate bond spreads are also functions of supply and demand, liquidity, convexity, and many other factors.

As mentioned in Chapter 4, to ascertain the probability of default from the credit spread we must be able to estimate the recovery value. If the spread is unknown or miscalculated, the recovery value cannot be determined.

Ratings-Based Models

Credit rating models are based on credit ratings (such as those issued by the credit rating agencies: Moody's and S&P).

These models assume that:

- The issue is rated.
- The present is like the past.
- All entities of the same rating are alike.

Using credit-rating-based models requires that the issuer be rated. This is quite likely the case when negotiating credit derivatives on corporate bonds. However, loan-based credit derivatives cannot directly rely on rating-based models because many loans are not rated.

CreditMetrics (see Chapter 11) relies heavily on the probability transition table. Such models assume that the probabilities in the table will continue to be valid in the future. They also assume that spread changes are due only to credit ratings changes.

In case of a general worsening of credit, all credit spreads might widen without a credit rating change. A credit-rating-based model may not be adequate in these situations. Another difficulty with these models is that they rely on credit rating changes. Credit ratings are subject to change based on an analyst's view. They are not fungible, tradeable instruments.

Credit-ratings-based models lump all AA issuers into one basket. General statistics that are collected on all AA issuers may not adequately reflect the particular issuer we are dealing with.

THE ACADEMIC QUESTION

One of the reasons for the profusion of models for credit derivatives is the existence of an unresolved academic question. There are at least three distinct approaches to modeling default:

1. Default as surprise: Default can occur at any time and it comes as a complete shock to market participants. Examples: Flesaker, Houghston, Schreiber and Sprung, 1994; the Hazard Rate Approach by Duffie.

   Example: Yamaichi went into default following a period of rising stock prices. In this case, default came as a total surprise to market participants.

2. Default happens when it is no longer rational for shareholders to make a payment. Default can occur only on coupon dates (Black, Scholes, and Merton, 1970s).

3. Default happens when share prices drop below a certain threshold (Longstaff and Schwartz, 1992; and Hull and White, 1992; KMV; the Merton model).

   Example: When Citibank got into trouble in the 1980s its share prices declined and bond spreads increased. Also UBS in October 1998.

Evidence from the Market

Most market participants would agree that a default is associated with a large drop in share prices. This was the basis of the Merton model. On the other hand, there are also cases in which default occurs as a complete surprise. In these cases, stock prices may not depreciate before a default.

- The last assumption implies that default is observable by looking at share prices.
- Under this assumption, short-dated paper has very little credit risk. There is not much chance of a large decline in stock prices in such a limited time.
- Under the first assumption, even very short-dated paper has a non-trivial default risk.

- Thus, there is anecdotal evidence for the first assumption as even very short-dated paper trades at spreads to Treasuries, for example, short-dated commercial paper.

One would like to think that the day before default, a credit would trade close to its expected recovery value. In practice this may or may not be the case, particularly in the high-grade sector where defaults are much harder to predict.

We have reviewed the main difficulties and academic questions related to the pricing of credit derivatives. Much useful work is being published on the subject. Undoubtedly, the models and the available data will improve.

CHAPTER 16

Analysis and Pricing

In this chapter, we consider several examples of credit derivatives. We analyze four structures to understand the logic behind the pricing. This chapter is written in a workshop format. The reader may find it useful to think about the questions posed here. Note that all the examples used are instructional. The spreads, recovery values, and data used in this chapter do not reflect actual market data.

BINARY STRUCTURE

Consider a binary structure with the following term sheet:

Term: One-year note

Issuer: Bankers Trust

Reference credit: International Business Machines (IBM)

Coupon: Zero coupon

Conditional payment at maturity: receive par if IBM has not defaulted; receive zero if IBM has defaulted.

Now we have to ask ourselves all the questions from Chapter 15 about this hypothetical security. Is there an interest rate view? What's the risk? What's the reward? How do I price it? We will not price the security to the last decimal place, but rather consider the concepts that are involved in pricing it.

Consider a company like IBM. There are many straight IBM notes and IBM bonds that already exist. One of these is chosen as the reference security. Now, Bankers Trust, for example, comes and issues a credit-linked bond.

The investor buys the bond from Bankers Trust. Assume you are the investor. You pay X to Bankers Trust and they give you the note. One year later, there are two possibilities.

1. IBM hasn't defaulted.

2. IBM has defaulted.

We have to be very specific and define what default is. For purposes of this exercise, we assume that the concept of default has been well defined and agreed upon by all parties.

If there is no default, the investor receives $100 from Bankers Trust. If IBM has defaulted, the investor receives zero.

Analysis

Let's consider the issues that you would look at as an investor if Bankers Trust offered this security to you. We know that it's a zero-one type of structure. Let's understand the pricing. There are two cases here. Either:

A. There is no default, or

B. There is a default.

First, we consider how one would price a one-year, zero coupon bond. How is a U.S. Treasury strip priced? With a treasury strip, you are guaranteed to receive your $100. If you were to price a U.S. Treasury strip bond that pays $100 in one year, all you would have to do is take $100 and discount it back. Take the $100 and if it an annual interest rate, divide it by 1+R. If it has a semiannual interest rate, as in the U.S., divide it by $(1+R/_2)^2$.

- $P = \$100 / (1+R)$, if R is an annual rate.
- $P = \$100 /((1+R/2)^2)$, if R is a semiannual rate.

That's how to price a zero coupon strip where R is the one-year zero coupon interest rate for government securities (the spot rate).

In what follows, we will assume annual compounding for simplicity. The price of the risk-free strip is $100 divided by $(1 + R)$. For example, if the interest rate is 6%, then you know that the price of the security is about $94, plus or minus. In our case it is $94.34.

Assume that the U.S. government is to issue the security. We have to consider the two scenarios, either default or no default. We can't just discount the $100 anymore because we are not even sure that we are going to receive that payout. Either we will receive $100 or we will receive zero. Let us designate P the probability of receiving zero, which is also the probability of default. Of course, 1 minus P is the probability of receiving $100.

The expected payout of the security is $100 * (1–P) + $0 * P = $100 * (1–P).

The price of the zero-one bond should be:

$$(\$100 * (1–P)) / (1+R)$$

Note that since we assumed that the note was issued by the U.S. government, we have to divide by the risk-free rate.

Let's return to the example of the IBM note that Bankers Trust issued. Assume that IBM does not default, but Bankers Trust does default; I still will not receive my $100. So I really should discount this note by (1 plus R plus the spread). This is the spread applicable to Bankers Trust zero coupon strips.

The price of the zero-one bond should be:

$$(\$100 * (1–P)) / (1+R+s)$$

where:

R = the risk-free rate

s = the Bankers Trust spread

P = the probability of default for IBM

We assume that the default correlation between IBM and BT is zero.

Let's see how to come to terms with this whole formula. The first key issue here is obviously the probability of default of the reference security, IBM. That's the most important piece of the whole puzzle. Whether the Bankers Trust spread is 20 over Treasuries or 40 over Treasuries is not going to cause a lot of difference in the price. But if we assume that the probability of default for IBM is 0.1% versus 5%, that is going to strongly affect the price. We must now assess the probability of default for IBM.

In general, there are two methods for estimating the probability of default.

1. The Historical Method: Given IBM's credit rating, we can examine how many issuers with this credit rating tend to default in one year. This information is given in the credit rating migration table. (See Tables 11-1 and 11-2.)

2. The Implied Method: Given IBM's corporate spread on a zero coupon bond and the recovery value for IBM, we can impute the probability of default.

These two methods are analogous to historical volatility and implied volatility. In what follows, we review the implied method. In real life, we would use both methods and compare results.

We look at the yield of an IBM one-year strip. Assume that the IBM spread is 50 basis points over a comparable U.S. strip. Let's also assume the recovery value for IBM is 70%. The U.S. Treasury strip rate is 6%. This is shown in Figure 16-1.

Probability of default for a one-year zero

Y	**6.50%** yield of the corporate zero
R	**70.00%** recovery value
F	**6.00%** yield of the Treasury strip
P	1.56%

Own 100 Tsy bonds	pay	$94.34 to receive	100
Owns 100 Corp bonds	pay	$93.90 to receive	$99.53
			P*R*100+(1–P)*100
	$94.34:	$100.00 =	0.943
	$93.90:	$ 99.53 =	0.943

Figure 16-1. Probability of default computation.

In Figure 16-1, we figure out the probability of default similarly to Table 4-4. A portfolio manager has a choice of buying 100 U.S. Treasury securities; each of these U.S. Treasury securities pays out $1 at the end. So this investor is going to receive $100 for sure. How much is each U.S. Treasury security priced? If the yield is 6%, then each U.S. Treasury strip is priced at $100 over 1.06, which is $94.34. If the investor were to buy 100 U.S. Treasury strips, its cost would be $94.34 and it would receive $100 in one year.

Now consider the following. The same investor buys 100 IBM strips. The yield on the strips is 6.50%, so the price for these strips is $93.90 (which is $100/1.0650). The IBM strips are IBM one-year bonds that pay no coupon and are going to pay $100 in one year.

Let's assume that IBM does not default. If IBM does not default, then each bond pays $1, so 100 bonds would pay $100.

If we were certain that IBM would not default, why would anybody buy U.S. Treasury strips, paying $94.34 to get $100, when they can buy IBM and pay $93.90 to get $100? In this case, no one would buy U.S. Treasury strips. Obviously IBM is not risk-free. In fact, it has some probability of default. If IBM defaults we are going to collect the recovery rate, or $0.70 on the dollar.

We can now say that the ratio of $94.34 to $100 has to be equal to the ratio of $93.90 to P*R*100+(1-P)*100.

We know that R is 0.70, as we obtain a proportion formula:

$$94.34 : 100 = 93.90 : P*70+(1-P)*100$$

There is only one probability of default, P, that will solve this proportion correctly. It is, in this case, 1.56%. The probability of default for IBM in one year is 1.56%. Now that we have a probability of default for IBM, we can price the security.

The expected payout of the IBM zero-one security is:

$$(\$100 * (1-P)) = \$98.44$$

We need to discount this to today's value at the Bankers Trust rate. Remember that if the government were to issue the bond, I would have to discount by 6%. But Bankers Trust is the issuer and cannot borrow at 6%, so I have to discount by one plus 6% plus the BT spread. Let's assume that the BT one-year zero coupon corporate spread is 20 basis points.

The price of the one-year security is:

$$\$98.44 / (1+6\%+0.20\%) = \$92.69$$

Note how we differentiate between IBM and BT. There are two spreads in this computation. The first one is the IBM spread, which was used to impute the probability of default. The second spread is the BT spread, which is used to compute the value of the zero-one bond.

To put it another way, suppose that I buy a Bankers Trust vanilla strip that has to do with the default of Bankers Trust. BT promises to pay $100 in one year. I would discount the $100 by dividing it by 1.0620. The discount rate includes the Bankers Trust spread, which is 20 basis points.

In this note, using the Bankers Trust spread is not sufficient. The investor is also taking a risk that the underlying (IBM) will not pay. So rather than discounting $100 by the BT rate, we discount $98.44 by 6.20%, where the 20 basis points is the Bankers Trust spread.

Note that the Bankers Trust spread is not necessarily the same as the IBM spread.

To price this note, we used a fundamental principal of finance: The price of any instrument is the present value of the expected value of the cash flows.

What we did not consider here is the correlation between IBM and Bankers Trust. We assumed there is no correlation of default. That is to say, this analysis is under the assumption that default by IBM is totally independent from default by Bankers Trust. Now we ask, what happens if there is correlation? What happens if IBM defaults together with Bankers Trust? What will this do to the price of the note?

If the correlation is high, that means that if either IBM or BT defaults, so does the other. If correlation is zero, then the default events are totally independent of each other. Now, let's assume for a moment that the recovery rate of BT is zero. If this were the case, we would have the following:

a. If IBM defaults, the investor receives nothing, as per the condition of the note.

b. If IBM does not default and BT does, the investor should receive $100, but because BT defaulted it cannot collect anything and receives zero.

c. Only if both IBM and BT survive will the investor receive $100.

High default correlation increases the chance that both will survive. Therefore, high correlation increases the price of the note. The structure will be worth more if there is positive default correlation between IBM and BT.

Now, assume that the recovery rate of BT is 50%.

In the general case, we have the scenario illustrated in Figure 16-2:

a. If IBM defaults, the investor receives nothing as per the condition of the note.

b. If IBM does not default and BT does, the investor will receive B, the recovery rate of BT.

c. Only if both IBM and BT survive will the investor receive $100.

		BT	
		Survive	**Default**
IBM	Survive	100	B
	Default	0	0

Figure 16-2. What the investor receives.

Later in this chapter we examine the effects of correlation further.

Motivation

Let us consider motivation. Who would buy this type of security? Why would somebody be willing to place the entire principal on the line only to save the difference between $94.34 (the price of the U.S. Treasury strip) and $92.69 (the price of the binary security)? Assume that you are the dealer who created this binary structure. Who would you sell it to?

It is clear that if a dealer went to somebody who had no view on IBM and said, You get a couple of extra basis points but you can lose your entire principal," that would be a very difficult sell.

- Consider the president of IBM. If IBM goes into default, the president has a lot worse problems than the $100,000 investment in this security. Therefore, the president of IBM would be a natural buyer. In general, a good buyer is someone who is going to have a lot more problems than just this note losing if IBM defaults. The sales pitch to such a buyer could proceed as follows: "Granted that if IBM defaults you lose your money; but that would be so bad for you anyway, that this note is the least of your worries. On the other hand, if IBM succeeds, you are going to get a very high return."

- Consider a competitor of IBM's. Such a company will make a huge profit if IBM defaults. In case IBM defaults, its competitors will become the dominant players in the market and will become very wealthy. On the other hand, if IBM survives, business will go on as usual. A competitor may be a potential client for this note. If IBM survives, it will receive a high return on its security. If IBM defaults, its other business activities will become so profitable that it will not mind losing the principal on this security.

In summary, the two types of clients are somewhat the opposite of each other. On the one hand we have someone whose interests are closely allied with the underlying company. This client has such a high exposure to the underlying already that it can take on more exposure, because it is like a drop in the bucket. The other investor is someone who is opposed to the underlying security. Such an investor will make such huge gains if the underlying company defaults that it can afford to lose the principal on the security.

A third type of investor is one who wishes to take a punt at the recovery value of IBM. This client might be of the opinion that in case of default, the recovery rate of IBM will be much lower than the market expects it to be. The security was priced in the marketplace with the assumption of a recovery rate of $0.70 per $1.00. But what if an investor thinks that the recovery value is more like $0.10 per $1.00? Such a client is willing to forgo the recovery value, invest in a zero-one security, and earn a higher return should IBM survive. Put another way, assume the investor agrees with the market that the probability of default for IBM is 1.56%. However, the investor estimates that the recovery value for IBM in case of default is only $0.10. Such an investor will not be willing to purchase IBM notes at $93.90, considering them too expensive. This is the type of investor who would be willing to purchase the zero-one securities. By giving up the recovery value (which it perceives as small) it will be earning a higher return on capital.

Hedging

Hedging binary securities is a difficult task in any market. For example, assume it is one day before a note expires and the reference creditor is hovering on the brink of bankruptcy. The entire value of the note depends on the precise bankruptcy date. If the issuer announces a credit event before the maturity of the note, the note pays out nothing. If the issuer announces a credit event just after the maturity of the note, the note matures and pays par. A trader who is hedging a note under these circumstances faces tremendous difficulties.

A CREDIT DEFAULT SWAP

To see the tremendous importance of default correlation, we analyze the pricing of a one-year credit default swap. Assume that we have purchased a one-year zero coupon bond from General Motors (GM) and are considering the purchase of a credit default swap from J.P. Morgan (JPM).

Notation and Assumptions

Let the probability of default of GM and its recovery value be labeled as P_{GM} and R_{GM}, respectively. A similar notation is established for JPM. The default correlation between GM and JPM is labeled ρ.

Assume that:

$P_{GM} = 0.50\%$ $\qquad\qquad$ $R_{GM} = 20\%$
$P_{JPM} = 0.75\%$ $\qquad\qquad$ $R_{JPM} = 10\%$

The zero coupon one-year risk-free rate is labeled r and assumed to be 5.50%.

We also define the four probabilities:

P00—Both GM and JPM survive.

P01—GM survives, JPM defaults.

P10—GM defaults, JPM survives.

P11—Both default.

Analysis

We have the following situation:

A default swap is the difference between buying the normal hM note and purchasing the hM note with a credit protection by JPM.

Probability	Scenario (GM)	Scenario (JPM)	Receive
P00	GM Survives	JPM Survives	Par
P01	GM Survives	JPM Defaults	Par
P10	GM Defaults	JPM Survives	Par
P11	GM Defaults	JPM Defaults	K

Table 16-1.

- If we only purchase the bond, we take the credit risk of GM.
- By purchasing the default swap, you have the situation depicted in Table 16-1.

The amount K to be received when both JPM and GM default is determined as follows. Since GM has defaulted, we have a claim against GM for par of which we will receive R_{GM}*Par. We also have a claim against JPM in an amount equal to $(1-R_{GM})$*Par. However, since JPM also defaulted, we are only going to receive R_{JPM} of that amount.

Thus:

$$K = (R_{GM}+R_{JPM} *(1-R_{GM}))*Par$$

In our example:

$$K= (20\%+10\%*(100\%-20\%))*\$100 = \$28$$

The price of the normal GM bond is computed as:

$$((P_{GM}*R_{GM}+(1-P_{GM}))*100)/(1+r) =$$
$$((0.50\%*20\%+99.50\%)*100)/(1+5.50\%) = \$94.407$$

The price of the bond with the default swap is computed as follows:

$$(P00*100+P01*100+P10*100+P11*K)/(1+r)$$

The price of the default swap is the difference between these two.

Our problem is, therefore, to determine the value of P11. We can set up a system of four linear equations in four unknowns:

- P00 + P01 + P10 + P11 = 1
- P10 + P11 = P_{GM}
- P01 + P11 = P_{JPM}

- An equation related to the correlation.

We create two random variables, Q_{GM} and Q_{JPM}. These random variables are set to 0 if there is no default and 1 if there is a default. The variable Q_{GM} is related to GM and Q_{JPM} is related to JPM.
Then, from the definition of covariance:

$$\text{Covariance} = P00*(0-E(Q_{GM}))*(0-E(Q_{JPM}))+P01*(0-E(Q_{GM}))*$$
$$(1-E(Q_{JPM}))+P10*(1-E(Q_{GM}))*(0-E(Q_{JPM}))+P11*(1-E(Q_{GM}))*$$
$$(1-E(Q_{JPM}))$$

However:

$$E(Q_{GM}) = P_{GM}*1+(1-P_{GM})*0 = P_{GM}$$

Similarly:

$$E(Q_{JPM}) = P_{JPM}$$

Therefore, we have:

$$P00*(0-P_{GM})*(0-P_{JPM})+P01*(0-P_{GM})*(1-P_{JPM})+P10*(1-P_{GM})*(0-P_{JPM})$$
$$+P11*(1-P_{GM})*(1-P_{JPM}) = \text{covariance}$$

The covariance is given by:

$$\text{Covariance} = \frac{\text{correlation}}{\sqrt{\text{Var}(Q_{GM}) * \text{Var}(Q_{JPM})}}$$

The variance is defined as:

$$\text{Var}(Q_{GM}) = E(Q_{GM}{}^2)-(E(Q_{GM}))^2$$

Now

$$E(Q^2{}_{GM}) = P_{GM}1^2 + (1-P_{GM})0^2 = P_M$$

So

$$\text{Var}(Q_{GM}) = P_{GM} - P_{GM}{}^2$$

And also:

$$\text{Var}(Q_{JPM}) = P_{JPM}-P_{JPM}{}^2$$

After some algebra we obtain:

$$P11 = \text{covariance} -$$
$$((1-P_{GM}-P_{JPM})*P_{GM}*P_{JPM}+P_{JPM}*(-P_{GM})*(1-P_{JPM})+P_{GM}*(1-P_{GM})*(-P_{JPM}))$$

The other probabilities may also be obtained:

$$P01 = P_{JPM}-P11$$

$P10 = P_{GM}-P11$

$P00 = 1-(P00+P10+P01)$

For example, the spreadsheet in Figure 16-3 shows the computation when the correlation is assumed to be 0.5.

Prob of Default			Recovery Values	
Reference (GM)	**0.50%**		**20.00%**	
Protection seller	**0.75%**		**10.00%**	
(JPM)				

Default correlation	**0.5000**	Risk-free rate	**5.50%**
Covariance	0.30%		

Reference	Prot Seller	Probability Receive		Vanilla Bond	
0	0	99.06%	$100.00	99.50%	$100.00
0	1	0.44%	$100.00	0.50%	$ 20.00
1	0	0.19%	$100.00		
1	1	0.3080%	$ 28.00		
		Price	94.57652	Price	94.40758

Default swap is worth
$0.1689

Figure 16-3. Computation of the present value of a default swap.

Note that the default swap has a positive present value even though the credit rating of the protection seller is well below that of the reference security. This is due to the less than perfect correlation between the reference security and the protection seller. Also, in the case of default, the recovery value is greater since the holder has a claim against two counterparties.

It is instructive to observe the values of the default swap for different correlation assumptions (see Table 16-2).

Note that the price of the structure is a linear function of the default correlation.

In our case, the default correlation cannot be greater than 0.82. For example, the correlation cannot be equal to 1. A correlation of 1 means that GM and JPM are bound to default together. However, as the probability of default of JPM is higher than that of GM, we must assume that there are some situations in which JPM

Default Correlation	Price of Swap
0	$0.376
0.1	$0.335
0.2	$0.293
0.3	$0.252
0.4	$0.210
0.5	$0.168
0.6	$0.127
0.7	$0.0859
0.8	$0.0443

Table 16-2.

defaults but GM survives. Therefore, the default correlation is less than 1.

Note that in this analysis we did not consider the cost savings to the lender in terms of regulatory capital. We assume that this is a lender who does not need to post regulatory capital.

Moral Hazard

Suppose that a bank has in fact made a loan and, without the borrower's knowledge, also purchased a default swap against the loan. Further, assume that the borrower got into financial trouble and came to the bank in order to renegotiate the terms of the loan. In a normal loan situation, the bank would be motivated to assist the borrower, possibly to extend some extra credit. In this situation, though, the borrower is in for a nasty surprise. The bank has two courses of action:

1. Let the borrower default and collect the proceeds of the default swap.
2. Renegotiate the loan and purchase a new default swap.

While it is a simple matter to renegotiate a loan, the bank is likely to have to abandon the existing default swap and purchase a completely new default swap. It could be in the bank's best interest to let the borrower default.

Credit derivatives have been blamed by many market participants for causing more defaults and more volatility in times of distress. Some even attribute to them a part in the collapse of the Asian debt markets in 1998.

CBO CREATION

Our next example simulates the work of the sell side. The financial engineering group is charged with the creation of a CBO. For the sake of simplicity, we assume the following structure.

No Default		Default	
100	106	100	106
100	106	100	106
100	106	100	85
100	106	100	106
400	424	400	403

Figure 16-4. The collateral.

There are four single-A-rated bonds in the collateral. There are equal amounts of each bond. For the sake of simplicity, we assume a risk-free rate of 5.75% and an annual coupon of 6% for the A-rated bonds. Thus the collateral is depicted in Figure 16-4.

We make the following assumptions for each of the bonds:

- If the bond does not default, it will pay $106 in one year at maturity.
- If the bond does default, it will pay a recovery value of $0.8018 \cdot \$106 = \$85$.
- At most, one bond will default.

The case of no default is depicted on the left-hand side of Figure 16-4, while a single default case is depicted on the right-hand side of Figure 16-4.

The challenge is to design three separate CBO structures. Each of the structures will have two tranches. The senior tranche will pay a coupon and principal even if one of the bonds in the collateral defaults. The junior tranche's characteristics will depend on the type of structure contemplated:

1. Upon default of an underlying security, the junior tranche loses its coupon and receives only $100 at maturity.
2. Upon default of an underlying security, the junior tranche loses its coupon and receives only the recovery value ($85) at maturity.

3. Upon default of an underlying security, the junior tranche loses its coupon and its principal. It will receive zero at maturity.

How many bonds can be created for each of the structures and what are the relevant coupon amounts?

Analysis

Let us begin with the third case.

- We have $400 worth of collateral. In one year, it will be worth either $403 or $424.
- Assume that we issue $x of the senior tranche. Therefore, we can issue $400–x of the junior tranche.
- In case of default, the junior tranche receives nothing, so we can direct all cash flows to the senior tranche.
- We issued $x of the senior tranche which will be worth $403 in one year.
- The annual yield on the senior tranche is $403/x-1$.
- We have issued $400–x of the junior tranche. The junior tranche only gets paid if there are no defaults. If there are no defaults, we still have to use $403 to pay the senior tranche. We are left with $21 to pay the junior tranche.
- The annual yield on the junior tranche will be $21/(400-x) - 1$.

In Table 16-3, we show possible coupon amounts and face values of both tranches. The mathematical relationships described above are all maintained by each of the possible solutions. Market conditions dictate the rest. For example, we cannot sell the senior tranche if it yields less than a risk-free security. Likewise, the junior tranche must yield quite a bit more than a risk-free security. The two reasonable solutions are highlighted.

Analysis of the other cases follows a similar path. Let's consider the second case, in which the junior tranche pays the recovery value upon default of any of the bonds in the collateral pool.

- We have $400 worth of collateral. In one year, it will be worth either $403 or $424.

Senior Tranche		Junior Tranche	
Amount	Coupon	Amount	Coupon
3.800	6.05%	0.20	5.00%
3.805	5.91%	0.20	7.69%
3.810	5.77%	0.19	10.53%
3.815	5.64%	0.19	13.51%
3.820	5.50%	0.18	16.67%
3.825	5.36%	0.18	20.00%
3.830	5.22%	0.17	23.53%
3.835	5.08%	0.17	27.27%
3.840	4.95%	0.16	31.25%
3.845	4.81%	0.16	35.48%
3.850	4.68%	0.15	40.00%
3.855	4.54%	0.15	44.83%
3.860	4.40%	0.14	50.00%
3.865	4.27%	0.14	55.56%
3.870	4.13%	0.13	61.54%
3.875	4.00%	0.13	68.00%
3.880	3.87%	0.12	75.00%
3.885	3.73%	0.12	82.61%
3.890	3.60%	0.11	90.91%
3.895	3.47%	0.11	100.00%

Table 16-3. Possible coupon amounts and face values; junior tranche pays nothing upon default.

- Assume that we issue $x of the senior tranche. Therefore, we can issue $400–x of the junior tranche.

- In case of default, the junior tranche receives 0.85 on the dollar, so we distribute the cash flows as follows: The junior tranche receives $0.85*(400–x) and the senior tranche receives the rest. There is $403–0.85*(400–x) to distribute to the senior tranche.

- We issued $x of the senior tranche which will be worth $403–0.85*(400–x) in one year.

- The annual yield on the senior tranche is (403–0.85* (400–x))/x–1.

- We have issued $400–x of the junior tranche. The junior tranche only receives a coupon if there are no defaults. If there are no defaults, we still have to use $403–0.85*(400–x) to pay the senior tranche. We are left with $21+0.85*(400–x) to pay the junior tranche.

- The annual yield on the junior tranche will be (21+0.85* (400–x)) / (400–x) – 1.

Senior Tranche		Junior Tranche	
Amount	Coupon	Amount	Coupon
3.000	6.00%	1.000	6.00%
3.005	5.97%	0.995	6.11%
3.010	5.93%	0.990	6.21%
3.015	5.90%	0.985	6.32%
3.020	5.86%	0.980	6.43%
3.025	5.83%	0.975	6.54%
3.030	**5.79%**	**0.970**	**6.65%**
3.035	**5.76%**	**0.965**	**6.76%**
3.040	5.72%	0.960	6.87%
3.045	5.69%	0.955	6.99%
3.050	5.66%	0.950	7.11%
3.055	5.62%	0.945	7.22%
3.060	5.59%	0.940	7.34%
3.065	5.55%	0.935	7.46%
3.070	5.52%	0.930	7.58%
3.075	5.49%	0.925	7.70%
3.080	5.45%	0.920	7.83%

Table 16-4. Possible coupon amounts and face values; junior tranche pays recovery value upon default.

Senior Tranche		Junior Tranche	
Amount	Coupon	Amount	Coupon
0.480	6.250%	3.520	5.966%
0.485	6.186%	3.515	5.974%
0.490	6.122%	3.510	5.983%
0.495	6.061%	3.505	5.991%
0.500	6.000%	3.500	6.000%
0.505	5.941%	3.495	6.009%
0.510	**5.882%**	**3.490**	**6.017%**
0.515	**5.825%**	**3.485**	**6.026%**
0.520	5.769%	3.480	6.034%
0.525	5.174%	3.475	6.043%
0.530	5.660%	3.470	6.052%
0.535	5.607%	3.465	6.061%
0.540	5.556%	3.460	6.069%
0.545	5.505%	3.455	6.078%
0.550	5.455%	3.450	6.087%
0.555	5.405%	3.445	6.096%
0.560	5.357%	3.440	6.105%
0.565	5.310%	3.435	6.114%
0.570	5.263%	3.430	6.122%
0.575	5.217%	3.425	6.131%

Table 16-5. CBO structure in which the junior tranche loses only its coupon.

In Table 16-4, we show possible coupon amounts and face values of both tranches. Two reasonable solutions are highlighted.

It is easy to analyze the case in which the junior tranche loses only its coupon. In Table 16-5 we show various coupon amounts and face values of both tranches. Two reasonable solutions are highlighted.

Note: Rather than examine many cases of the amount of the senior tranche, we can proceed in another way. First, determine a reasonable coupon for the senior tranche. Then, figure out the amounts and the coupon available to the junior tranche.

Comparison

The first case in which the junior tranche loses only its coupon results in a structure in which there is a larger outstanding amount of the junior tranche than of the senior. This is not a likely structure. It is difficult to sell the junior tranche of a CBO, so we would like to keep the face value amount small.

The structure in which the junior tranche loses everything also looks difficult to sell. Will an investor agree to accept a coupon of 7.69% or even 10.53% and risk losing the entire principal?

The middle structure looks the most promising. We can offer an above-average coupon of 6.017% or even 6.026%. In case of default, the investor will still receive the recovery value.

Commission

The above analysis was done on a perfect cash flow matched basis. In real life, a commission would be included in the CBO structure. The coupon amounts that were calculated would then be reduced to account for the commissions.

A STRUCTURED NOTE

Our next example is a structured note. Assume that Bankers Trust issues a six-year floating-rate note that pays Libor flat. This will be our underlying reference credit. We also assume that the floating-rate note is priced at par.

Bankers Trust now wishes to create a new one-year floating-rate security with a higher coupon (e.g., Libor+spread). The new security has the provision that it will immediately go to zero if the reference security should ever deteriorate in price to below $90. So if the underlying security ever trades below $90, all coupon payments cease and the new security will immediately redeem at zero.

Question: What is a reasonable spread to offer on the new security?

Analysis

To determine an adequate spread, the main question that needs to be answered is,

"What is the probability that the reference security will trade below $90 in the next year?"

Roughly speaking, assume that it is determined that the probability is 1%. This means that the investor in the structured note has a 1% chance of losing the entire investment. To compensate for this, we need to pay the investor a coupon that is higher than normal.

Assume that Libor is 5.75%. The structured note has:

- 99% probability of returning 100+5.75+spread, and
- 1% probability of returning zero.

The expected return from the structured note is 0.99*(105.75+spread). A one-year floating-rate bond will pay 100+5.75 = $105.75.

Equating the two, we have:

$$0.99*(105.75+spread) = 105.75$$

Where:

$$Spread = 1.07\%$$

Therefore, the structured note will have a spread of about 107 basis points.

We now consider what would cause the original note to decline to $90. Since the reference security is a floating-rate note, its price is not affected by interest rate changes. The price of the reference security will be determined by the credit spread of the issuer.

The issuer's credit spread will widen if:

a. The rating of the issuer declines.

b. All spreads in the market widen out.

At the time of issuance, the issuer pays a coupon of Libor. If during the lifetime of the reference security the issuer's credit rating declines, it will have to offer a higher coupon. If the issuer were

FRN			Maturity	Six years	Effective margin
Pays index plus		**0** bps	Reset every six months		0
			Market price	**100**	

Time	Index	Cash Flow	Discount R	PV
0.5	**5.75%**	2.875	5.75%	2.794654
1	5.75%	2.875	5.75%	2.716553
1.5	5.75%	2.875	5.75%	2.640635
2	5.75%	2.875	5.75%	2.566838
2.5	5.75%	2.875	5.75%	2.495104
3	5.75%	2.875	5.75%	2.425374
3.5	5.75%	2.875	5.75%	2.357593
4	5.75%	2.875	5.75%	2.291707
4.5	5.75%	2.875	5.75%	2.227662
5	5.75%	2.875	5.75%	2.165406
5.5	5.75%	2.875	5.75%	2.104891
6	5.75%	102.875	5.75%	73.21358
				100

Table 16-6. A floating-rate note paying Libor flat is priced at $100 if the effective margin is zero.

to issue a floating-rate security paying a higher coupon than Libor, that new security would be sold at par. However, the original security that pays Libor will be priced below par. On the other hand, if the issuer's credit rating were to strengthen, it could offer new securities with a sub-Libor coupon. Thus a floating-rate bond paying Libor would be priced above par.

The question becomes: What spread would cause a Libor-paying security to be priced at $90?

Floating-rate notes are typically priced with the use of an "effective margin." In Table 16-6 we show that a floating-rate note paying Libor flat is priced at par if the effective margin is zero.

FRN			Maturity	Six years	Effective margin
Pays index plus		**0 bps**	Reset every six months		212.3207
			Market price	**90**	

Time	Index	Cash Flow	Discount R	PV
0.5	**5.75%**	2.875	7.87%	2.766109
1	5.75%	2.875	7.87%	2.661343
1.5	5.75%	2.875	7.87%	2.560544
2	5.75%	2.875	7.87%	2.463564
2.5	5.75%	2.875	7.87%	2.370256
3	5.75%	2.875	7.87%	2.280482
3.5	5.75%	2.875	7.87%	2.194109
4	5.75%	2.875	7.87%	2.111007
4.5	5.75%	2.875	7.87%	2.031053
5	5.75%	2.875	7.87%	1.954126
5.5	5.75%	2.875	7.87%	1.880114
6	5.75%	102.875	7.87%	64.72732
				90.00002

Table 16-7. To be priced at $90, the effective margin of the security must be 212 basis points.

The effective margin is used to determine a discount rate. In Table 16-6, all cash flows are generated by determining the Libor rate plus a spread. Then the cash flows are discounted by an interest rate that is Libor plus the effective margin.

Table 16-7 shows that to bring the price of the security down to $90, the effective margin must be 212.32 basis points.

Our question becomes: Given an issuer whose credit rating allows it to issue at Libor flat, what are the chances that the spread of that issuer will increase by 212 basis points?

Chances of Spread Increase

There are two primary methods for determining the chances that the spread will increase by 212 basis points, from Libor flat to Libor+212.

As mentioned previously, the spread may increase as a result of two factors:

1. A worsening of the issuer's credit rating, or
2. A general spread widening.

We may assume that a general spread widening will be reflected in a corresponding TED spread increase. As the coupon is tied to Libor (and not, for example, to the Constant Maturity Treasury), the price of the floating-rate security will not decline. Hence, we can assume that we are actually trying to determine the probable worsening of the issuer's credit rating.

The historical method relies on the use of the credit migration table. Assume, for example, that a Libor flat spread corresponds to an AA credit rating. Also, assume that an issuer rated BB could issue a six-year floating-rate note at Libor+212.

Next, we consult the probability transition table shown in Table 11-1. The probability of a rating downgrade:

- From AA to BB is 0.06%.
- From AA to B is 0.14%.
- From AA to CCC is 0.02%.
- From AA to default is 0.0%.

The sum of these is 0.22%.

We conclude that the structured note could be constructed. A fair value for the coupon on the structured note would be approximately Libor+22 basis points.

An alternative methodology requires the creation of a statistical model of credit spreads. Given such a model, we can deduce the probability of a rate change.

The Longstaff and Schwartz Model

One model of credit spreads is given by Francis Longstaff and Eduardo Schwartz, UCLA, May 1995. In the model, spreads are modeled directly. They are assumed to be stationary and mean reverting.

In their paper, the authors derived simple closed-form formulas for call and put options on the credit spread:

- Calls and puts on the credit spreads can have prices below their intrinsic value.

- Credit spread calls have negative convexity and the delta of a call can be higher for OTM calls and ATM calls than for ITM calls.
- The delta of both calls and puts converges to zero as the time until expiration increases. This implies that long-term credit derivatives may be useless to hedge against current shifts in credit spreads.

Here are the steps the authors took:

1. The authors examined the Moody's Aaa, Aa, A, and Baa industrial bond indices and Moody's Aaa, Aa, A, and Baa utility bond indices. They compared monthly spread data versus U.S. Treasury bonds. The data set used was from 1977 to 1992.

2. Because the spread is always positive, the authors chose to build a model for X, the logarithm of the spread.

3. Take the time series X and perform a regression analysis on it. The authors assumed a linear function of the form: $\Delta X_{t+1} = \gamma_0 + \gamma_1 {}^* X_t + \varepsilon_t$.

4. The numbers γ_0 and γ_1 are the intercept and slope coefficients of the regression, respectively.

5. The authors performed a regression analysis for each series.

6. In most cases, the slope variable is negative. This shows that credit spreads are mean reverting.

7. Create a differential equation for the credit spread. The equation is of the form $dX = (a-bX)\, dt + c\, dZ_1$, where a, b, and c are parameters and dZ_1 is a normal Wiener process.

8. These dynamics imply that X is mean reverting and homoskedastic are in agreement with the empirical data.

9. Credit spreads are positive and conditionally lognormally distributed.

10. Now add a random interest rate component. The authors chose the Vasicek model given by $dr = (\alpha - \beta r)\, dt + \sigma\, dZ_2$.

11. The reason for choosing the Vasicek model is that interest rates have very similar dynamics to credit spreads.

12. The correlation coefficient between dZ_1 and dZ_2 is ρ.

13. The authors allow for the possibility that both interest rate risk and credit spread risk are priced by the market.

14. The market price of risk premiums is incorporated into the a and α measures.

15. Therefore, a and α are equilibrium or risk-adjusted parameters rather than empirical parameters.

16. Obtain that X(t) is conditionally normally distributed with a mean and a variance.

17. From this, the authors derive a PDE that credit spread options must satisfy.

18. Solving this equation, they then find a closed-form expression for the option whose payoff function is H(X) = max(0,exp(X)–K).

19. The result is a closed-form formula.

Surprising Results

The authors compared the option price versus intrinsic value and noted that the value of the option is less than intrinsic value even when the call option is slightly in the money. This is due to the fact that credit spreads are mean reverting. For example, if the spread is ITM now, it may be less likely to remain ITM at expiration. Hence, ITM call options are less likely to remain ITM over time.

The value of an ITM call option can be less than its intrinsic value because of the expected decrease in credit spreads and because of the time value of money. This cannot happen in the standard Black-Scholes model, because the underlying asset must appreciate at the risk-free rate and is not mean reverting.

The authors looked at the delta of a credit spread option. It is always positive, between 0 and 1. However, as time to expiration increases, the delta goes to zero. This is due to mean reversion. Changes in the current value of the credit spread have little to do with its expected final value. A change in the current credit spread is expected to be canceled by the time expiration arrives. Therefore, long-term credit spread options may not be useful tools for hedging the risk of changes in the current credit spread. Short-term credit spread options are much more practical.

The prices of call options on credit spreads behave quite differently than those for options on tradeable assets. If we apply put–call parity, we obtain the discounted forward value of the credit spread. This is different from options on a traded asset, for which the put–call parity involves today's price. The traded asset's discounted forward price is simply today's price: It grows at the risk-free rate and gets discounted back at the same rate.

The authors note that the results of mean reversion should be carefully considered when designing options on credit spreads.

Back to Our Problem

Consider a model for credit spread behavior (e.g., the Longstaff and Schwartz model). Given the dynamics of the credit spread, we can formulate an algorithm (for example, a two-factor Monte Carlo simulation) to simultaneously track both the credit spreads and the interest rates. The simulation would be repeated many times and the number of occurrences of spread widening counted. From this number, it would be possible to deduce the probability of the relevant spread widening.

Note that the Longstaff and Schwartz model is calibrated to spreads above risk-free rates. Thus the model will also incorporate the possibility that spreads widened out in general. In our case, we are not interested in that aspect of the security.

SUMMARY

The analysis of credit derivatives remains quite challenging.

Glossary

Contingent capital note. A security normally issued from a special purpose vehicle or trust. It is collateralized with Treasuries in which a company pays a premium from the outset for the right, at any time during the specified period, to substitute its own notes for the Treasuries.

Credit event. Public information of a receivership, bankruptcy, insolvency, winding up, or failure to meet payment obligations. Often coupled with a **materiality** clause.

Credit spread forwards. A bilateral financial contract in which the **protection buyer** receives the difference between the yield of the reference security and some benchmark yield (usually Treasuries) and the strike, if positive, and pays the difference, if negative.

Credit swap. The credit swap is a bilateral financial contract in which one party (the **protection buyer**) pays a periodic fee, typically expressed in basis points of the notional amount, in return for a **contingent payment** by the other counterparty (the **protection seller**) after a **credit event** of the **reference credit**. The **contingent payment** is designed to mirror the loss incurred by the creditors of the **reference security** in the event of its default. The settlement mechanism depends on the liquidity and availability of the reference securities.

Contingent payment. Payment by the **protection seller:**

Recovery linked—Usually calculated as the fall in price of a reference security below par, as established by polling reference dealers.

Physical delivery—Full notional in exchange for defaulted **reference securities.**

Binary—Payment of a predetermined fixed amount.

Credit-linked note. A security normally issued from a collateralized special purpose vehicle or trust with redemption linked to the occurrence of a **credit event** by the **reference security.**

Materiality. A significant price deterioration in a **reference security** following a **credit event.**

Protection buyer. A counterparty who wishes to be protected from a deterioration in the credit quality of the **reference security.**

Protection seller. The counterparty who sells protection against a deterioration in the credit quality of the **reference security.**

Reference credit. A specified entity that may be a sovereign, financial institution, corporation, or one among a basket of such specified entities.

Reference security. Typically, a public security issued by the reference credit, alternatively a "reference asset" such as loans or other financial assets (including swaps, trade receivables, indemnification letters, and so on).

Swap guarantee. A credit swap with a dynamic notional that matches the mark to market on any given day of a specified swap (or other market-sensitive instrument).

Total return swap. A bilateral financial contract in which the total return of an asset is exchanged for another cash flow. One counterparty (the TR payer) pays the total return (interest plus fees plus price appreciation) of the reference security and (usually) receives Libor plus a spread from the other counterparty (the TR receiver). Price appreciation or depreciation may be calculated and exchanged at maturity or on an interim basis.

Index

Analysis and pricing, 281-305
  binary structure, 281-289
  CBO creation, 294-298
  credit default swap, 289-293
    moral hazard, 293
  Longstaff and Schwartz model, 302-304
  structured note, 298-302
  structures, four, 281
  zero-one structure, 281-289
    hedging, 288-289
    motivation to buy, 287-288
Anniversary polling, 76
Annual Credit Provisioning (ACP), 236-237
Asia, credit risk management in, 193-203
  Bankers Trust, 197
  after its catastrophe, 200-202
  collateralization, 197-198
  courts, 195
  credit derivatives, 199-200, 203
  credit mediation, 200
  credit neutral strategies, 202-203
  credit quality, lower, 194
  cross border legal risk, 195
  data, historical, dearth of, 193-194
  dealing with, 199
  default models, 195-196
  disclosure requirements, loose, 194
  government intervention, 197
  illiquidity, 196-197
  introduction, 193
  legal system, 195
  managers, shortage of, 198-199
  recovery rates, 195
  speculation, 198
  staff, 198-199
  summary, 203
  "unwinding the position," 196
  vulture funds, 201
Asset swap put, 164-166

Asset swap put credit spread, 119-122
At-the-money put option, 24

BAKred, 95-97
  and banking book, 95-96
Bank, locating CD function within, 189-192
  alternatives, five, 189
  as decentralized unit, 191
  in derivatives unit, 190-191
  as independent group, 191
  introduction, 189
  in loan portfolio department, 190
  in loan syndication and trading unit, 191
  requirements, 189-191
  summary, 191-192
Bank for International Settlements (BIS), 9,
    169, 253
  Basle Committee of, 79
Bank loans, credit derivatives and, 239-263
  attraction of loans, 248-249
    Sharpe ratios for alternative invest-
      ments, 248
  capital, return on, 249-255
  correlation, 260
  credit derivative trade, 256-257
  credit line restraints, addressing, 258-259
  credit paradox, 257-258
  cultural changes within bank, 261-263
    credit derivatives as risk management
      tool, 263
    dynamic credit risk management, 261
    mark to market of portfolio, 261-262
    RAROC, compensation based on, 262-
      263
  exposures, managing, 243-245
    index, use of, 243
    securitization, 244-245
  holder of loans, 247-248
    hedge fund, 248, 249-252

Bank loans *(cont.)*
  internal conflict, 255
  introduction, 239
    secondary market, growth of, 239
    pooled investment vehicles, 239
  joint default, 256-257
  nontraditional investors, opening loan
      market to, 249-252
  off-balance sheet credit risk, increasing,
      260-261
  originators of loans, 246-247
  regulatory capital, return on, 252-255
  returns, improving, 240
  risk capital, 245-246
  risk management, using CDs for, 241-242
  role, 239-240
    risk-adjusted return on capital
        (RAROC) approach, 240, 246, 247,
        257
  swap guarantees, 259-260
  volatility of defaults in loan book, 242-
      243
Bankers Trust, 11, 14
  in Asia, 197
Bankruptcy credit event, 62-63
Basket credit-linked notes, term sheets for,
    134-139
Basle Committee of Bank for International
    Settlements (BIS), 79
Binary bonds, term sheets for, 129-134
Black-Scholes formula, 275, 304
Brady Bond index, 184
BTPs, 49-50
Buyer, 12-13

Capital Adequacy Directive (CAD), 80
Cash settlement, 77-78
Chase Manhattan, 11
Citibank in Asia, 199
CLN, 43-47 *(see also* Credit-linked notes)
Collars, 122-126
Collateralization in Asia, 197-198
Collateralized bond obligations (CBOs),
    175-187
  and Collateralized Loan Obligation
      (CLO), 177
  as complementary vehicles to credit
      derivatives, 179
  credit rating agencies, 187
  difficulties, 179
  fees, 181
  financial engineering, 180

history, 178
introduction, 175
junior tranche, 181-185
  call risk, 184-185
  correlation of default events, 184
  default, probability of, 183
  size of, 183-185
junk debt, 177-178
market size, 180
and mortgage-backed security (MBS),
    175-177
risk, 179
sample deal, 185-186
summary, 187
sweetener, 185
tranches, 176, 177
  junior, 181-185 *(see also* ... junior)
Collateralized Loan Obligation (CLO), 177
Commission Bancaire, 96-97
Condition to Payment (CTP), 61
Convertibility risk products, 50-51, 59
  "sovereign credit event," 59
Credit default products, 59-61
  options or swaps, 60
  swap as unfunded credit derivative, 84
Credit default swap trade, 141-157
Credit derivatives, 1-14
  in Asia, 199-200, 203
  bank, location in, 189-192
  and bank loans, 239-263 *(see also* Bank
      loans)
  buyer and seller, 12-13
  CBOs as complementary to, 179 *(see also*
      Collateralized bond)
  credit paradox, 3-4
  credit swap, 14, 15-16
  default swap, 14, 15-16
  definition, 173
  estimating, difficulties in, 9-10
  financial engineering, 1-2
  globalization and democratization of
      finance, 7-8
  "growing pains" of, 10-11
  history, 13-14
  instruments, types of, 54-61 *(see also*
      Legal)
  investment banks, needs of, 13-14
  legal issues, 1, 53-100 *(see also* Legal)
  liquidity, lack of, 10-11
  market, one-sided nature of, 4-5
  market for, potential, 8-9
  market size, 9-10

players in, 11
poaching mechanism, 11
rationale of, 11-12
regulatory aspects, 53-99 (*see also* Legal)
and regulatory capital issues, 12
relationship issues, 2-3
and repo markets, 167-173 (*see also* Repo)
risk measurement, 6-7
special purpose vehicles (SPVs), 14
structured, creation and analysis of, 265-
    273 (*see also* Structured)
structures, 5, 15-52 (*see also* Structures)
supply and demand, relationship
    between, 11-12
trends, current, 6
types, three main, 52
valuation of, 275-279 (*see also* Valuation)
volatility, 1-2
weather-linked, 1-2
yield, search for, 5-6
Credit Equivalent Amount, 93
Credit Event upon Merger, 63 (*see also*
    Legal)
Credit exposure default swap, 158-160
Credit-linked notes (CLN), 43-47
advantage, 43
investor in, 45-47
structured note, 43-44, 45
Credit Manager, 237
Credit mediation in Asia, 200
CreditMetrics of J.P. Morgan, 109, 205-223,
    237, 277
acceptance, 208-209
bond, value of, 212-215
correlation, 222-223
credit risk vs. market risk, 207-208, 216
default, downgrade or upgrade, proba-
    bility of, 211-212
default, probability of, 216-217
elements of, three, 205-207
goals, 206-207
historical data, use of, 218
introduction, 205
"market-driven exposures," 221
Markov chains, 215-216
methodology, 209
Monte Carlo algorithm, 214, 228
Moody's Investor Services, 218
portfolio, 214-215
    advantages of, 219
questions, 217-218
recovery values, 221-222

risk limits, 218
RiskMetrics, 205, 208
schematic, 221
skewed distribution, 208
summary, 222
swap, credit risk of, 210-211
system, architecture of, 220-221
traditional credit allocation, 219
what-if questions, 217-218
Credit paradox, 3-4, 257
CreditPortfolio View, 237
Credit risk vs. market risk, 207-208, 216
CreditRisk+, 1, 109, 225-237
Annual Credit Provisioning (ACP), 236-
    237
continuous variable approach, use of,
    226-227
credit provisions, 235-237
of Credit Suisse Financial Products, 1,
    109, 205, 225
default events and default losses, 232
default rate, 226-227
    and correlation, 229-232
default risk as focus, 226
economic capital, 234-235
economy, tying default risk to, 229-230
Incremental Credit Reserve (ICR), 236-
    237
leptokurtic distribution, 230
loans, credit risks in, 226
management practices, current, 227-228
model, three methods of using, 233-234
model inputs, 228-229
output reports, 227
Poisson distribution, 231-232
portfolio, four products to measure and
    manage risk of, 237
risks in designing model, three, 225
sector analysis, 233
summary, 237
time horizon, 227
volatility of default rate, 229
Credit spread options, 34-40, 56, 57
BTPs, 51-52
call option, 37
currency, 49-50
duration, 37-38
forwards, 38-40
hedging difficult, 37
put, example of, 36-38
volatility, 40
Credit spreads, analysis of, 101-107

Credit spreads, analysis of *(cont.)*
   forward spread, computation of, 102-104
   probability of default, 105-107
   recovery value, 105-107
   spread curve, example of, 101-102
   volatility, estimation of, 104-105
Credit Suisse:
   in Asia, 199
   Financial Products (CSF), 1, 11
Credit swap, 4, 15-52 *(see also* Structures)
   credit intermediation swap, 26-28
Cross acceleration and cross default, 63-65
   Reference Obligation, 63
Cross border legal risks, 195

Default models in Asia, 195-196
Default Requirement, 64
Default swap, 14, 15-52
   default substitution swaps, 28-29
Deliverable Obligations, 73-74
Democratization of finance, 7-8
Derivatives unit in bank, CDs as part of,
   190-191
Digital option, 24-26
Digital spread options, term sheets for, 118-
   119
   "step," 119
Downgrade, 65-66
Downgrade options, 26
Duration (DUR), 37-38, 117, 124, 126
Dynamic credit risk management, 261

Economic capital, 234-235
Edgar database, 194
Emerging market debt, 177-178
Equity swap, 31-33, 141
   and TROR, difference between, 31
Equity value models in valuation of credit
   derivative, 275-276
European Union, 9
Exposure to credit desired, 34

Failure to pay, 66-70
Financial engineering, 1-2, 265-273 *(see also*
   Structured)
Financial Services Authority (FSA) of
   United Kingdom, 82-98
   asset mismatch, 86
   Banking Book treatment for credit deriv-
     atives, 86
   basket products, 88-89
   capital charges, three, 90-94
   Chapter CD, 82-83, 89-90

   counterparty risk charge, 90, 93-94
   Credit Equivalent Amount, 93
   currency mismatch, 87
   "first past the post" structures, 89
   funded or unfunded, 84-85
   general market risk charge 90-91
   "green bottle structures," 89
   maturity mismatch, 87-88
   payout structure, 85-86
   potential future credit exposure (PFCE),
     93-94
   product categories, three, 90
   risk transfer requirements, 94
   Securities and Futures Authority (SFA),
     81-82, 83
   specific risk charge, 91, 92-93
     "double whammy," 92
     offset, 92-93
   trading book treatment, 89-90
"First past the post" structures, 89
Foreign exchange and credit combined,
   term sheets for, 126-129, 130
   structured products, 129, 130
Forwards, 52
France, regulatory treatment of credit
   derivatives in, 96-98
Funded credit derivative, 84

Germany, regulatory capital treatment in,
   95-96
   BAKred, 95-96
   and banking book, 96
Globalization of finance, 7
Glossary, 307-308
Goldman Sachs, 14
Government intervention in Asia, 197

Hedge fund, 31, 248, 249
   opening loan market to, 249-252
Hedging, 23-26
   zero-one securities, 288-289
High-yield corporate debt, 177-178

Illiquidity in Asian markets, 196-197
   "unwinding the position," 196
Incremental Credit Reserve (ICR), 236-
   237
Interest rate swap, 31-33
   credit risk of, 210-211
International Swaps and Derivatives
   Association (ISDA), 9, 60, 62
   Multi-Currency-Cross-Border Master
     Agreement, 62-63

Investment banks, needs of as source of credit derivatives, 13

J.P. Morgan, 11, 195, 197
Brady Bond Index, 184
CreditMetrics system, 1
Wal-Mart CLNs, 48-49
Junior tranche, 181-185 (see also Collateralized bond)
Junk debt, 177-178

Legal and regulatory aspects, 53-99
Credit Event upon Merger, 63
ISDA Master Agreement definition, 60, 62
cross acceleration and cross default, 63-65
Reference Obligation, 64
"documentary basis" risk, creating, 53
downgrade, 65-66
failure to pay, 66-67
instruments, types of, 54-61
convertibility products, 54, 59
credit default products, 59-61 (see also Credit default)
credit-linked notes, 54
credit spread products, 55
total rate of return swaps, 55-59
materiality, 71-72
notices, 69-70
payout profile, 61-63
bankruptcy credit event, 61-62
"buyer" and "seller," 61
Condition to Payment (CTP), 61
ISDA Multi-Currency-Cross-Border Master Agreement, 62
publicly available information (PAI), 68-69
regulatory capital treatment, 78-82 (see also Regulatory)
repudiation, 67
restructuring, 67
settlement terms, 72-78 (see also Settlement terms)
summary, 78
written documents critical, 53
Legal test in credit swap, 22-23
Leptokurtic distribution, 230
Libor plus spread, 30, 31-33
Libor rate, 41, 43-47, 50, 102
in structured note, 298-302
Liquidity in Asia, 196-197

Loan portfolio department of bank, CDs as part of, 190
Loan syndication and trading unit, CDs as part of, 191
Loans, credit derivatives and, 239-263 (see also Bank loans)

Management practices for credit risks, current, 227-228
Managers in Asia, shortage of, 199
Market:
one-sided nature of, 4-5
size, 9-10
"Market-driven exposures" of CreditMetrics, 221
Market risk vs. credit risk, 207-208, 216
Market test in credit swap, 22-23
Markov chains, 215-216
Materiality, 71-72
clause, 16
Maturity, 33-34
MBS, 175-177
Merton model, 278
Monte Carlo algorithm, 214, 228
Moody's Investor Services, 218, 228, 277
Morgan, J.P., 12 (see also J.P. Morgan)
Mortgage-backed security (MBS) and collateralized bond obligations, 175-177

Net interest margin (NIM), 240, 246, 256
Nontraditional investors, opening loan market to, 249-252
Notices of Publicly Available Information, 69

Obligations, 64
One-year default swap, 160-164
Options, 52
Out-of-the-money put option, 24

PAI, 68-69
Payout profile of credit swap, 61-62
bankruptcy credit event, 61-62
Physical settlement amount (PSA), 73
Poaching mechanism, 11
Poisson distribution, 231-232
PortfolioManager, 237
Potential future credit exposure (PFCE), 96
Power options, 25
Price materiality, 71-72
Publicly available information (PAI), 68-69
Put credit spread, term sheet for, 115-118
asset swap, 119-122

Ratings-based model in valuation of credit derivative, 275, 277
Recovery value, 21
Reference Obligation, 65
Regulatory aspects, 53-100 (*see also* Legal)
  Basle Committee of Bank for International Settlements (BIS), 79
  Capital Adequacy Directive (CAD), 80
  Financial Services Authority (FSA) of United Kingdom, 82-98 (*see also* Financial)
  France, regulatory capital treatment in, 96-98
  Germany, regulatory capital treatment in, 95-96 (*see also* Germany)
    BAKred, 95-96
  regulatory capital treatment, 78-80
  Solvency Ratio Directive (SRD), 80
  in United Kingdom, 80-94 (*see also* Financial Services)
Repo markets, credit derivatives and, 167-173
  classic, 167-169
  emerging and developed, difference between, 169
  selling credit risk, 172-173
  summary, 173
  vs. total return (TR) swap, 169-173
    balance sheet consideration, 172
    length of deal, 172
    similarities, 171-172
Repudiation, 67
Restructuring, 67
Revenue-neutral diversification, 109-114
  background, 110
  caveat, 114
  credit risk measurement, 109-110
  equivalent position, 113-114
  portfolio theories, 109
  trade, 111-113
Reverse engineering, 265 (*see also* Structured)
Risk-adjusted return on capital (RAROC), 240, 246, 247, 257
Risk capital, 245-246
Risk measurement, 6-7
RiskMetrics, 205, 208 (*see also* CreditMetrics)

Scheduled Termination Date, 69
Secrecy issues, 21-22

Securities and Futures Authority (SFA) 80-81, 82 (*see also* Financial Services)
Securitization, 244-245
Seller, 12-13
Settlement terms, 72-78
  anniversary polling, 76
  cash, 74-78
  Deliverable Obligations, 73-74
  physical, 73-74
Sharpe ratios for alternative investments, 248
Solvency Ratio Directive (SRD), 80
Sovereign credit event, 59
Special purpose vehicles (SPVs), 14
Speculation in Asia, 198
Spread-based model in valuation of credit derivative, 275, 276-277
Spread options, 34-38 (*see also* Credit spread options)
Spread materiality, 72
Square option, 25
Staff in Asia, 198-199
Standardization, 41
Structured credit derivatives, creation and analysis of, 265-273
  creation process of note, 267-273
    buy-and-hold strategy, 271
    conceptual stage, 267-268
    identification stage, 267, 269-273
    structuring stage, 273
    trading strategy, 271-272
  financial engineering, 265
  note, analysis of, 265-266
    "buy side" issues, 265-266
    "sell side" issues, 266
  reverse engineering, 265
Structures, 15-52
  at-the-money put option, 24
  contingent payment, 20
  convertibility risk products, 50-51
  correlation of default between reference credit and protection writer, 18-20
  credit-linked notes, 43-50 (*see also* Credit-linked notes)
  credit swap, 15-20
  credit intermediation swap, 26-27
  credit spread options, 34-40 (*see also* Credit spread options)
  default substitution swaps, 28-29
  default swap, 15-20
  digital option, 24-25

downgrade options, 26
equity swap, 31
exposure to credit desired, 34
hedge fund, 31
hedging, 23-26
interest rate swap, 31-33, 34
legal test, 22-23
Libor plus spread, 31-33
market test, 22-23
materiality clause, 16
maturity, 33-34
moral hazard, 23
out-of-the-money put option, 24-25
power options, 25
premium, 16-18
protection provider, credit rating of, 17
recovery value, 20, 21
requests, special, 44
secrecy issues, 21-22
square option, 25
standardization, 41
total return swap, 29-34
   corporations, use of by, 42-43
   credit-linked notes, 43-49 (*see also*
    Credit-linked)
   credit risk in, 31-33
  trade, example of, 51-52
Swap guarantee, 259-260
Swaps, 52

Term sheets, examination of, 115-166
asset swap put, 164-166
asset swap put credit spread, 119-122
basket credit-linked notes, 134-139
credit default swap trade, 141-157
credit exposure default swap, 158-160
digital spread options, 118-119
  "step," 119
foreign exchange, combining credit with,
  126-129, 130
  structured products, 129, 130
one-year default swap, 160-164
put credit spread, 118
  asset swap, 119-122
summary, 166
total return swaps, 139-141
zero premium collars, 122-126

Total rate of return swaps (TROR), 55-58
  (*see also* TROR)
Total return swap, 29-34 (*see also* Structures
  and TROR)
  vs. repo trade, 169-173
   balance sheet consideration, 172
   length of deal, 172
   similarities, 171-172
  term sheets for, 139-141
Tranches, 176, 177
  junior, 181-185 (*see also* Collateralized
   bond)
TROR, 29-34
  corporations, use of by, 42-43
  credit-linked notes, 43-49 (*see also* Credit-
   linked)
  credit risk in, 31-34
  and equity swap, difference between, 31
  maturity, 33-34
  payer and receiver, 55-58
  Reference Obligations, 55-58
  tax issues, 58

Unfunded credit derivative, 84, 93-94
United Kingdom, regulatory capital treat-
  ment in, 80-94 (*see also* Financial
  Services)
"Unwinding the position," 196

Valuation of credit derivatives, 275-279
  academic question, unresolved, 278
  equity value models, 275-276
  introduction, 275
   Black-Scholes formula, 245
  ratings-based models, 275, 277
  spread-based models, 275, 276-277
Vulture funds, 201

Weather-linked derivative, 1-2

Yield, search for, 5-6

Zero cost collars, 123-126 (*see also* Zero premium)
Zero coupon note, 51
  strip, 282-283
Zero premium collars, term sheets for, 122-
  126

About the Author

Israel Nelken, Ph.D., is president of Super Computer Consulting, Inc., which specializes in software development, exotic options, convertible bonds, fixed income mathematics, and statistical analysis. Dr. Nelken is a lecturer in the University of Chicago Master of Science in Financial Mathematics program, and hosts sold-out options-related seminars in New York and London. His books include *The Handbook of Exotic Options, Volatility in the Capital Markets,* and *Option Embedded Bonds.*